Between Voters and Eurocrats

Between Voters and Eurocrats

How Do Governments Justify Their Budgets?

Johannes Karremans

OXFORD
UNIVERSITY PRESS

OXFORD
UNIVERSITY PRESS

Great Clarendon Street, Oxford, OX2 6DP,
United Kingdom

Oxford University Press is a department of the University of Oxford.
It furthers the University's objective of excellence in research, scholarship,
and education by publishing worldwide. Oxford is a registered trade mark of
Oxford University Press in the UK and in certain other countries

Published in the United States of America by Oxford University Press
198 Madison Avenue, New York, NY 10016, United States of America

British Library Cataloguing in Publication Data

Data available

Library of Congress Control Number: 2023945771

ISBN 9780192886583

DOI: 10.1093/oso/9780192886583.001.0001

Printed and bound in the UK by
Clays Ltd, Elcograf S.p.A.

To Mara

Preface and Acknowledgements

Fiesole, 23 October 2022

This book takes up the challenge of distinguishing two drivers for public decision-making that in reality are often closely intertwined. It places the demands of voters in contraposition to long-term state interests. This distinction may seem odd because in democracies state interests and voters' preferences are meant to coincide. Governments are appointed through democratic elections at which political parties present different political programmes and voters may reward or punish incumbent governing parties. Electoral programmes, however, are certainly not the only criteria by which governments pursue their policies. Governments must also take into consideration the financial sustainability of the state. In an internationally integrated economy, maintaining this sustainability is becoming increasingly complex and is tied to international obligations. This sometimes raises the concern that financial considerations have become more important than meeting people's demands for legitimating public policy. This book investigates whether this proposition is true focusing on five European countries, namely Austria, France, Germany, Italy, and Spain.

The present manuscript is the outcome of a long intellectual and empirical journey. On a foggy autumn morning in 2011, as a Master student at the Vrije Universiteit Brussel, I was meeting Professor Kris Deschouwer to discuss the possibility of applying for a doctoral programme. I had some vague ideas about combining debates in international political economy about whether globalization was reducing states' power and authority, with debates in comparative politics about how since the 1980s political parties were struggling to fulfil their role as representatives of citizens' demands. During the meeting I was given a paper to read that would define my research for the next ten years: it was the working paper by Peter Mair *Bini Smaghi vs the Parties*. After the meeting, I proceeded to write a research proposal that allowed me to join the doctoral programme of the European University Institute in Florence.

Supervised by Professor Pepper Culpepper and co-supervised by Professor Hanspeter Kriesi, I had the privilege to write my doctoral thesis not only under the best possible guidance, but also in direct conversation with the highest standard of research into political economy and political parties.

More precisely, the conversations I had with Professor Culpepper stimulated me to think in terms of the power structures within which political actors operate. In parallel, from Professor Kriesi I learned how to systematically collect data on political communication in a way that allows meaningful comparative inferences. The research featured in the present book is precisely this: the presentation of systematically collected data on budget speeches from which comparative inferences emerge on the power structures within which governments and parties operate. Five years after defending my doctoral thesis, I remain greatly indebted to my two main supervisors for their invaluable guidance.

My doctoral thesis turned out to be largely an intellectual exercise through which I taught myself a method for comparatively studying the criteria by which governments operate. It was thus the beginning of an intellectual journey and, in my view, it was not sufficiently developed to be turned into a monograph for a wider audience. I wanted to further advance my method and apply it to more contemporary cases. I wanted to reframe my research question and design in a way that would allow me to be more focused on the power structures that are built into European economic governance. With these new ambitions, I started writing a new research proposal.

The transition from doctoral to post-doctoral research can be surprisingly challenging, and I cannot overstate the incredible amount of help I received from Professor Zoe Lefkofridi in this particular phase. I am indebted to her for most of my post-doctoral achievements. Without her support I doubt whether I would have found the energy and motivation to push through the walls that academia often puts between a draft and a finalized recognizable product. It was thanks to her support and encouragement that in 2018 I successfully submitted my new research proposal to the Austrian Science Fund and was awarded a 'Lise Meitner' grant (M 2591). With these research funds I became a post-doctoral researcher at the University of Salzburg (2019–2021) and was able to hire three excellent student assistants who helped me in coding the empirical material that is presented in Chapter 2. It was after finalizing this project, that I finally felt ready to write a monograph.

When writing a monograph, it is extremely valuable to be surrounded by a stimulating intellectual environment. I am therefore very grateful to Professor Anton Hemerijck for bringing me back to the European University Institute and taking me on board in his 'Wellsire' research project, funded by the European Research Council (grant agreement No 882276). In this setting, I had the good fortune to be constantly surrounded by seminars and informal conversations about how social spending can be financially sustainable in the long term. As will become clear in Chapter 7, this is also the question that European policymakers seem to be increasingly asking themselves. Discussing these matters with colleagues on an almost weekly basis has certainly influenced this manuscript for the better.

Beyond my direct work environment, I was blessed with having the possibility to reach out to scholars and friends, for advice, comments, suggestions, reviews, or chats. Among these, I would like to mention Fabio Bulfone, Alice Cavalieri, Koen Damhuis, Björn Bremer, Barry Colfer, Robert Huber, Diego Garzia, Professor Adrienne Héritier and Professor Ferdinand Müller-Rommel. Special thanks also to Eve Leckey for being the best English language editor one could wish for.

Finally, the success of a research endeavour is inevitably and intrinsically tied with one's own direct personal sphere. The quality of my work would be much lower if I were not married to Ilze, who is a true antidote to my own complacency and constantly raises the standards in everything I do. Our daughter Mara came into our lives early enough to consciously witness me writing this book. Hence, I am dedicating this work to her.

Contents

List of Figures

List of Tables

1
How can governments legitimize their budgets?

Introduction

Giving and taking. Like most entities of a society, governments too are expected to strike a balance between these two actions. Similarly to a business activity, governments are recognized, appreciated, and contested for the quality and quantity of the goods and services they deliver, and for the price they ask for them. Governments produce a variety of goods and services that are needed or widely demanded in societies, including the building and maintenance of crucial infrastructure, the organization and delivery of mass-scale education, the enforcement of legislation, the provision of health services, and the payment of social security schemes. In the long run, governments need to raise sufficient revenues to ensure the financing of their activities. If they don't raise enough revenues, in order to prevent national bankruptcy governments may need to lower the quality and quantity of their goods and services. This, in turn, is likely to trigger public discontent and may even lead to a crisis of legitimacy. The mechanisms by which governments meet citizens' demands are referred to in political science as responsiveness (Powell, 2004), while the preservation of the long-term financial interests of the state is often referred to as responsibility (Bardi et al., 2014; Karremans and Lefkofridi, 2020a; Mair, 2014; Sartori, 1976). This book is about how the balance between responsiveness and responsibility remains a fundamental legitimizing principle in the ever more complex environment in which contemporary governments operate, as is the case for the member states of the European Union (EU).

As can easily be imagined, compared to most entities in societies, a government's 'giving and taking' is constituted by a much larger multitude of actors, interactions, and activities. Governments' actions generally involve large amounts of deliberation, formal procedures, and votes. The evaluation of a government's actions often undergoes highly articulated processes.

Between Voters and Eurocrats. Johannes Karremans, Oxford University Press. © Johannes Karremans (2024).
DOI: 10.1093/oso/9780192886583.003.0001

What goods and services should governments deliver, and how much revenue should they raise to this end? There are no straightforward answers to these questions. In Europe and many other parts of the world, societies have organized themselves to answer these through two main means: democracy on the one hand and a market economy on the other. The latter entails that goods are allocated through mechanisms of demand and supply. Democracy instead involves electoral procedures to decide by whom should governments be constituted and which direction should their actions take. Governments deliver goods and services that are demanded of them through electoral processes but are partially dependent on the functioning of the market economy for the generation of sufficient revenues. The legitimacy of governments thus rests on both their ability to satisfy democratic demands and their ability to cope with a market economy to keep public finances sustainable.

As we shall see below, expectations about the balance between responsiveness and responsibility are an inheritance from the early twentieth century and largely persist today. In the meantime, though, societies and economies have changed. In Europe, the rise of the service sector and the decline of large national industries has brought important changes in the services and goods demanded by national electorates (Gingrich and Häusermann, 2015; Häusermann and Kriesi, 2015; Kitschelt and Rehm, 2015). In parallel, international economic integration has changed the environment in which governments operate, as they need to be accountable to a growing number of public and private institutions that have regulatory competence over important sections of the economy (Genschel and Zangl,. 2014). In the context of the financialization of the economy, governments increasingly draw resources from financial markets to finance their running expenditures, a situation that may create additional long-term pressures for raising sufficient revenues to repay the loans from private investors (Lagna, 2016). In the context of the European Economic and Monetary Union (EMU), the European Commission, the European Central Bank, and national governments are pressured to maintain the confidence of financial markets in member states' public finances in order to preserve the stability of the common currency (De Grauwe, 2016). Under these circumstances, and particularly under the circumstances of European economic integration, the question emerges about the extent to which governments operate to meet the domestic electorates' expectations regarding the delivery of public goods and services, or whether instead they become predominantly focused on the stability of their finances.

This book investigates this question in five eurozone countries, namely Austria, France, Germany, Italy, and Spain. As the eurozone is arguably the world's most internationally economically integrated area and the EU is certainly the most elaborate existing system of supranational governance, this book also engages with questions about the relation between globalization and national democracy. Empirically, the study consists of comparative analyses of how, in their dealings with parliaments, governments legitimize their decisions about national budgets, which comprise the whole of their expenditures and revenues. Drawing on earlier research with this empirical focus (Karremans and Damhuis, 2020; Karremans and Kaltenleithner, 2021), the study first illustrates how comparisons between governments operating before and after the entry into force of the European common currency reveal no major cross-time differences in the extent to which they justify their budgets in terms of meeting domestic demands or meeting institutional responsibilities. The study then focuses on the period ranging approximately from the global financial crisis of 2008 until 2020, the first year of the coronavirus disease (Covid-19) pandemic. During this period, the rules of European economic governance (EEG) were strengthened to ensure governments' compliance with European budgetary targets. In parallel, virtually all EU member states witnessed a growth of populist parties that fiercely campaigned against the EU's economic rules (Hobolt and Tilley, 2016). How did European governments cope with these pressures? Did the European rules induce them to become gradually more preoccupied with public finance stability, or were governments instead more preoccupied with responding to the growing social discontent?

As we shall see, between 2009 and 2013 governments were primarily focused on the sustainability of public finances, and to a considerable extent neglected domestic electoral demands. Nonetheless, the rules of European economic governance do not seem to have structurally impeded governments to deliver according to domestic democratic demands. The main finding of the book is that in all five countries from 2014 onwards there is a progressive increase of the share of budgetary decisions designed to expand domestic goods and services. This progressive increase received a boost in the year of the coronavirus pandemic, when governments went beyond their means to finance domestic health and social services as a response to the pandemic. These findings run counter to the idea that under increasing levels of European economic integration, governments are induced to focus only on financial stability. The results instead suggest that governments operate under certain economic paradigms, intended as the dominant ideas within a policy community about how governments should balance their expenditures and revenues (Baumgartner, 2013; Cavalieri and Karremans, 2022). These paradigms may be all-encompassing during their climax, but they may wither away with time, especially when they lead to policies producing negative socio-economic outcomes. At the same time, the findings also confirm that an excessive imbalance between responsiveness and responsibility indeed leads to a legitimation crisis of the democratic system. In Europe, these challenges have taken the form of populist challenger parties and technocratic forms of governance.

This opening chapter outlines the conceptual foundations of this study, and underscores the relevance of measuring the balance between governments' main legitimizing principles. It then proceeds to illustrate how the balance between responsiveness and responsibility as a legitimizing principle is rooted in tortuous historical processes in which political parties played a key role. The subsequent section illustrates conceptually how imbalances between responsiveness and responsibility may alter the nature of democracy as we know it, leading towards either populist or technocratic forms of rule. The discussion then turns to how in Europe these challenges have become real, increasing the need for analysis and understanding of these developments. After having clarified the operational distinction between responsiveness and responsibility, the chapter ends by illustrating the logic of the case selection and the structure of the book.

Democratic legitimacy and its historical roots

The peculiarity of the goods and services delivered by governments is that they generally serve the entire community and are accompanied by binding legislation. For example, the provision of large-scale education is crucial for the formation of young individuals as active members of civil society. It requires that schools in different parts of the territory follow the same or similar didactic programmes, and that these are consistently attended in large numbers. With the help of law-enforcing institutions, governments provide this and similar services. To fulfil these tasks, they collect and spend resources from and to the community. The procedures through which these activities are made acceptable to the community constitute the edifice of a polity's legitimacy (Bartolini, 2005, pp. 165–166). As anticipated, in most European countries what makes these procedures publicly acceptable is their democratic nature.

Like most social constructions, however, democracies are in a constant flux. The current form of democracy as we know it is the outcome of a dialectic historical process (Keman and Woldendorp, 2020; Sartori, 1976; Schneider et al., 2010). After having served for several centuries as the executive hand of European monarchies, in the nineteenth and early twentieth centuries governments throughout Europe were increasingly expected to be accountable to national parliaments. These chambers were at first representative of the main national business organizations. With the introduction of universal suffrage, however, parliaments became representative of the entire national population. In this process, political parties became the solution to the problem of representing the preferences of a heterogeneous population composed of different 'parts' (Sartori, 1976), which coincided on the one hand with religious dividing lines and on the other with the contrasts between business owners and working-class population (Rokkan, 1977).

As governments were until then mainly organizations that acted on behalf of monarchies, for political parties the simple monitoring of government activities was not enough. In order to meet the expectations of their constituencies, political parties had to enter government and take full charge of public policy. By entering governing institutions, political parties gained the power to be *responsive* to the demands of their constituencies. At the same time, they became *responsible* for running the state apparatus for the whole nation (Sartori, 1976, pp. 18–24). Party government gradually became the legitimate expression of democratic government (Manin, 1997, pp. 195–196), and democracy without political parties became 'unthinkable' (Schattschneider, 1942). Democracy as we know it is still today a system in which political parties stand their candidates for election and organize parliamentary and government activities (Dalton et al., 2011).

Today, the combination of responsiveness and responsibility is not only the essence of the functioning of democracy as we know it but it is also the *raison d'être* of political parties themselves. If they represented without governing, political parties could be replaced with opinion polls, whereas if they governed without representing they could be substituted with technical experts (Sartori, 1976, p. 28). The balance between responsiveness and responsibility is therefore at the heart of the legitimacy of western democracy. This balance guarantees that the interests of the 'part' represented *by* the governing parties will be served only to the extent that it does not undermine the 'whole' *for* which they govern. If this balance were not there, government by the representatives of a 'part' of the population would turn the polity into a tyranny of the majority. Representative government, therefore, is to be understood neither as merely self-government *by* the segment of society represented by the party in office nor as a government by an elite *for* the people. Instead, it is meant to be a complex mix of these two notions in which, through the processes of representation and accountability, government is simultaneously *by*, *for*, and *with* the people.

This complex mix unfolds through a circular process that runs from the citizens to public policy through a chain of responsiveness (Powell, 2004) and back from public policies to the citizens through a chain of accountability (Bühlmann and Kriesi, 2013; Karremans and Lefkofridi, 2020a). Political parties are fully operative at each stage. The process begins with an aggregation and institutionalization of citizens' preferences into coherent sets of policy packages. At elections parties compete and if they are successful they place their candidates in public office. They are in turn expected to ensure that the policies produced by the executive somehow reflect the preferences for which the party was voted in (Bühlmann and Kriesi, 2013, p. 47). In public office, however, the party mandate becomes only one of the criteria for decision-making. When making their decisions, legislators must consider a wide range of factors, for example, constitutional and other types of laws, policy legacies, the feasibility of new policies, and constraints coming from the international sphere (Schmidt, 1996). Legislators and policymakers, therefore, are at the same time partisan and state actors. Responsibility involves a commitment to fulfil the state's obligations, and thus also the recognition and acceptance that sometimes governments' hands are tied (Mair, 2011, p. 11). As the democratic process continues with the chain of accountability, legislators and policymakers are expected to provide information about their decisions and justify them to the parliament and the public. Such justifications can regard their party's mandate, domestic demands, constraints encountered during the policy process, criteria related to the national interest such as national security, the state of the economy, or the state of public finances. As these justifications serve the purpose of asserting the legitimacy of the government's actions, they offer a window into the responsive–responsible dilemma.

In western democracies, public decisions can be evaluated from the perspective of two legitimizing principles. As famously argued by Fritz Scharpf (1975, p. 21), on the one hand there are those processes through which governments receive their democratic inputs and on the other there is the quality of outputs that they produce. Even though this distinction between input and output legitimacy is not an exact synonym for the responsive–responsible dilemma, it runs parallel to the distinction between government *by* and *for* the people. When Scharpf speaks of the democratic preferences that are at the basis of input legitimacy, he conceives the community as what Sartori calls a 'whole'. Political parties' responsiveness is instead about meeting the preferences of a 'part'. Through alternation in government, partisan democracy is expected to be responsive to the entire population. The responsive–responsible dilemma is therefore the way that modern-day representative democracies integrate input and output legitimacy, where the responsive side ensures that the preferences expressed at elections matter in policymaking and the responsible side safeguards the general interest from being jeopardized by partisan interests.

Populist and technocratic challenges

As it is a result of a dialectic historical process, the balance between responsiveness and responsibility is prone to lead to suboptimal outcomes, both in terms of meeting people's short-term demands and in terms of the state's long-term interests (Linde and Peters, 2020; Powell, 2004). A government that is both responsive and responsible is not necessarily the best representative of the people's will or the most efficient administrator of public resources. From the perspectives of both government and representation, these shortcomings have often been acknowledged (Mair, 2008). On the governmental side, the administrative quality of party-affiliated politicians has often been called into question, resulting in a growing sphere of government activities being delegated to independent agencies and sectoral experts (Bovens and Wille, 2017; Majone, 1994). On the representative side, the growing entrenchment of traditional governing parties in the government sphere has turned them into bureaucratic machines that are too complex to adapt to the changing demands of societies (Katz and Mair, 2009). This has in turn triggered the rise of populist challenger parties, claiming a better and more direct representation of people's demands but often presenting unfeasible or under-specified policy programmes (Bickerton and Accetti, 2017; De Vries and Hobolt, 2020). The crises that hovered over Europe between 2008 and 2020 put the legitimacy of representative democracies under even more severe stress, with critiques emphasizing either the role of electoral considerations in preventing effective policy solutions or—on the contrary—the technocratic nature of many key decision-making processes (Karremans and Lefkofridi, 2020a).

In response to the apparent ineffectiveness of party democracy in fulfilling either its representative or its governmental tasks, during the 2010s populism and technocracy increasingly emerged as two alternative visions of governance (Caramani, 2017; Urbinati, 2014). Building on critiques of the representative and governmental qualities of party governments, both visions oppose the compromise between responsive and responsible policy criteria, and give exclusive importance to responsiveness in the case of populism and responsibility in the case of technocracy (Caramani, 2017).

By respectively claiming to know the will of the people and presuming to know what is best for the country, both populists and technocrats have an aversion to the intermediary role played by political parties. At the same time, the two challenges tend to fuel one another, as technocratic rule strengthens the populist appeal for representation of the people's will, while ineffective populist rule may strengthen the appeal of technocratic experts.

Populism and technocracy are the extreme extrapolations of responsive and responsible government respectively. As populism conceives democracy as the direct implementation of the will of the people in policy outputs, populist *parties* are inclined to govern only for the part of the electorate they represent, and to delegitimize the norms and procedures that induce governments to be responsible state administrators. In the technocratic vision of democracy, instead, government action must be entirely embedded in norms, procedures, competences, expertise, and best practices, while the preferences coming from the electorate should not interfere with the policymaking process. Representative democracy, instead, aims to respect both input- and output-oriented principles, with governments being responsive to democratic preferences within the limits prescribed to them by the duties of responsible government. A loss of equilibrium between the two foundational principles would entail a move towards populism in cases where responsibility is excessively undervalued and a move towards technocracy where responsiveness is neglected. Figure 1.1 illustrates this idea.

This responsive–responsible dimension represents the different expectations one may have of democratic governments. The left-hand side of the dimension is dominated by the notion of input legitimacy, where government is conceived as being *by the people*, emphasizing that it must be

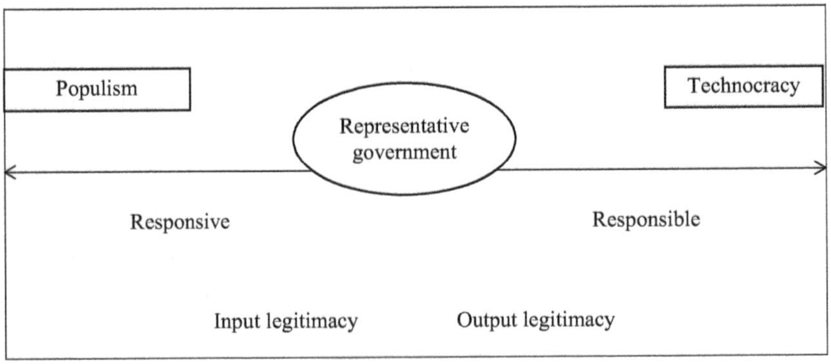

Figure 1.1 The legitimacy of representative government

Source: Author's illustration

responsive to the voters. This is the most *political* side of the dimension, in which government activity is under the spell of the different representative claims of political parties. The more we move to the right of this dimension, the more there is the idea that responsiveness to partisan voters must be counterbalanced with responsibility to the national community, namely the responsibility of producing and delivering collective goods. An appropriate delivery of collective goods requires technical competence and awareness of constraints on achieving certain policy goals. On the right-hand side of the dimension, therefore, stands output legitimacy, in which technical competence gradually replaces political confrontation. A responsible government, therefore, is less political than a responsive government, and the more it emphasizes its output legitimacy the more it moves towards resembling a technocratic government.

Figure 1.1 does not merely present an abstract theoretical construct but it is also illustrative of the challenges faced by European democracies in recent years. To give a few examples, in 2011 the ineffectiveness of the Italian centre-right government in handling the country's economic and financial problems induced the head of state, Giorgio Napolitano, to replace it with a government of technical experts led by Mario Monti (Culpepper, 2014). Similarly, during the years of the eurozone crisis, the technical expertise of supranational actors such as the European Commission and the International Monetary Fund (IMF) constituted a significant challenge to the output legitimacy of various European national governments. In parallel, populist parties across Europe continue to directly challenge the input legitimacy of traditional governing parties, accusing them of being overly concerned with European requirements regarding public finance and economic growth, and too little with the demands of the people. The critique that these parties generally receive in turn in public debates is that they lack the competence to govern (see for example Heinisch, 2003).

Despite the democratic shortcomings of populist and technocratic rule, among citizens there seems to be a growing appreciation of the two alternative forms of governance. On the one hand, between 2000 and 2020 populist parties have gained a more prominent position in European party systems, while the traditional European party families—the Christian democrats, social democrats, and liberals—have increasingly lost ground (De Vries and Hobolt, 2020). At the same time, among citizens there is a high demand for technocratic expertise for solving collective action problems (Bertsou and Caramani, 2020). These developments pose serious questions about whether, how, to what extent, and how long democracy as we know it will remain the main form of governance of advanced industrial countries.

Are we losing the balance?

Recent research has found evidence of how responsiveness generates a 'reservoir of goodwill' that makes citizens more willing to entrust governments with the authority to make unpopular decisions in economic hard times (Linde and Peters, 2020). In established democracies, citizens tend to recognize that the collective interest may not always align with their preferences and entrust the government with serving this interest if they perceive it will again serve their preferences when circumstances are more favourable. When governments pursue unpopular policies over a prolonged period of time, however, citizens are likely to lose trust in the governing parties. Taking the populist and technocratic challenges into account, the question at stake is whether a structural process is occurring that affects governments' autonomy to decide about the production and delivery of goods and services, and that creates new necessities for technical competence in the design of public policies.

In relation to this question, a lot of scholarly attention has been devoted to the homogeneity of policy responses among European governments to the global financial crisis of 2008 and the subsequent sovereign debt crisis (Pontusson and Raess, 2012; Schäfer and Streeck, 2013). After first bailing out their national banks, governments pursued policies of fiscal consolidation largely in line with the austerity prescriptions of international or supranational institutions like the International Monetary Fund and the European Union. The electoral losses of mainstream parties and the successes of populist challenger parties in Europe during the 2010s can be seen as a result of successive years of unpopular austerity measures justified as being in the collective interest (Alonso and Ruiz-Rufino, 2020; Bojar et al., 2021; Karremans and Lefkofridi, 2020a). What needs to be assessed, however, is whether the lengthy austerity of the 2010s was a contingency of the aftermath of the global financial crisis, or whether instead it was part of a structural process in which governments are increasingly induced to design their policies as functions of the global post-industrial economy, regardless of domestic electoral demands (Scharpf, 2015).

Populist and technocratic critiques of party democracy intensified after the global financial crisis of 2008, but they have their sociological roots in the shift from a national industrial to a globalized post-industrial economy that started in the 1980s (Dalton, 2018; Kriesi, 2014). This economic change brought substantial alterations to the societal divisions that political parties represented during the post-war period and to the rules on how governments could redistribute socio-economic resources at the domestic level. Post-industrialization and globalization created new sets of winners and losers, with the winners being those with the ability to take advantage of the economic changes and the so-called losers being those for whom the decline of the industrial economy entailed losses in socio-economic status (Kriesi et al., 2008). This new division cut across the traditional electoral blocs (Häusermann and Kriesi, 2015; Kitschelt, 1994). As a consequence, the modes of representation changed, with mainstream political parties shifting from representing distinct material societal interests to representing different views on how to best run government (Saward, 2008). In the logic of the populist critique of party democracy, these developments are interpretable as a disappearance of representative commitments from government action: the political elite is only interested in securing a place in governing institutions and has moved away from the interests and demands of 'real' people. In the technocratic critique, instead, these developments can be seen as a persistence of dysfunctional electoral pressures that prevent the pursuit of efficient policies: at the end of the day politicians still need to win elections, and to do so they may make unfeasible promises for which they will be held accountable.

The governance innovations introduced in the eurozone during recent decades are in many ways an effort to reduce the unpredictability that elections may bring to governments' actions. More broadly, they represent an intensification of a global pattern of increasing numbers of supranational institutions to which governments are expected to be accountable (Genschel and Zangl, 2014). In this context, the technical expertise demanded from governments is certainly more articulated and possibly more influential. It is possibly not unrelated that, over time, the career profiles of prime ministers in Europe have become increasingly technical and less political, in that their curricula are built less and less on the basis of experience in leadership positions in political parties, and more and more on the basis of experience in international organizations, state bureaucracies, and private enterprises (Müller-Rommel et al., 2022). In documenting the career profiles of political leaders, some scholars even go as far as characterizing European democracies as 'diploma democracies', as leadership positions in governments are increasingly occupied by university graduates (Bovens and Wille, 2017). The electoral growth of populist parties needs also to be seen as a counter-reaction to this trend (Kriesi, 2014).

The growing weight of technical expertise as a criterion for policymaking can act as a constraint on democratic responsiveness, particularly when such expertise is about the management of public finances. Despite the changing contents of political competition, and the cultural differences between the 'winners' and 'losers' of globalization (Kriesi et al., 2012), redistributive issues are the main theme structuring election campaigns. Political parties still largely distinguish themselves and win votes on the basis of their advocacy for either redistribution through social transfers or for private economic action through tax reductions (Hutter and Kriesi, 2019). The competition between welfare- and liberal-oriented political programmes entails that governing parties, depending on which side of the political spectrum they belong to, are expected by voters to serve either social- or private-ownership-oriented goals. Depending on how policies are designed, the pursuit of these goals may turn out to be burdensome on public finances, either in the form of excessive expenditure or of insufficient revenue. The achievement of political goals often requires policies that may temporarily overburden public finances. Under the conditions of European economic integration, however, governments are confronted with more and more rules that are designed to prevent imbalances in public accounts (Rodrik, 2011; Schäfer and Streeck, 2013; Scharpf, 2015).

EU and eurozone membership involves strict fiscal rules which were introduced with the Treaty of Maastricht in 1993 and further strengthened and formalized through a series of pacts between 2009 and 2013 (Laffan, 2014; Verdun, 2015). The formalization of the European Semester in 2010 and the strengthening of the Stability and Growth Pact between 2011 and 2012 brought substantial constraints on the ways in which governments make decisions on their spending policies. With these reforms the European Commission gained tighter control over national budgetary decision-making processes and the formal power to sanction governments that fail to comply with European budgetary agreements. As a result of these reforms, between 2009 and 2013 most EU member states introduced a series of fiscal stringency rules in their national legislation to make sure that the governments' budgetary policies were in line with European criteria (Doray-Demers and Foucault, 2017). The aim of these reforms was to ensure that EU member states would not spend beyond their means, not least to send signals to financial markets about the credibility of European public finances. If financial markets doubt such credibility, in fact, this may have negative effects on the country's sovereign bond rates. In a common currency area, divergence in sovereign bond rates can trigger capital flight from more risky to more secure countries (De Grauwe, 2016). Managing public finances in the eurozone thus involves coping with European rules and the pressures of financial markets, and consequently requires a considerable amount of financial expertise.

The recent experience of the coronavirus crisis, however, shows that EU agreements are not always and only about financial stability, but may also be about socio-economic recovery. The Next Generation EU, more commonly known as Recovery Fund, was agreed upon by EU member states and the Commission in the summer of 2020 and involves €750 billion of European funds to be invested in national economies. The conditions attached to the funds, however, are that these must be productive investments and, as a result, ensure future economic returns. Under this generous programme, questions therefore persist about governments' autonomy in making decisions relating to the domestic delivery of goods and services (D'Erman and Verdun, 2022). These questions need to be answered by measuring the balance between the main legitimizing principles that guide governments' action.

Finding responsiveness and responsibility

While the distinction between responsiveness and responsibility may appear clear at the conceptual level, empirically it leaves space for several ambiguities, to the extent that even the empirical manifestations of populism and technocracy may to some extent coincide (Bickerton and Accetti, 2018). Acting in function of the state's interests may in many cases coincide with being responsive to citizens' demands. In the context of a country's economics, the state's finances are more easily sustainable when there is economic growth. Enhanced economic activity, in turn, brings more wealth for those directly participating in it and creates more resources for the government to redistribute. Actions targeted at improving the country's economic performance can therefore be legitimized both in terms of responsiveness as well as of responsibility. Scholarly efforts to move down from the general concepts of responsiveness and responsibility to empirical reality often stumble on this realization,[1] raising doubts about the usefulness of the conceptual distinction (Enroth, 2017).

The challenge of the operational distinction, however, should not obscure the importance and relevance of the two concepts, nor their pertinence to empirical reality. The two concepts capture two clearly different logics for government action. The fact that in practical terms the two logics may coincide to some extent needs also be seen as a virtuous outcome of several decades in which political parties have been *combining* responsiveness and responsibility. As argued above, this combination is at the heart of their *raison*

[1] This sentence is inspired by Giovanni Sartori's seminal article, 'Concept Misformation in Comparative Politics' (Sartori, 1970).

d'être and of the legitimacy of democracy as we know it. In empirical reality, therefore, responsiveness and responsibility are meant to be blended. Their distinction is an academic exercise aimed at better understanding the values driving societies and governments. Understanding such values is one of the key tasks of social and political sciences (Flyvbjerg, 2001).

At the level of governments and public policy, the distinction between responsiveness and responsibility is particularly difficult to grasp. When it comes to political parties and their representation, the distinction can, to some extent, be captured by coding whether—in their manifestos and media appearances—political parties stress their capabilities as prospective governors more than their sincerity concerning distinct material or ideal values. The coding strategy would thus resemble that adopted for capturing different modes of representation (Saward, 2008, 2006). When it comes to public policy, however, understanding whether this is embedded more in responsive or responsible criteria is much more problematic, certainly in the socio-economic sphere.

Spending and tax policies can easily generate confusion for the characterization of a government's action as either responsive or responsible. Such policies may have the simultaneous aim of both giving resources to domestic socio-economic groups and of triggering the growth necessary for future fiscal returns. A tax reduction for companies may be responsive to centre-right political preferences, but may at the same time also be seen as an effort to enhance economic activity and therefore overall fiscal returns. Similarly, spending in active labour market policies may be responsive to certain social needs, but its overall employment effect may improve the overall sustainability of the welfare state (Hemerijck, 2012). By the same token, tax increases and expenditure cuts may serve the purpose of finding enough resources for meeting certain societal demands. As will be argued more elaborately in Chapter 2, clearly policy outputs do not offer a sufficiently complete picture to capture the criteria by which governments operate. As is also recognized by scholars measuring the magnitude of policy change in public budgets (see, for instance, Baumgartner, 2013), spending outputs do not offer insights into the political dynamics behind policy change.

To overcome these difficulties, the required approach is one that takes strength from studies on political representation and which at the same time captures the actual policies that governments produce (Karremans, 2021a; Karremans and Lefkofridi, 2020a). For this reason, the study presented here focuses on the arguments by which governments justify their actions. This approach is rooted in the insight that '[a]ny legitimate authority—even if coercive, institutional, or structural—requires legitimation' and 'this demands a different kind of power: the power of ideas and discourse' (Schmidt, 2020a, p. 17). The discourse by which policymakers legitimize their decisions contains crucial information about the shared understanding between rulers and ruled about what the ruler should do. In the context of the current populist and technocratic challenges to democracy, analysing governments' legitimation discourse can offer a glimpse into the extent to which this shared understanding moves towards responsiveness or towards responsibility. In turn the advantage of studying legitimation discourse in established democracies is that politicians are expected to speak in conformity with their actions and that therefore discourse that is produced in the institutional context can be a valuable proxy of governments' policy intentions (Veen, 2011, p. 31).

As democratic governments need to provide explanations of how their policies are in line with either their party mandate or their 'legitimate constraints' (Powell, 2004), the justifications that governments provide in the institutional context to fellow policymakers and legislators are a valuable proxy for the criteria that were followed in pursuit of their policies. The sphere of budgetary policy offers an ideal setting for studying this type of discourse, as every year governments are expected to explain to parliament their yearly budgetary measures. As will be described in more detail in Chapter 2, these speeches allow for a measurement of responsiveness and responsibility that takes into account both the types of policies proposed each year by the government and the arguments with which they are supported.

As they inevitably involve choices about how burdens and benefits are distributed among the national population, government budgets are highly political and their annual presentation is a recurrence in which the internal contradictions of democratic governance regularly clash. In countries with a market economy, budgetary choices generally involve either expansion or retrenchment of the public sector, with the former being generally more associated with egalitarian ideals and the latter with more meritocratic and entrepreneurial ideals (Beramendi et al., 2015; Kitschelt et al., 1999; Kriesi et al., 2012). Both political choices involve giving resources to domestic socio-economic groups, either in the form of expenditure increases or tax reductions. Therefore, they may potentially lead to imbalances in the public accounts, namely a situation in which expenditure is not backed by sufficient revenue. Under the budgetary rules of European economic governance framework, governments have an institutional commitment to reduce this risk as much as possible (Laffan, 2014). The justifications for the annual budget thus provide insights into the shared understanding between the government, the parliament, and public, regarding whether socio-economic policies are more about responding to demands expressed during election campaigns or responsibly following existing budgetary rules.

In this book, the operationalization of responsiveness and responsibility is designed to measure the weight these intentions and commitments have in governments' annual budgets. The dividing line between the two central concepts is represented as an effort to either give resources to domestic socio-economic groups or to improve the state's financial situation. The inevitable ambiguities between the two concepts are solved using this benchmark. For instance, to the extent that it is true that parts of European electorates may favour a fiscal consolidation policy (see for example Bansak et al., 2021), this study presumes that such preference is based on a promise of (future) compensating benefits, such as tax reductions. When justifications for fiscal consolidation focus on the state's public finances they are then categorized as responsible. When they focus on, for example, how the policy generates lower tax levels for citizens it is categorized as responsive. The relative frequencies of the different types of policy justifications in the annual budget presentations offer a proxy of the extent to which responsiveness or responsibility matter more in the shaping of a government's overall socio-economic policy.

Besides enabling consistent choices about the categorization of ambiguous manifestations of responsiveness and responsibility, the focus on policy justifications also allows the identification of unequivocal cases of commitment towards either 'giving' to domestic socio-economic groups or towards 'taking' in the state's financial interests. When increases in social spending are justified as meeting certain social demands, these are coded as unequivocal instances of responsiveness. When fiscal consolidation policies are justified with arguments about the need to reduce public deficit levels, these are unequivocal manifestations of responsibility. As will be described in Chapter 2 and shown throughout the book, the focus on policy justifications helps to capture these nuances and therefore to provide informative assessments about the extent to which different governments are comparatively more or less responsive or responsible.

Five eurozone countries in a tumultuous decade

The distinction between responsiveness and responsibility acquired a substantial amount of both academic and public attention in the years between 2008 and 2016, years that comprised the global financial crisis, the European sovereign debt crisis, technocratic governments in Greece and Italy, success of populist parties across Europe, and the British Brexit referendum (e.g. Telegraph, 2014). These events were critical moments that highlighted the tensions between institutional and electoral commitments (Mair, 2013). In economic terms, these tensions were relatively more acute in southern European countries (Matthijs, 2017), whereas northern European countries such as Austria, Germany, and the Netherlands witnessed a 'hardening' of their export-led growth models (Baccaro and Benassi, 2014; Regan, 2017). As will be emphasized in several chapters of this book, the tension between responsiveness and responsibility observed in these years is difficult to disentangle from the crisis-ridden context, making it difficult to make inferences about whether such tension is caused by long-term structural processes. The study presented here tries to overcome this challenge through several comparative 'tricks'. The first one resides in the logic of case selection.

The five countries selected for this study capture two different groups of member states in which European economic governance seems to be having different socio-economic consequences (Johnston and Regan, 2018; Matthijs, 2017). After 2008, in France, Italy, and Spain public debt rose sharply, towards or even far beyond 100 per cent of national gross domestic product (GDP) (Figure 1.2). In Germany and Austria instead, as well as in other northern European countries like the Netherlands, (Hemerijck et al., 2022a) public debt rose only marginally between 2008 and 2010, and declined visibly between 2014 and 2019. This divergence has been attributed by several scholars to the compatibility between European budgetary rules and national economies (Matthijs, 2017; Regan, 2017). By capturing both sets of countries, the case selection allows to explore whether the rules of European economic governance have a structural effect on responsiveness and responsibility in all democracies, or only in certain economic contexts.

At the same time, these countries did not undergo the most dramatic consequences of the sovereign debt crisis. While countries such as Cyprus, Greece, Ireland, and Portugal were drawn into a bailout programme that forced them for several years to design their budgets according to the prescriptions of the EU and IMF Memorandum of Understanding (MoU), all countries of the case selection remained relatively sovereign over their public finances. The most critical cases in this regard were Spain and Italy. In the aftermath of the global financial crisis, the Spanish government had to spend a substantial amount of its budgets on bank bailouts, which made public debt rise from around 40 per cent of national GDP in 2008 to 90 per cent in 2012 (Figure 1.2). To finance the recapitalization of its banks, in 2012 Spain was allocated a €100 billion grant by the EU, which brought it under strict

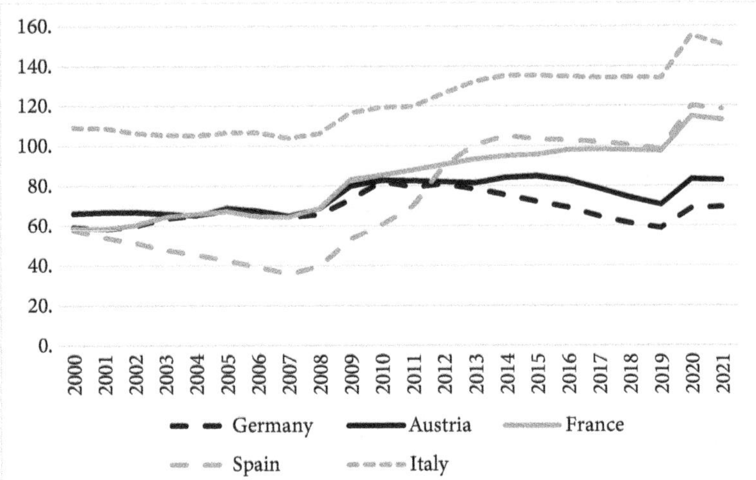

Figure 1.2 Public debt in Austria, France, Germany, Italy, and Spain, measured as a percentage of GDP
Source: Eurostat data

surveillance as regards its efforts to reduce public debt. In Italy, as anticipated, in November 2011 the technocratic Monti government was appointed by President Giorgio Napolitano, with the mandate to introduce measures that would avoid the critical situation in which the country would have to apply for a bailout from the EU and the IMF. Nonetheless, Italy and Spain survived the sovereign debt crisis under relatively less severe circumstances than in Cyprus or Greece. The overall case selection therefore seeks to avoid extreme circumstances of crisis and capture the links between deepening European integration and national democracy.

Structure of the book

The analysis presented in this book is a novel contribution to an old debate about the relationship between international economic integration and national democracy. The novelty is constituted largely by the empirical focus on the justifications that governments provide for the policies contained in their annual budgets which, unlike previous research focusing on either policy outputs or the contents of political competition, allows making comparative assessments of the criteria by which governments pursue different types of policies. The book thus first describes the added value of this particular empirical focus, and then gradually explores the empirical insights generated by this research on how international economic integration affects national democracy.

Chapter 2 first discusses why the analysis of governments' justifications for their annual budgets can be fruitful for answering questions about responsiveness and responsibility. The chapter argues that while talk may be 'cheap' in many cases, it can have high policy relevance in others. Especially in institutional settings, policymakers are expected to speak in conformity with their actions. This is particularly true in the case of governments' annual presentations of their budgets, because these are an institutional recurrence that forces them to explain the rationale and objectives of their budgetary policies to an audience that—besides the majority and the opposition—also includes international stakeholders and local constituencies. The chapter proceeds by illustrating how these texts can be coded and transformed into indicators for responsiveness and responsibility. The coding of these texts consists in a two-step procedure in which first a policy proposal is identified and codified and then the justifications for the policy are gathered and categorized according to their theme of reference. While the broad distinction between responsiveness and responsibility largely follows a deductive reasoning, the chapter describes how the same distinction was achieved through inductive data collection. In sum, this chapter describes how fifty-eight annual budget presentations were coded into a dataset that constitutes the basis for the analysis presented in Chapters 4 to 7.

Before diving into the analysis of the 2007–2020 period, Chapter 3 deals with the question whether the intensification of international economic integration that occurred between the 1980s and 2010s brought major changes to the balance of criteria in governments' decision-making. After discussing several macro-economic indicators, the chapter reports descriptive inferences derived from my earlier research on cross-time comparisons between governments facing challenging economic circumstances. It shows how the cross-time comparisons of annual budget plans of governments during the 2010s with those of governments in preceding decades provides ambivalent evidence about globalization reducing responsiveness (Damhuis and Karremans, 2017; Karremans and Damhuis, 2020; Karremans and Kaltenleithner, 2021). On the one hand, there is some evidence for financial commitments playing a greater role in shaping governments' criteria; on the other there is no strong evidence for a substantial decline in responsiveness. This chapter thus sets the scene for further exploring the question of how international economic integration affects national democracy, and thus for testing several theoretical propositions about the consequences of a strengthened European economic governance for the balance between responsiveness and responsibility.

Chapter 4 dives directly into this question and the testing of the related theoretical propositions. Building on the discussion in Chapter 3, it hypothesizes one scenario in which the balance between responsiveness and responsibility was only altered by the context of the crisis, and one in which the strengthening of European budgetary thresholds had a lasting effect throughout the subsequent decade. A statistical analysis of the policy justifications collected in the five eurozone countries between 2007 and 2019 finds substantive evidence of the former scenario, as responsibility was the dominant criterion during the years of the sovereign debt crisis, and responsiveness instead became gradually more and more dominant in subsequent years. The chapter also introduces findings from the coding of budget speeches delivered after the outbreak of the coronavirus pandemic and shows a continuation of a trend that started in 2014 in which governments progressively became more committed to delivering resources to domestic socio-economic groups rather than reducing public deficits.

Chapter 5 explores the extent to which the sharp variations in the balance between responsiveness and responsibility documented in Chapter 4 can be considered as deviations towards technocratic and populist forms of rule. The analysis is based on the Italian case which, between 2008 and 2019, experienced an alternation between populist, technocratic and mainstream coalition governments and therefore allows testing the empirical implications of the theoretical dimension sketched in Figure 1.1. The analysis finds evidence that, all things being equal, technocratic governments tend to be substantially more responsible and populist governments substantially more responsive than coalition governments featuring mainstream parties. At the same time, the chapter also provides qualitative evidence of how the accountability mechanisms of the parliamentary system induce technocratic governments to focus part of their attention on how their action delivers resources to socio-economic groups, and populist governments to ensure that their policy course does not lead the country out of the prescribed budgetary parameters. Over time, in terms of the balance between responsiveness and responsibility, Italy featured similar patterns to the other cases studied. The chapter thus argues that mature democracies have an inbuilt resilience to technocratic and populist challenges which is based on the accountability mechanisms that force governments to report on their actions to a variegated audience of stakeholders.

After having shown that from 2014 onwards responsiveness increased in all the selected cases, Chapter 6 dives into the qualitative contents of these increases, investigating whether the higher shares of responsive policy justifications also reflect the redistributive preferences advocated by the governing parties. The chapter shows how the contents of the responsive policy justifications are, to a large extent, in line with the redistributive preferences advocated during election campaigns, but at the same time are also partially shaped by the policy legacies of previous governments. In any case, it confirms that the strengthening of European budgetary rules did not prevent governments pursuing policies according to distinct political preferences.

Chapter 7, in turn, shows how notions of responsibility have changed over time and how this impacts on the extent to which governments can or cannot pursue fiscal stimulus policies. The chapter argues that the dominant notions of responsibility are contingent on the consensus reigning at European level and that even though governments have substantial influence in shaping this consensus they do not have control over which notion of responsibility they are expected to comply with.

The book ends by highlighting that despite their political, institutional, and economic diversity, the five countries feature an almost identical trend in the annual budget plans, namely that of a dominance of fiscal responsibility between 2009 and 2013 and a gradual increase of responsiveness afterwards. Chapter 8 reflects on the evidence gathered in this book regarding mechanisms that explain this common trend, and sets out a future research agenda for a fuller understanding on the determinants of the balance between responsiveness and responsibility in systems of supranational governance.

2

The coding of annual budget plans

Introduction

Most of the time, talk is cheap, particularly from a policymaking perspective. Politicians give speeches continuously, in the media and at public events. In many of these speeches, they seek to legitimize their positions from a variety of angles. Neoliberal politicians may appear at a trade union event and make statements about how their policies are best fit to serve the interests of workers. Socialist politicians, for their part, can give interviews to the *Financial Times* about how they are committed to preserve the competitive advantage of their country's most important firms. The extent to which these words matter is obviously questionable, and most of the time they remain unrelated to what happens in the world of public policy.

Sometimes, however, talk can matter a great deal. On 26 July 2012 the then president of the European Central Bank (ECB) Mario Draghi, was one of the most eagerly awaited speakers at a conference hosted by the British Prime Minister David Cameron in London. At the time, the whole world was anxious to know what the ECB was going to do to tackle the sovereign debt crisis and therefore to save the common currency. It was on that occasion that, Mario Draghi pronounced the famous phrase that the ECB was ready to do 'whatever it takes'. These words changed the course of the sovereign debt crisis that was plaguing Europe since 2009, as they expressed the commitment of Europe's most powerful central bank to actively support governments against financial speculation (Randow and Speciale, 2018). A similar, yet different, incident took place in March 2020, a few weeks after the outbreak of the coronavirus pandemic, with the new president of the ECB, Christine Lagarde, who stated that the growing spreads between the yields of German and other European bonds could only be reversed through national governments' fiscal policies. This immediately created financial turbulence, as capital markets took this as a signal that the ECB would not support the economic recovery of member states facing the consequences of the pandemic. The ECB had to quickly correct this statement, and consequently commit

Between Voters and Eurocrats. Johannes Karremans, Oxford University Press. © Johannes Karremans (2024).
DOI: 10.1093/oso/9780192886583.003.0002

itself to the purchase of sovereign bonds, continuing de facto the policy initiated by Mario Draghi. The statement announcing this correction quickly calmed down the markets and kept the spread between German and Italian bonds temporarily in check.

Sometimes the whole world seems to hang on the lips of key decision makers. Even if sometimes talk may be 'cheap', it is one of the key elements that make public policy and democracy work. Public policymaking involves communication between different actors. Especially in established democracies, policymakers are required to be accountable to a variety of actors, including various overseers, different types of stakeholders and the public at large. Discourse can be considered as the glue that keeps together the various actors involved in—and affected by—the policymaking process. To some extent, discourse may at times also reflect the characteristics of a polity (Schmidt, 2010), tending for example to be more conflictual in majoritarian democracies and more consensus-seeking in proportional parliamentary systems (Karremans, 2017). At moments when the audience includes watchdogs and stakeholders *and* in which key public policy decisions are discussed, the analysis of decision makers' discourse can be highly revealing about the criteria driving the decision-making process. On such occasions, policymakers cannot escape explaining their actual actions (Veen, 2011, p. 31).

In national socio-economic policymaking, this takes place on an annual basis. Every year the finance minister is expected to appear in front of parliament to illustrate the government's expenditure and taxation policies, and to provide an explanation of the government's actions. On these occasions, the minister's discourse is not only followed by all parties in the parliament, but in the context of European economic governance, it is also closely followed by European institutions (see for example Mérand, 2021). Furthermore, as the policies presented have direct fiscal implications, through media coverage the discourse also reaches the attention of financial markets, businesses, local constituencies, and the public at large. Budgetary debates represent a point of central importance in national political disputes (Maatsch, 2017, p. 693).

Given this context, when presenting the annual budget, finance ministers are pressured to both prove their technical competences *and* to make political statements in order to win the votes of a parliamentary majority and maintain the support of large sections of the electorate. Their discourse in these contexts is indicative of which set of criteria they tend to favour in order to legitimize their actions. Annual budget plans and their presentation are therefore valuable proxies for grasping how governments interpret their double role as electoral representatives and responsible state administrators.

In order to make inferences about whether and how decision-making criteria vary from one government to the other, or from one year to the next, it necessary to apply a method for analysis that is replicable in a consistent way across time and countries. This chapter illustrates a method that not only zooms into the parts of the discourse in which the finance minister justifies the government's policies, but also transforms these policy justifications into countable units, on the basis of which it is subsequently possible to perform statistical analyses.

Selecting comparable and relevant texts

In order to be comparable across different states and situation, the texts selected for analysis need to have the same communicational purpose, a similar level of institutional formality, and cover the same subject (Schmidt, 2008). For public policy discourses, this entails first identifying communications produced at a particular stage of the chain of democratic accountability, featuring therefore a specific communicational purpose and institutional format (Bühlmann and Kriesi, 2013; Karremans and Lefkofridi, 2020a). Second, it entails identifying a subject of communication that is not country- or time-specific, but that is a universal subject of debate in democratic societies.

In addition to being an event that captures the attention of many audiences, the presentation of an annual budgets is a perfectly suitable text for comparative research. In parliamentary democracies, the presentation of the government's budget is a key moment in which the balance of power between governments and parliaments is exercised. The former have executive power over the budget, but need to secure a reliable majority in the parliament in order to effectively continue their action. Through their vote, members of parliament can express their formal approval or disapproval of the government's budget and therefore, as a collective, they have the power to secure continuation or to put an end to the government's socio-economic policy. In terms of their place in the democratic accountability chain, the presentation of annual budget plans belongs to that stage in which the government provides information to the parliament—and by extension to the voters—about its actions.

As regards the content of communication, the budget captures the variety of actions a government undertakes in the socio-economic sphere, ranging from taxation to capital gains in financial markets, to the payment of family benefits. The budget comprises the sum of public revenues and expenditures, and therefore has a central role in a government's socio-economic policy.

Even though it may not be directly about the more regulatory aspects of socio-economic policy, such as labour market regulation or wage-setting, when presenting the budget the government is induced to explain how its spending and taxation policies relate to such regulatory measures. For example, the government may need to explain how certain market regulations generate additional state revenues and improve the fiscal balance. The regulatory aspects of socio-economic policymaking generally involve measures directly or indirectly affecting tax and expenditure rates or levels. For example, labour market regulations may involve changes in the taxes paid by employers and employees, or changes in the retirement age may have substantial implications for pension expenditures in the medium term. Presentation of the annual budget is therefore a moment when the government is expected to clarify its choices regarding the country's economy, social policy, and the balance of its finances (Schiavo-Campo, 2017).

Being a key instance of executive–legislative relations, the annual presentation of the government's budget is something that occurs in every advanced democracy. In the United Kingdom, for instance, each year in spring there is 'budget day', in which the Chancellor of the Exchequer appears in front of parliament to present the expenditure and taxation policies for the upcoming fiscal year, which ends on 5 April each year. In most Continental European countries, instead, the fiscal year runs from January to December. The presentation of the annual budget therefore generally takes place in autumn. In the context of the European Semester, there is an increasing harmonization of the annual budgetary process, as member states have specific deadlines for sending their plans to the Commission, receiving recommendations and having the budget approved by the parliament (Verdun and Zeitlin, 2018). Being such a similar annual recurrence across countries, presentations of annual budgets lend themselves very well for comparative analyses.

In France, Germany, and Spain, the presentation of annual budgetary plans follows largely the same format, with the finance minister appearing in front of the parliament between August and October, in order to give a speech that marks the beginning of a week of parliamentary debates about the government's plans for the upcoming fiscal year (Karremans, 2021a). In Austria, the procedure is also very similar, even though sometimes the finance minister presents a double budget, stating a plan for the upcoming two fiscal years. On such occasions, the speech may take place in spring rather than autumn (Karremans and Kaltenleithner, 2021). In other eurozone countries like Italy or the Netherlands, the annual procedure for budget approval follows a similar temporal scheme as in Germany, France, and Spain, but the finance minister generally only appears in parliament to answer questions, and does not always provide a structured speech. In these cases, the best comparable text is the written document provided by the government to parliament to illustrate the budgetary plan. Most importantly the text must be representative and illustrative of the government's overall budgetary policy, and be central in the communication exchanges between government and parliament on this issue.

Table 2.1 lists the speeches and documents that were analysed for the purpose of the present study. The selection seeks to capture the annual budget plans for three consecutive legislatures in Austria, France, Germany, Italy, and Spain, and therefore to cover the roughly twelve-year period that runs from the global financial crisis of 2008 to the coronavirus pandemic of 2020. For Austria, the legislatures covered are five because of the short-lived legislatures of the Kern government in 2016–2017 and the first Kurz government in 2018–2019. For Spain, the analysis ends in 2018, because between the elections of that year and 2020 no structured budget speeches were held in autumn. In Germany, the analysis starts from the second Merkel

Table 2.1 List of texts analysed

	Text type	Dates	Budget years	Governments / Presidencies	Finance ministers
Austria	Finance minister's speech in Nationalrat	21-04-2009	2009	Faymann I	Josef Pröll
			2010	Faymann I	
		30-11-2010	2011	Faymann I	Josef Pröll
		19-10-2011	2012	Faymann I	Maria Fekter
		16-10-2012	2013	Faymann I	Maria Fekter
		29-04-2014	2014	Faymann II	Michael Spindelegger
			2015	Faymann II	Hans Jörg Schelling
		14-10-2015	2016	Faymann II	Hans Jörg Schelling
		12-10-2016	2017	Kern	Hartwig Löger
		21-03-2018	2018	Kurz I	
			2019		Gernot Blümel
		14-04-2020	2020	Kurz II	
France	Finance minister's speech in Assemblée Générale	16-10-2007	2008	Sarkozy	Éric Woerth
		20-10-2008	2009	Sarkozy	Éric Woerth
		20-10-2009	2010	Sarkozy	Éric Woerth
		18-10-2010	2011	Sarkozy	François Baroin
		18-10-2011	2012	Sarkozy	Valérie Pécresse
		16-10-2012	2013	Hollande	Pierre Moscovici

	Text type	Dates	Budget years	Governments / Presidencies	Finance ministers
		15-10-2013	2014	Hollande	Pierre Moscovici
		14-10-2014	2015	Hollande	Michel Sapin
		13-10-2015	2016	Hollande	Michel Sapin
		18-10-2016	2017	Hollande	Michel Sapin
		17-10-2017	2018	Macron	Bruno Le Maire
		15-10-2018	2019	Macron	Bruno Le Maire
		14-10-2019	2020	Macron	Bruno Le Maire
		12-10-2020	2021	Macron	Bruno Le Maire
Germany	Finance minister's speech in Bundestag	19-01-2010	2010	Merkel II	Wolfgang Schäuble
		14-09-2010	2011	Merkel II	Wolfgang Schäuble
		06-09-2011	2012	Merkel II	Wolfgang Schäuble
		11-09-2012	2013	Merkel II	Wolfgang Schäuble
		30-01-2014	2014	Merkel III	Wolfgang Schäuble
		09-09-2014	2015	Merkel III	Wolfgang Schäuble
		08-09-2015	2016	Merkel III	Wolfgang Schäuble
		06-09-2016	2017	Merkel III	Wolfgang Schäuble
		15-05-2018	2018	Merkel IV	Olaf Scholz
		11-09-2018	2019	Merkel IV	Olaf Scholz
		11-09-2019	2020	Merkel IV	Olaf Scholz
		20-09-2020	2021	Merkel IV	Olaf Scholz
Italy	Documento di Economia e Finanza, signed by finance minister and prime minister	18-06-2008	2008	Berlusconi IV	Giulio Tremonti
		15-07-2009	2009	Berlusconi IV	Giulio Tremonti
		29-09-2010	2010	Berlusconi IV	Giulio Tremonti
		13-04-2011	2011	Berlusconi IV	Giulio Tremonti
		18-04-2012	2012	Monti	Mario Monti
		10-04-2013	2013	Monti	Mario Monti
		08-04-2014	2014	Renzi	Pier Carlo Padoan
		10-04-2015	2015	Renzi	Pier Carlo Padoan
		08-04-2016	2016	Renzi	Pier Carlo Padoan
		11-04-2017	2017	Gentiloni	Pier Carlo Padoan
		26-04-2018	2018	Gentiloni	Pier Carlo Padoan
		09-04-2019	2019	Conte I	Giovanni Tria
		24-04-2020	2020	Conte II	Roberto Gualtieri
Spain	Finance minister's speech in the Congreso	21-10-2008	2009	Zapatero II	Solbes Mira
		20-10-2009	2010	Zapatero II	Salgado Méndez
		19-10-2010	2011	Zapatero II	Salgado Méndez
		24-04-2012	2012	Rajoy I	Montoro Romero
		23-10-2012	2013	Rajoy I	Montoro Romero
		22-10-2013	2014	Rajoy I	Montoro Romero
		14-10-2014	2015	Rajoy I	Montoro Romero
		25-08-2015	2016	Rajoy I	Montoro Romero
		03-05-2017	2017	Rajoy II	Montoro Romero
		25-04-2018	2018	Rajoy II	Montoro Romero

government (2009–2013) which featured its first budget speech in January 2010. As German elections take place in September, the first budget speech of a new government is always postponed to the winter or spring of the following year. For France, the selection includes a budget speech for every autumn between 2007 and 2020. For Italy, the selection includes every *Documento di Economia e Finanza* (DEF) published by the government between 2008 and 2020.

An important aspect to highlight is that the fiscal year for budget speeches delivered in autumn—which are the vast majority of texts analysed in this book—is the year after that in which the speech is taking place. This entails that for speeches delivered in autumn 2009, for example, the budget year is 2010. In cases where the speech or the document is produced in the first half of the year—as in the case of the Italian DEFs or for some speeches in the German, Austrian, and Spanish cases—the budget year coincides with that in which the speech is delivered. Most references in the analyses here are to the budget years.

Distinguishing relevant from 'cheap' talk

Having identified the presentation of annual budget plans as the object of study, the next question to reflect on is whether every passage within these texts is relevant. The answer to this question is simply no. Also in the presentation of annual budgets, there is a lot of talk that is relatively 'cheap' included in annual budget presentations, in the sense that it is unrelated to the government's policies. The first analytical task, therefore, is to separate the 'cheap' from the talk that matters.

As anticipated, in order for talk to become relevant for policy analysis, addressing it to stakeholders and watchdogs is not enough: it must also include statements about policy choices. In the context of annual budgetary plans, this means that when the government expresses its opinion about the state of international affairs, for example, these statements are 'cheap', unless they are linked to actions undertaken by the government. When, in autumn 2008, finance ministers expressed their opinions about how the collapse of the Lehman Brothers bank in the United States was affecting the world economy, for instance, most of these statements were irrelevant for understanding the criteria behind their actions, unless these statements were directly used as an argument to justify specific policies. In short, in understanding the criteria behind policymaking, talk becomes relevant when decision makers make binding statements about their policy choices. Table 2.2 lists several passages

Table 2.2 Distinguishing between hard and cheap talk: Examples of relevant and non-relevant passages

Examples of relevant passages	Examples of irrelevant passages
'This Budget is about equipping Britain for the times ahead and making sure that everyone, no matter what their circumstances, can exploit their full potential. It is about building a fairer society, offering more opportunity—a fair Britain in which everyone can succeed.'[a]	'Throughout the world, economies have benefited from the globalisation of trade and investment, which has delivered strong world growth. Here in Britain, our openness, our global reach and our history of scientific invention and creative success make us uniquely placed to succeed in the global economy. But with the benefits of globalisation, we see, too, how problems in one part of the world can quickly spread to another. Turbulence in the global financial markets, which started in the American mortgage market, has affected all economies, from the United States to Asia, as well as Europe.'[e]
'In addition, we were forced—I mean forced—to increase VAT. It was best to do so, in order not to be passively observing that the country was the very cause of a crisis of the euro.'[b]	'Ladies and gentlemen! The economic situation that is embedded in every budget consultation is overshadowed this year by the crisis of confidence, which can in short be named Euro-crisis. Even if we are on course, the crisis is not over. Problems due to excessive public debt, instability in the banking sector and, as a consequence, periods of uncertainty in the real economy will unfortunately continue to affect Europe and the world in the coming months.'[f]
'A considerable fortune, no one can deny, confers a particular contributory faculty. This is the first reason for which it is legitimate to impose taxes on large fortunes. Such taxation is also justified by the need to correct inequalities, which are superior in terms of assets to those already considerable in terms of income.'[c]	
'The 2017 budget will also make 3 additional billion euro available for schools and higher education. Thanks to our action since 2012, the school system of the Republic is once again able to educate our fellow citizens in the changes of today's and tomorrow's world, and to play its emancipatory role so that everyone, whatever one's social origin, can fully participate in public life.'[d]	

Notes: [a] Alistair Darling, House of Commons, 12 March 2008.
[b] Montoro Romero, Spanish Congreso, 25 August 2015.
[c] Laurent Fabius, Assemblée nationale, 27 October 1981.
[d] Michel Sapin, Assemblée nationale, 18 October 2016.
[e] Alistair Darrling, House of Commons, 12 March 2008.
[f] Wolfgang Schäuble, German Bundestag, 11 September 2012.

from budget speeches of different European governments, including both cases that will be analysed in this book as well as cases from earlier studies (Karremans, 2017; Karremans and Damhuis, 2020). In the left column, the table reports examples of passages that are relevant for understanding policymaking criteria. In the right column, instead, examples of non-relevant passages are reported.

What distinguishes the passages on the left from the passages in the right column is that the former have a direct reference to a government's policy that is accompanied by one or more arguments justifying it. The passages in the right column give an assessment about the economy, without however referring to something that the government is doing. The passages in the left column, instead, refer to 'this budget', 'increase VAT', 'taxes on large fortunes', and '3 additional billion euro'. All passages in the left column, thus, refer to a government's policy. These policies are justified respectively with arguments about 'building a fairer society', avoiding 'a crisis of the euro', 'correcting inequalities' and ensuring that everyone 'can fully participate in public life'. From the passages in the left column there is something to learn about policymaking criteria. From the passages in the right column, not really. The coding of policy justifications starts by collecting statements that directly refer to the government's policies, intended as any action that the government has done, is doing, or is intending to do. The policies being referred to, in turn, can be categorized according to whether they involve more or less expenditures, or revenues.

The categorization of policy references

The policies referred to in the annual budget plans can range from general references to the government's overall budget to references to more specific measures, such as an increase of VAT or cuts in unemployment benefits. As we shall see below, distinguishing between references to different types of policies is crucial for establishing whether the government is engaging in 'hard' talk by being assertive in its policy choices, or whether instead it engages in relatively 'cheaper' talk by refraining from disclosing the direction of its policy. For instance, when a budget speech presents a specific expenditure increase as part of a programme to increase the number of school teachers in the country, the audience is better informed about the criteria for policymaking than when the speech simply says that in its budgetary policy the government is doing something for education. When justifications refer to clear policy choices, the related justifications have greater weight, because they give the audience an argument allowing them to hold the government accountable for its choices. In the example of a statement justifying expenditure increases for hiring more teachers, the parliament is being given the possibility to evaluate whether the said increases in expenditure effectively meet the given purpose. If the parliament is only told that in the budget there are resources for education, it has fewer instruments to evaluate the government's choices.

To grasp the distinction between responsiveness and responsibility, the relevant information to be coded from the policy references is whether the policy choices are targeted more at 'giving' or 'taking' resources from domestic socio-economic groups. Therefore, in those instances where the policy reference is precise enough, it is important to code whether the policy choice involves increases or decreases in public spending, or increases or decreases in taxation. In some cases, the policy reference may be to a policy package or a regulation involving the combination of different measures in terms of spending and taxation. In these cases, it is important to distinguish whether the policy package involves (a) more spending and more taxes, (b) less spending and less taxation, (c) less spending and more taxation, or (d) more spending and less taxation. The first two policy packages can be coded respectively as Keynesian and neoliberal, where the former reflects the traditional social democratic welfare-oriented policies involving progressive taxation and relatively high public spending, whilst the second reflects economic policies favoured by the political right involving low taxes and a relatively small public sector. The third and fourth policy packages reflect respectively an effort of fiscal consolidation and of fiscal stimulus, with the former having a strong accent on 'taking' resources to rebalance the state's finances and the latter a strong accent on 'giving' resources at the risk of affecting the balance between expenditures and revenues. When the policy reference is about expenditure or tax in/decreases, or about one of these policy packages, the budget speech (or document) is giving information about the government's choices as regards the direction of socio-economic policy.

Table 2.3 lists the various types of policy references that were coded from the annual budget plans in the selected cases[1]. The categories are listed from the most precise to the most general references to the government's policy choices in terms of expenditure and taxation. The policy references coded as 'general' are those from which it is not possible to infer the direction of socio-economic policy. Among these, there are also references to government actions undertaken at the EU level, such as the positions expressed at an EU summit. Even though in some cases certain types of stances on EU-level policies go hand in hand with different choices regarding expenditure policies (Karremans, 2021b, pp. 521–522)—for example a government promoting more solidarity at EU level may also pursue more expansive policies

[1] For online access to the dataset, please see Karremans (2023).

Table 2.3 Different types of policies referred to in annual budget plans

Level of policy choice	Policy type	Description
Specific policies	Expenditure increase	Explicit references to an increase in expenditure
	Expenditure reduction	Explicit references to a reduction in expenditure
	Tax increase	Explicit references to an increase in taxation
	Tax reduction	Explicit references to a reduction in taxation
Policy packages	Keynesian	Combinations of or regulations involving tax and expenditure increases
	Neoliberal	Combinations of, or regulations involving, tax and expenditure reductions
	Fiscal consolidation	Combinations of, or regulations involving, tax increases and expenditure reductions; policies of debt and deficit reduction
	Fiscal stimulus	Combinations of, or regulations involving, expenditure increases and tax increases
General policies	Budget general	General budgetary policy (e.g. 'this budget'); references to government action with no further specification about taxation or expenditure
	Expenditure general	References to expenditure or spending, but no specific details about increases or decreases
	Tax general	References to taxation (or fiscal policy) but no specific details about increases or decreases
	Administrative reforms	Broad reforms in state assets (e.g. reform of judicial system) that do not directly involve changes in expenditure or taxation
	EU level	Actions taken at the European level
	Other	Regulatory policies that cannot be classified as part of one of the policy packages listed above

domestically—taken by themselves these measures are not directly informative about budgetary policy choices. In this study, these references are thus considered in the same way as references to the government's overall actions.

The categorization of the different types of policies helps make more sense of the statements justifying them. As we shall see below, the coding of responsiveness and responsibility is achieved precisely by combining the information on the types of policies referred to with the information on the content of the justifications.

The coding of justifications

The ultimate step in capturing policymaking criteria from annual budget plans is to identify statements that justify the actions undertaken by the government. In social relations, a justification is understood as a 'legitimation process that normalizes unexpected, untoward acts' (Zelditch, 2001, p. 7). As discussed in Chapter 1, legitimation processes are about the principles through which collectivized decisions are accepted by the community (Bartolini, 2005, pp. 165–166). Justifications are those arguments used by an actor to explain to an audience how or why its actions are suited in a certain circumstance. In the case of governments, justifications are those arguments with which policies are being presented as proper and therefore as acceptable to the parliament and the wider (inter)national community. Justifications are thus informative about the common understanding between politicians and their audiences about what governments are expected to do. By studying these arguments, we learn about how governments profile themselves and, thereby, we get a closer insight into 'what they are about' (Robinson, 2005, p. 51), as well into the 'logic of appropriateness' of their actions (March and Olsen, 2009).

When presenting the budget, the arguments governments use to explain their policies give some hints about why such policies ought to be accepted. In the example of explaining an increase in expenditure as being necessary to hire more school teachers, the explanation is a reason for the audience to accept (or refuse) such expenditure increase. In annual budget plans, the statements that clarify the criteria behind, or the purpose of, the policy can be seen as a justification. These statements can subsequently be analysed through the following lens:

This *policy* is just because ⟶ justification

The justification statements can be collected inductively. In the following excerpt from the budget speech of the German finance minister Olaf Scholz on 11 September 2018, for instance, there are two justification statements referring to one policy. The justification statements are underlined and the policy reference is italicized.

> One of the things we need to get underway, which we have prepared in the Federal Government, which is now up for decision and for which we have made provision in this budget, is that we want to do something for the children who are

> growing up in this country. The *Gute-KiTa-Gesetz* is not only a good quality law that we will discuss, but it is also something that we can finance and that we will finance.
>
> **Olaf Scholz, Bundestag, 11 September 2018**

The policy referred to regards a provision in relation to the *Gute-KiTa-Gesetz*, which is Germany's childcare scheme. The provision foresees more public spending in this area. The government provides two reasons for this increase of spending, namely the desire to improve services for children, and the availability of sufficient financial resources. The statement that emphasizes children can be categorized as a socially oriented argument, while the statement that emphasizes affordability can be seen as a financial argument.

The following excerpt from the budget speech of French Finance Minister Bruno La Maire features three justification statements:

> The long-term objective of *this budget* is indeed the new French prosperity, which must concern all French people and all territories. It must not be based on ever-increasing public expenditure but must be the result of the creation of value by the French and by our companies. Indeed, the path to prosperity based on public spending leads us straight to the increase in public debt and taxes, where we want to *reduce spending, reduce debt, reduce our taxes.*
>
> **(Bruno La Maire, Assemblée Générale, 15 October 2018)**

The first two justifications refer to the overall budget, with the first one emphasizing how it will bring prosperity to the entire country, and the second one how it aims to promote the entrepreneurship of private companies. The third statement refers to the choice for a policy of expenditure and tax reduction, justifying it with the argument that this is the best way to reduce debts and deficits. The first statement simply underlines how the budget is designed to contribute to the country's economic well-being, and can thus be categorized as an argument about the macro-economy. The second statement can be seen as an example of ideological support for private economic freedom, as it emphasizes that wealth should be created by creative private companies. The third statement is another example of a financial argument, in the sense that it expresses a concern about the state of public finances.

Through this inductive coding procedure, justification statements can be categorized according to their main theme of reference. From the budget speeches and documents listed in Table 2.1, the following types of justifications were identified:

- *Social*: Address social issues related to: education, health, equality, family, unemployment, vulnerable groups, social inclusion, integration, redistribution, helping people into work, etc.;
- *Environmental*: Address environmental issues, e.g. climate change, pollution, etc.
- *Security*: Policy is about providing law and order, police, military;
- *Private economic freedom*: Promote the private market, support the free market, stimulate private entrepreneurship, promote private ownership (e.g. heritage), etc.;
- *Macroeconomic*: Address the country's macroeconomic issues such as: gross domestic product, growth rates, competitiveness, productivity, prosperity, overall employment, etc.;
- *Financial*: Address public finances: public debt, public deficit, government balance sheet, long-term sustainability of public finances, stability of public finances;
- *International commitments*: Referring to international commitments to e.g. the European Union, G20, International Monetary Fund;
- *State polity*: Organization of finances across different state levels;
- *Demography*: Policy driven by demographic developments such as birth rates or ageing;
- *Sovereignty*: Policy is about maintaining national sovereignty;
- *Other/bureaucratic logics*: Various kinds of bureaucratic logics.

The statements underlined in the examples above from the speeches of Olaf Scholz and Bruno La Maire are the units of observation of the study presented in this book. The counting is based on full grammatical sentences: each justification corresponds to a sentence that explains why the policy is just. However, as discourse is extremely fluid, breaking it down into consistent countable units is not a straightforward task. In earlier research using this same research approach (Damhuis and Karremans, 2017; Karremans and Damhuis, 2020), the counting was more centred on references to actors or objectives. This strategy can be problematic in the case of the German language, as there may be multiple references to actors within one word, or the reference may be 'hidden' in a pronoun. In an effort to have a more consistent counting strategy across the cases, for this study all speeches were coded by focusing on grammatical sentences. Even though the speeches of the Hollande presidency had been coded for earlier studies (Damhuis and Karremans, 2017; Karremans and Damhuis, 2020), the analyses presented from Chapter 4 onwards are based on an entirely new coding based on grammatical sentences (instead of actors or objectives). This also provided an additional, and successful, reliability test.[2] The coding for the earlier study with Koen Damhuis had produced 474 observations from the speeches of the Hollande presidency (to be discussed in more detail in Chapter 3). For the study presented here, 488 observations were collected from the same speeches, featuring highly similar identical patterns, particularly with regard to the annual shares of socially and financially oriented justifications.

Table 2.4 reports the matrix of policy justifications coded by their policy reference and justification theme, for the total of 7,806 observations collected from the fifty-eight annual budget plans listed in Table 2.1 (for the dataset, see Karremans, 2023). The table shows that of the total 7,806 policy justifications, 1,669 concern social themes. Of these, 549 emphasize social themes *and* justify an expenditure increase. Similarly, 2,150 policy justifications are about financial themes and of these 371 serve to justify expenditure reductions. When dividing these numbers by the total, one already has an indication of how much governments between 2008 and 2020 in the five countries focused on social, financial, or macroeconomic issues, or how much their justification discourse was about expenditure increases or fiscal consolidation. The codification of responsiveness and responsibility is built by matching the information from the rows and columns of this table.

The codification of responsiveness and responsibility

In terms of distinguishing between responsiveness and responsibility, the analytical distinction should capture, on the one hand, policy choices that are tailored to deliver resources for the benefit of domestic constituencies—whatever these may be—and on the other, policy choices targeted at improving the sustainability of the state's finances. The matrix of Table 3.4 provides a bird's-eye view of both the frequency of the references to the actual policy choices and of the theme of the related justification arguments. The policy reference categories allow to distinguish between policies that *give* to domestic constituencies in the form of expenditure increases and tax reductions, and policies that *take* resources in the form of spending cuts and tax increases. The related justifications are informative about whether these policies are actually intended to serve domestic socio-economic groups or—for example—reduce public deficits. In some instances though, the policy justification statements do not provide inferences about governments' choices.

[2] For more info on the technicalities of the coding procedure and reliability tests, please see also the Online Appendix of Karremans (2021a).

Table 2.4 Matrix of policy justifications from fifty-eight annual budget plans, in absolute numbers

	JUSTIFICATION THEME											
	Social	Environ-mental	Security	Private economic freedom	Macroeco-nomic	Financial	International commit-ments	State	Demo-graphy	Sover-eignty	Other	Total
Exp increase	550	42	61	67	218	178	42	58	6	0	30	*1252*
Exp reduction	48	2	6	28	44	371	20	9	1	2	10	*541*
Tax increase	56	11	0	10	18	91	7	4	0	0	10	*207*
Tax reduction	113	7	2	194	87	41	15	4	0	0	4	*467*
Keynes	12	3	0	0	2	4	3	0	0	0	0	*24*
Neolib	9	0	0	24	18	45	1	1	0	0	1	*99*
Consolidation	45	0	0	15	94	295	51	12	3	1	12	*528*
Generous	31	0	0	22	22	7	2	0	0	0	1	*85*
Budget	458	26	23	199	925	618	135	98	7	4	153	*2646*
Exp general	145	22	9	50	131	231	38	39	5	2	21	*693*
Tax general	71	0	3	76	25	92	20	15	0	0	26	*328*
Administrative reform	45	0	0	34	37	27	3	23	0	0	37	*206*
European policy	34	6	5	13	139	95	126	3	0	2	13	*436*
Other	53	6	1	34	64	55	36	13	1	0	31	*294*
Total	*1670*	*125*	*110*	*766*	*1824*	*2150*	*499*	*279*	*23*	*11*	*349*	*7806*

In these instances, the statements are to be considered as neutral, in the sense that they do reveal the government's propensity to be either responsive or responsible. At the broadest level of abstraction, therefore, the policy justifications can be divided into three categories: neutral, responsive, and responsible.

The neutral statements are those in which there is no indication of policy choices on the allocation of public finances. Statements expressing how the overall budget serves broad macroeconomic objectives, for instance, provide no information about responsiveness and responsibility. Justifications focusing on macroeconomic aspects such as growth rates, overall employment rates, prosperity, or productivity, are functional to both responsive and responsible purposes, as higher growth rates give more resources for domestic redistribution and ensure a larger pool for future governments to draw revenues from. The very first sentence from the Bruno La Maire excerpt analysed above refers to providing prosperity but features no information about policy choices and the related justification theme is functional both to domestic redistributive purposes and to guaranteeing sufficient state revenues in the long run. The same logic applies to justifications about sovereignty and those that were coded as 'other'. In these cases, policy justifications cannot be coded as either responsive or responsible. Justifications from the 'macroeconomic', 'sovereignty', and 'other' categories can be coded as manifestations of responsiveness and responsibility only when clear policy choices are disclosed. These neutral statements amount to 21 per cent of the total observations.

It is not by chance that statements focusing on macroeconomic aspects are the core of the 'neutral' category. In socio-economic policymaking, economic growth is the glue between responsiveness and responsibility. Yet there are different ways in which economic growth can be pursued, and these may be either more or less responsive to different political preferences, or be part of an institutionalized consensus about the mutual relationship between economic performance and public finances. When economic growth is pursued through expenditure increases, this can be seen as responsive to the preferences of the political left, while growth strategies based on tax reductions can be seen as responsive to the preferences of the political right. On the other hand, the idea that fiscal consolidation is a necessary precondition for economic prosperity is inherent to the ideational framework by which European fiscal rules were developed (Matthijs, 2016). Statements presenting fiscal consolidation as the only option for economic performance can therefore be seen as manifestations of responsibility.

The government's inclination towards responsiveness or responsibility becomes even more unequivocal when the justification statements express commitment to a particular policy goal and at the same time present coherent policy choices. The categories 'social', 'environment', and 'security' contain arguments about improving social justice, ameliorating the quality of life, or facilitating the functioning of domestic societies. These goals often require increases in public spending. The category 'private economic freedom' contains statements that reflect the preferences of liberal-oriented voters and requires resources in the form of a reduction of fiscal burdens. The combination of either one of these four justification categories with references to expenditure increases or tax cuts are unequivocal manifestations of responsiveness towards distinct political or redistributive preferences.

On the other hand, the categories 'financial' and 'international commitments' contain statements that profile a government's policy clearly in more responsible terms. When these justifications are about policies of fiscal consolidation, they can be seen as unambiguous manifestations of responsibility, as they reflect shared understanding between EU institutions and national authorities about the importance of sound public finances. Justifications about the allocation of financial resources among different state levels ('state polity') can be considered as part of this rationale. The collected justifications about demographic developments are essentially reflections about the financial implications of democratic ageing and can therefore also be added to the 'responsible' side of the dividing line. In sum, manifestations of responsibility are those statements that highlight the web of institutional and financial constraints in which the government operates. These manifestations are the most unambiguous when they refer to acts of fiscal consolidation.

The matching of information between policy references and justification themes enables a consideration of governments' potential rhetorical strategies, by giving greater weight to statements that unambiguously commit resources to domestic social groups, or that clearly express a commitment towards fiscal sustainability. The statements can be placed on a dimension ranging from the most responsive to the most responsible. Figure 2.1 illustrates this idea.

At the left extreme of the dimension illustrated in Figure 2.1, arguments are unequivocally about how the government uses public resources in order to serve certain social or private interests. These may be increases in social benefits justified with arguments about the importance of providing the unemployed with support or tax reductions justified with arguments about the inalienable right to home ownership. At the right extreme, policies of

Responsive policy:	Responsive economics:	Responsive discourse:	Responsive rhetoric:	Responsible rhetoric:	Responsible discourse:	Responsible economics:	Responsible policy:
Fiscal stimulus justified with social and/or private-sphere arguments	Fiscal stimulus justified with economic arguments	General budget justified with social and private-sphere arguments	Fiscal consolidation justified with social and/or private-sphere arguments	Fiscal stimulus justified with institutional arguments	General budget justified with institutional arguments	Fiscal consolidation justified with economic arguments	Fiscal consolidation justified with institutional arguments
4	3	2	1	1	2	3	4
← Responsive				Responsible →			

Figure 2.1 The responsive–responsible continuum
Source: Author's illustration

fiscal consolidation are justified with arguments about deficit levels or international agreements, for example. These are unequivocal examples of fiscal responsibility that one would imagine hearing from a technocratic executive, but certainly not from a populist party claiming to represent the will of the people. In between, there are different gradations of responsive and responsible justifications. At one level, moving inwards, in columns marked with the number 3, justifications express how the government's policy serves the country's economic growth. On the responsive side, they are associated with distinct policies that are attributable to Keynesian or neoliberal ideologies, involving fiscal stimuli in the form of either public investments or tax reductions. As they reflect the government's autonomy in designing its budgetary policy, the more these arguments occur the less valid is the claim that European economic governance constrains choice in macroeconomic policy. By the same token, when fiscal consolidation is justified with macroeconomic arguments, it indicates that the government's criteria are in line with the supranational logic that low debt and deficit levels are the conditions *sine qua non* for economic prosperity to be achieved. Further towards the middle, in the columns marked with number 2, the justifications clearly express political or institutional arguments but refer only to the overall budget and not to distinct policies that confirm a certain commitment. They give an indication on whether the government seeks to be evaluated in either responsive or responsible terms, without however disclosing information on clear policy choices. Finally, at the most ambiguous level, in the columns marked with number 1, the responsive and responsible justifications feature an internal contradiction, as on the one hand they justify fiscally responsible policies with political arguments and on the other they justify fiscally less responsible policies with arguments of fiscal responsibility.

The scheme presented in Figure 2.1 indicates a clear and consistent dividing line, which is necessary for carrying out meaningful comparative research. In addition, it allows development of insights on the extent to which the observed variations in responsiveness or responsibility genuinely reflect a real change in approach to budgetary policymaking. The various levels of categorization of the justification statements enable tracking how the contents of responsiveness and responsibility change from one government to another. While it is relatively straightforward that governments of different partisan compositions are likely to feature different types of responsiveness because they respond to different socio-economic groups, with regard to responsibility it is less clear whether and how this may be interpreted differently by different governments. In principle, as will be discussed in Chapter 7, there are different ways of serving the principle of fiscal sustainability. The extent to which this is also the case under European economic governance is an under-explored question that can be tackled through this categorization of policy justification statements.

Ready to start comparing

The categorization of policy justifications presented in this chapter allows us to gain comparative insights into the extent to which, in the shared understanding between governments and parliaments, budgetary policy ought to be evaluated in terms of what it delivers domestically, or in terms of how it is compliant with several financial thresholds. The different subcategories in which responsive and responsible statements are divided reflect different levels of ambiguity towards different policy goals. This differentiation reveals whether the vocal commitments are associated with clear policy initiatives. The distinction of subcategories according to the clearness and cohesion of the policy justifications allows us to separate 'hard' discourse that matters from talk that is relatively 'cheaper'. Faced with parliaments that closely follow the choices regarding the allocation of public resources, and in front of polarizing electoral demands and mounting institutional commitments, governments' unambiguous statements about the purpose of expenditure increases or fiscal consolidation are highly informative about the criteria by which they perceive their actions ought to be evaluated.

The policy justifications gathered from annual budget plans contain clear signals to international audiences and local constituencies about whether the government intends to pay more attention to domestic demands or whether it is more concerned with the sustainability of public finances. Based on this data, it is possible to gain insights into the extent to which international economic integration makes governments focus more on fiscal sustainability and less on domestic responsiveness, and into whether European economic governance strengthens this trend further.

At this stage, everything is set for exploring the extent to which governments, after the introduction and strengthening of European economic governance, have become less responsive and more responsible. Before zooming into how the consequences of reforms introduced during the sovereign debt crisis, the next chapter first illustrates whether during the 2010s the overall balance between different types of policy justifications was substantially different than during the 1980s and 1990s, at the dawn of the intensification of European integration. The subsequent chapters exploit the data presented in this chapter more fully, seeking to grasp the extent to which the strengthening of European economic governance had an effect on the balance between responsiveness and responsibility.

3
Is globalization reducing responsiveness?

Introduction

Since its appearance in the political science literature, the word 'globalization' has been associated with big questions about how it impacts the very foundations of national democracies (Schmitter, 2011, 2009). Particularly when intended as deepening international economic integration, globalization has raised the question whether it reduces the room for manoeuvre of democratically elected governments (Rodrik, 2011, 2000; Scharpf, 1998, 1991). International economic integration requires a certain level of coordination among governments on their economic policies. This coordination may spill over into supranational policy prescriptions for other spheres as well, such as social policy provisions. In addition, under the conditions of free movement of capital, goods, services, and workforce, there is a risk that resourceful individuals and firms move to the countries where they are taxed the least. This, in turn, may trigger governments into a 'race to the bottom' in terms of taxation levels, causing a reduction of the financial resources at their disposal to deliver goods and services (Genschel and Schwarz, 2013; Rodrik, 2000). Theoretically, therefore, the proposition that international economic integration may be incompatible with democratic responsiveness is plausible.

Towards the end of the twentieth century, this proposition started finding partial empirical support in several electoral developments. International economic integration was flourishing in the 1990s and 2000s, particularly in advanced industrial countries, mainly countries that are part of the Organisation for Economic Co-operation and Development (OECD). During this same period, scholars focusing on political parties documented declining levels of voter turnout and party membership (Dalton and Wattenberg, 2002). In parallel, mainstream governing parties' vote share experienced a gradual decline. For the first time since 1945, during the 2010s the joint vote share of the traditional centre-right and centre-left parties was less than 50 per cent in several European elections (Hobolt and Tilley, 2016). Many of the new

Between Voters and Eurocrats. Johannes Karremans, Oxford University Press. © Johannes Karremans (2024).
DOI: 10.1093/oso/9780192886583.003.0003

votes went to parties that advocated for the interests of the so-called 'losers of globalization', namely citizens who perceive they are losing from the increasingly internationalized economy (Kriesi et al., 2012). In addition, several countries witnessed the development of extra-parliamentary movements, many of which protested against the status quo and government policies. The most violent example was perhaps the *gilets jaunes* movement in France, which created widespread public disorder between 2018 and 2020 in protest against the policies of the Macron presidency. Are these indicators and developments confirming that globalization is indeed causing a decline of responsiveness?

Recent research on how political parties represent changing preferences within the electorate suggests that this is not necessarily the case. In the example of the *gilets jaunes*, the discontent expressed by this movement is against a set of policies—such as raising taxes on fuel—that are against the interests of a certain section of the electorate, but are at the same time supported in large numbers by other large groups of citizens. For many party scholars, the case of the *gilets jaunes* exemplifies the emergence of new electoral cleavages, to which the political supply offered by parties has been largely responsive (Hutter and Kriesi, 2019; Kriesi et al., 2012). These new electoral cleavages are narrowly related to changing socio-economic structures.

The rise of international economic integration in OECD countries happened largely simultaneously with the increasing relevance of the service sector in national economies and a decline of the number of jobs in the industrial sector (Oesch, 2015). This changing occupational structure triggered changing electoral preferences, involving also a change from material to post-material values, which explains also the rise of environmentalist parties (Inglehart, 2008; Luther et al., 2002). By and large, highly skilled citizens employed in the service sector started demanding different kinds of policies than those traditionally demanded by the industrial working class (Häusermann and Kriesi, 2015). Following up on these changing demands, social democratic parties started to increasingly advocate for policies such as active labour market policies, lifelong learning schemes, and childcare provisions to capture the preferences of the new, better skilled parts of the labour force (Gingrich and Häusermann, 2015). Similarly, parties on the centre-right also started reorienting their supply according to changing demands. New challenger parties, instead, voiced the discontent of those parts of the electorate that did not recognize their preferences in these reorientations of the traditional centre-left and centre-right parties. As a result of this process, the overall political supply offered by political parties continues to match the preferences of an increasingly diversified electorate (Kitschelt and Rehm, 2015). From this perspective, the declining levels of voter turnout and vote shares of mainstream parties should be interpreted as part of a process of realignment between voters' demands and parties' supply (Dalton et al., 2011; Kitschelt and Rehm, 2015).

Despite such studies showing how parties adapt their supply to changing electoral demands, the question about the extent to which political representation is still channelled through the policymaking process is not yet fully answered. Qualitatively, the world in which governments and parties operate has undoubtedly changed. In a fully internationally and economically integrated area like the EU, governments clearly have more institutional and procedural obligations than governments operating outside these systems (Genschel and Zangl, 2014; Rose, 2014). Institutional innovations such as the European Semester force national governments to operate at both the European and national level in the development of their policies (Verdun and Zeitlin, 2018). What is also clear, is that the institutions established to safeguard international economic integration—such as the EU or the IMF—actively engage with governments about the best ways to shape public expenditure. Even though the implementation rates of supranational recommendations tend to be relatively low (Bekker, 2016), certain structural reforms in socio-economic policies—such as increases in retirement age or labour market flexibilization—have occurred in virtually all EU member states and beyond, in line with the advocacy of international institutions (Howell, 2019). This advocacy is particularly concerned about the sustainability of governments' public finances in a global market economy. As the episode of the European sovereign debt crisis made clear, in an economic and monetary union the potential financial collapse of a member state is highly dangerous for the entire system, as its detrimental effects would quickly spread cross-nationally (De Grauwe, 2016). In sum, in the context of international economic integration, governments are also accountable to additional inter- and supranational actors, most of whom demand fiscal responsibility.

Whether, how, and to what extent this affects democratic responsiveness, is still open to debate. This chapter illustrates the unanswered questions. After having discussed the limitations of spending and taxation data in shedding further light on this matter, it is argued that to understand whether international economic integration affects responsiveness and responsibility, it is necessary to collect comparable information on the criteria by which governments design and pursue their socio-economic policies. Identifying comparable data for this purpose, however, is rather difficult. The focus on budgets presented in Chapter 2 offers a solution to this challenge.

This chapter discusses the advantages of comparing governments facing challenging economic times and presents evidence from cross-time comparisons. Based on insights from my earlier research (Damhuis and Karremans, 2017; Karremans and Damhuis, 2020; Karremans and Kaltenleithner, 2021), the chapter concludes by reflecting on what a study on budgetary discourse in five eurozone countries between 2008 and 2020 can contribute to our understanding of the relationship between globalization and representative democracy.

The ambiguity behind macroeconomic trends

In macroeconomic terms, a decline in responsiveness would entail a reduction in resources that governments provide to their domestic constituencies. Following the argument that globalization affects democratic responsiveness, the mechanism behind such a reduction could imply either that the requisites for international economic policy integration are incompatible with large domestic public expenditure programmes, or that the logics of economic integration will trigger governments into lowering their tax rates and therefore collect insufficient revenues to finance large expenditures. Both mechanisms bear the empirical implication that the more international economic integration grows, the more likely it is that public spending will decline, and an increase will remain highly unlikely. As international economic integration has increased in OECD countries from the 1980s to the 2010s (Gygli et al., 2019), this would entail a decline of public spending over time.

Contrary to this conjecture, however, over the last decades public spending in OECD countries has increased rather than decreased. Measured as a percentage of GDP, public spending gradually grew on aggregate from around 20 per cent in the 1970s to more than 25 per cent from the 2000s onwards, with even further increases after the coronavirus pandemic (Figure 3.1). In line with theories of policy change, public spending grew in a 'punctuated' manner, with big changes concentrated in a few single years, while most years are characterized by small incremental changes (Baumgartner, 2013). The punctuated increases of public spending coincide with years featuring sharp declines in economic growth rates (dotted line in Figure 3.1, right axis). Considering that, for the most part, public spending involves running expenditure programmes, these sharp increases need to be seen partially as the result of the decline in the denominator of the percentage by which public spending is measured: as negative growth entails a smaller GDP, the overall spending is divided by a smaller denominator. At the same time, these sharp increases generally also reflect governments' efforts to compensate for the negative effects of an economic downturn (Gourevitch, 1986; Pontusson and Raess, 2012). On top of this, a large economic downturn may cause a deeper change in the economic problems and priorities addressed by the government, triggering therefore new spending programmes (Baumgartner, 2013; Hall, 1993). The trends reported in Figure 3.1 suggest that international economic integration has not disrupted these policymaking regularities. They also show that while public spending grows in a punctuated manner, the share of government revenues grows with a relatively steady trend, seemingly catching up with the growing public spending revenues.

The evidence for international economic integration *not* necessarily causing a reduction of public spending is even stronger when considering that the levels of public expenditure and revenues are even higher in the countries of the eurozone (Figure 3.2). Despite a highly integrated market and a common currency area, in these countries public spending is on aggregate higher than 45 per cent of GDP. In addition, in eurozone countries half of public spending is dedicated to social purposes, including various types of social protection and social services. As can be seen in Figure 3.2 (dotted line), social spending was a key component of the rise in public expenditure registered in 2009, the year of the Great Recession caused by the financial crisis of 2008. This increase reflects how, in the twenty-first

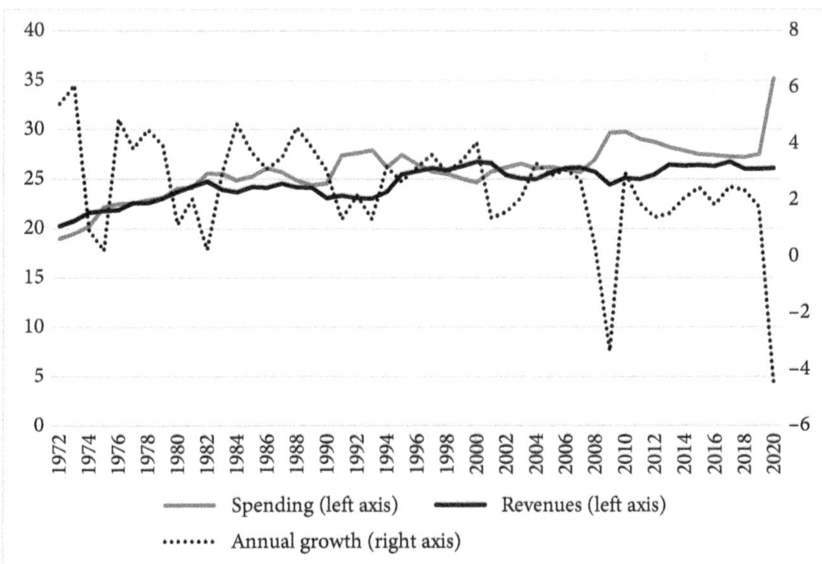

Figure 3.1 Public spending, revenues, and economic growth rates as percentage of GDP in OECD countries from 1972 to 2020

Source: World Bank Data

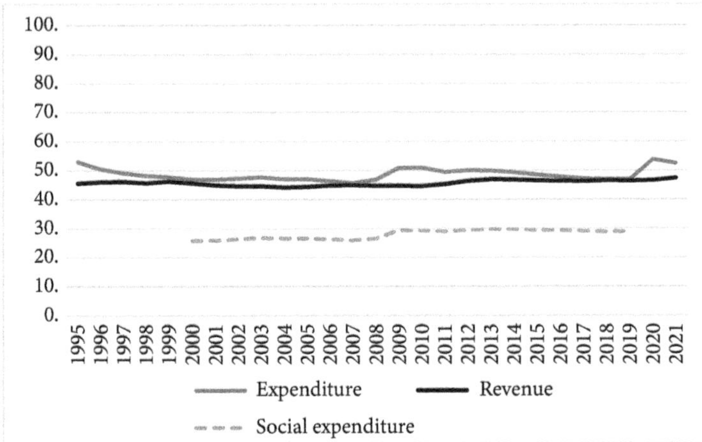

Figure 3.2 Public spending, revenues, and social expenditures as percentage of GDP in eurozone countries from 1995 to 2020

Source: Eurostat
Note: Time ranges are selected according to data availability

century, European welfare states still play an important role in absorbing the social shocks of major economic downturns (Hemerijck and Matsaganis, forthcoming).

Another interesting observation on social expenditures in Europe is that, over time, in many countries their composition has changed from being almost entirely composed of traditional social protection schemes such as pensions and unemployment benefits, to being gradually more composed of investments in human capital, such as active labour market policies or child-care subsidies (Ferragina, 2019; Ronchi, 2018). These changes are aligned with the changing preferences of many citizens who, in their transition from industrial to service sector jobs, became less supportive of income replacement schemes and more favourable to social policies targeted at improving work–life balance (Gingrich and Häusermann, 2015; Häusermann and Kriesi, 2015). Despite deepening levels of international economic integration, governments therefore still seem to redistribute resources according to the preferences and demands of citizens (Beramendi et al., 2015).

There is, however, an alternative way of interpreting the macroeconomic trends reported in Figures 3.1 and 3.2, namely that of a permanent austerity (Pierson, 1996; Schäfer and Streeck, 2013; Streeck, 2015). Except for those instances of major economic downturns, public spending tends be relatively flat on the revenue line. While on the one hand this can be seen as a virtuous effort of governments acting within their means and thus of being 'responsible', at the same time it also suggests that over the last few decades governments did not try to go *beyond* their means to be responsive to domestic preferences.

The high levels of public spending registered in advanced industrial countries are not necessarily reflective of governments' responsiveness to voters' short-term demands, but need also to be seen as the path-dependent accumulation of lasting commitments, that are increasingly difficult to finance. Old-age pensions, for instance, are one of the biggest areas of public spending in most countries, particularly in Europe where demographic ageing is increasing virtually everywhere. With a growing share of the population becoming entitled to a pension, these expenditures increasingly put the sustainability of public finances at risk. To reduce the financial burden of pensions, between the 2000s and 2010s most European governments felt compelled to increase the retirement age. These initiatives were highly unpopular among the public (Alonso and Ruiz-Rufino, 2020). At the same time, they were the flagship policies initiated by technocratic governments (Culpepper, 2014) and were insistently advocated by international institutions (Lefkofridi and Nezi, 2020). While pension expenditures were on the rise in recent decades, policy initiatives in this area were mostly directed at reducing them, with technocratic considerations about fiscal sustainability seemingly overshadowing popular preferences.

The example of pensions is illustrative of how public spending levels may offer a misleading picture about the criteria driving governments' actions, and thus about the levels of responsiveness and responsibility. Focusing solely on expenditures, one would be induced to think that governments during the 2000s and 2010s were highly responsive to the demands of pensioners, as spending increased in line with demographic ageing. However, the policy initiatives of governments in this area were rather targeted at reducing the costs, in order to maintain the monthly payment of pensions affordable in the long term. The fulfilment of lasting commitments, and thus the securing of their financing, is a key aspect of responsibility.

In European democracies, where—decade after decade throughout the twentieth century—new commitments were made, the weight of past policy legacies has become highly burdensome. These legacies are a considerable constraint on government actions, as they reduce the space for discretionary spending, namely the part of the budget which they can freely decide how to allocate (Schmidt, 1996; Streeck, 2015). In a context where public spending is increasing in a path-dependent manner, international economic integration becomes a constraint that induces governments to limit this increase as much as possible. Considering that there is also evidence of a race to the bottom in terms of the taxation of large corporations (Genschel and Schwarz, 2013)—reducing income from a substantial source of revenue—international economic integration may indeed be acting as a brake on democratic responsiveness. Taking this perspective into account, simple public spending figures cannot provide a definite answer. What is needed, instead, is a comparative research design that provides insights on the weight of different decision-making criteria under different levels of international economic integration.

Lessons from policymaking in hard times

As anticipated in Chapter 1, the proposition that international economic integration affects democratic responsiveness gained particular attention in the aftermath of the global financial crisis of 2008. Peter Mair's articles about responsiveness and responsibility (2014, 2013, 2011) resulted largely from a reflection on the events surrounding the harsh austerity measures imposed on Ireland by the EU and the IMF. The argument about responsibility increasingly overshadowing responsiveness resonated with the empirical observation that in the early 2010s governments across the western world were subscribing to the paradigm of austerity in the name of long-term national interest (Blyth, 2013; Pontusson and Raess, 2012). Between 2009 and 2012, governments from both the right and the left across Europe introduced restrictive measures to popular welfare provisions, such as pensions and unemployment benefits, emphasizing their duties in terms of fiscal responsibility (Alonso and Ruiz-Rufino, 2020). The events surrounding the European sovereign debt crisis seemed to be the ultimate confirmation that international economic integration was reducing governments' attention towards domestic democratic demands (Rodrik, 2011).

Major crises offer a unique window into the beliefs and constraints that policymakers hold and face. To back a broader argument about the causal link between globalization and the functioning of national democracy, though, a comparative perspective is needed on the beliefs and constraints that governments were holding and facing in times when international economic integration was less developed. Generally, during economic crises, governments need to act according to a clearly defined policy recipe in order to steer their countries out of the recession (Gourevitch, 1986). During the sovereign debt crisis, austerity was the main recipe that most governments followed. As will also be discussed in Chapter 4, the lack of alternatives observed in those years is not necessarily attributable to the logics of European economic integration, but can also be considered as being merely crisis-specific. In order to establish the accuracy of Mair's and similar claims, it is necessary to comparatively assess whether during and after the sovereign debt crisis there was something fundamentally different in how governments combined responsiveness with responsibility.

Despite their peculiar nature, economic crises offer important insights in the dynamics behind socio-economic policymaking across different historical periods. In his highly influential study, Peter Gourevitch (1986) studied the responses of governments to the five main economic crises between the end of the nineteenth century and the 1980s in five major western countries, namely France, Germany, Sweden, the United Kingdom, and the United States. The study reveals a recurrent pattern. In all cases analysed, Gourevitch finds that crises confront governments with a limited number of policy options. When making their choices, governments need to ensure that their policy strategies will have adequate levels of support to ensure successful implementation. This support may come from various angles, including large business organizations or electoral coalitions. Domestic political processes determine the formation of the support base according to which governments design their crisis response. Once the policy strategy is defined, governments need to stick to it in order to ensure a successful way out of the recession. In this process, we may identify responsiveness in the politics of defining the crisis response strategy, and responsibility in the recognition that the available policy options are limited, as well as in a consistent pursuit of the chosen crisis response strategy. This insight allows to reflect more concretely about whether the response of European governments to the sovereign debt crisis follows the same dynamics as crisis politics in previous historical periods, or whether instead there are substantial differences that are attributable to deepened levels of economic integration. The analyses of Chapter 4 will build on these reflections.

Another important aspect emerging from Gourevitch's comparative study is that international stakeholders played a relevant role in governments' economic policy decisions also before the rise of international economic integration experienced since the 1980s. This aspect is emphasized strongly by Dorothee Bohle (2014), who illustrates several striking parallels between Germany in the 1920s and 1930s and the developments surrounding the European sovereign debt crisis of the 2010s. These parallels largely coincide with the tension between responsiveness and responsibility described by Mair (2014) which, Bohle argues, is closely linked with the incompatibilities between globalizing capitalism and national democracy. As observed during the European sovereign debt crisis, during the 1920s and 1930s too there were several incompatibilities between the policy requirements of international economic integration and national electoral demands. Between 1924 and 1929, the German government pursued several policies that were aimed at securing inflows of foreign capital by, for example, strengthening the independence of the central bank and introducing a cap on government lending. The rise of capital inflow ensured a period of economic prosperity, but when the country entered a period of economic recession in 1929, the tensions between international obligations and national political demands became increasingly difficult to manage. One of the elements of tension was that international lending was given on the condition of repayment of debts from the First World War, a condition that for various nationalist political forces was difficult to digest. As is known, these nationalist political forces gained increasing political support in the early 1930s. Even though the bitterness over war repayments that was widespread in certain parts of the German electorate of the 1930s cannot be compared with the social discontent of the 2010s, this cross-time comparison is illustrative of how the tension between responsiveness and responsibility is not peculiar to the EU or the twenty-first century, but is a recurrent feature of the troubled relation between capitalism and democracy.

Besides their substantial insights, the studies of Gourevitch (1986) and Bohle (2014) are also illustrative of how moments of economic crisis offer a setting in which the decision-making processes of governments operating in different historical periods become comparable. In several scholarly contributions, in fact, governments' responses to the crises of the 2008–2012 period are discussed against the background of governments' responses to the economic stagnation that plagued various European countries between the 1970s and the early 1980s (e.g. Hemerijck et al., 2022a; Pontusson and Raess, 2012). The crisis of the 1970s started with the oil crisis in 1973 and continued with several years of stagflation. Under the pressure from their governments, national central banks would increase the money supply with no positive effects on economic growth, unwillingly creating stagflation, a situation of high inflation in a context of economic stagnation. In this context, most European countries started to make their central bank independent of political influences, in order to make the money supply more predictable and more aligned with economic cycles, a practice that by the 1990s was a mandatory condition for joining the European Economic and Monetary Union. In parallel, from the mid-1970s several countries entered a negative spiral in which larger numbers of citizens started demanding the benefits of expanding welfare states, while the industrial sector increasingly struggled to remain a source of job growth and thus of social contributions for financing the welfare state (Scharpf, 1991). Consequently, from the 1970s onwards governments came increasingly under pressure to reduce access to welfare benefits, which were becoming a growing burden on the public purse (Allan and Scruggs, 2004). Similarly to the early 2010s, governments were operating in a context of economic stagnation that was linked to an international economic crisis, and were under pressure to reduce public expenditure.

An illustrative example from the 1970s of the incompatibility between domestic political programmes and international constraints is the case of the British Labour government that was in office between 1974 and 1979, led first by Harold Wilson and after 1976 by James Callaghan (Harmon, 1997; Karremans, 2017). The Labour Party won the spring election of 1974 with a majority so narrow that a second election in October of the same year was needed. In its electoral manifesto, the Labour Party had promised massive redistribution of wealth and income in order to help the poor and weaker parts of society, such as the low paid, families in poverty, pensioners, and the disabled. With Denis Healey as Chancellor of the Exchequer, the first budget was introduced between the two elections held that year. By implementing many of the electoral promises, the budget increased the popularity of the government to the extent that Labour won the October elections by a considerably more secure margin (Denver and Garnett, 2014, p. 53). At the same time, implementation of the electoral promises entailed a substantial rise in public spending, inducing the government to borrow substantial amounts of money. After the initial expansive policy attitude, from 1975 onwards the pressures regarding public finances started to increasingly set the tone of budgetary policymaking (Harmon, 1997). During the same year, Denis Healey started to seek help from the IMF. The negotiations started in 1975 and in autumn 1976 a deal was reached for a loan to cover the government's short-term expenses. The conditions attached to this loan were commitments to substantially reduce the deficit in the balance of payments. In the period between 1976 and 1979, the Labour government not only had to deal with increasing deficits, but also had the institutional commitment to reduce these. By the time of the 1979 elections, the party conference was accusing the government of not being sufficiently 'socialist' (Denver and Garnett, 2014, p. 59). To these accusations, Prime Minister James Callaghan responded that it was no longer possible to 'spend your way out of a recession' (Callaghan, 1976).

This case features several parallels with various crisis-ridden governments of the 2010s. The creed that it is impossible to use public spending as a way out of a recession typifies the conditions that the EU and the IMF attached to their bailout programmes for Cyprus, Greece, Ireland, and Portugal from 2009 to 2015 (Matthijs and Blyth, 2018). As with the Callaghan government, these conditions forced several governments to make a U-turn on their electoral promises. In Greece, for example, after having won the 2015 elections with a radical redistributive programme that even contemplated an exit from the monetary union, the Tsipras government eventually had to renounce most of them and abide by the supranational policy prescriptions (Lefkofridi and Nezi, 2020). The precedent of the Wilson/Callaghan government reduces the anecdotal strength of the bailout programmes of the 2010s as evidence of international economic integration being the cause for (temporary) reductions in government responsiveness.

As actors operating in a market economy, governments inevitably have extra-electoral obligations to fulfil. The assessment of whether international economic integration makes these obligations become more stringent requires a comparative investigation into whether governments from past decades were relatively more constrained than more recent governments within the same country, featuring the same partisan composition and similar macroeconomic challenges. There are, however, only very few cases that fulfil these selection criteria. In earlier research, I have sought to identify governments with such cross-time similarities (Karremans, 2017). Among the most comparable cases, there are the French governments led by the Parti socialiste under the presidencies of respectively François Mitterrand (1981–1986) and François Hollande (2012–2017) (Damhuis and Karremans, 2017; Karremans and Damhuis, 2020), and the Austrian Christian-democratic and social democratic coalition governments of 1992–1998 and 2009–2017 (Karremans and Kaltenleithner, 2021). The next section illustrates the main insights derived from these comparisons.

Cross-time comparisons in France and Austria

The cross-time comparison of governments of the same partisan composition operating in relatively similar macroeconomic circumstances offers a window into the extent to which different levels of embedment in a system of international economic governance is associated with different decision-making criteria. The analysis of policy justifications for annual budget plans allows to comparatively collect such information. The institutional practice by which governments each year appear in front of national parliament to present their budgetary policy existed also in previous decades (see also Karremans, 2017, pp. 31–37). As these speeches have maintained the same institutional format over time, they are particularly suitable for cross-time comparisons.

The argument that international economic integration brings additional layers of constraints entails that the governments of the 2010s should feature relatively more statements about financial commitments, while the governments of the 1970s, 1980s, or 1990s should feature relatively more statements about domestic socio-economic goals. More precisely, under most similar circumstances, the expectation is that centre-left governments from past decades should be more focused on socially-oriented goals while similar governments from the 2010s should be relatively more concerned with meeting financial targets. Similarly, centre-right governments from the 1980s or 1990s should dedicate a substantial part of their budgets for the sole purpose of benefiting economically domestic entrepreneurs or homeowners, while centre-right governments from the 2010s should place more emphasis on their virtues in maintaining low debt and deficits (Karremans, 2017: 152–166). In short, governments from the 2010s should feature relatively less justifications framing budgetary policy as an effort of meeting social goals and of meeting economic benefits to domestic actors, and more justifications referring to financial and international commitments.

The cross-time comparisons between centre-left governments in France and between grand coalition governments in Austria captures executives that in each country feature a most similar political composition and that face relatively similar economic challenges. In the French case, the comparison regards the governments operating under the first Mitterrand presidency (1981–1986) and the Hollande presidency (2012–2017), which were both led by the Parti socialiste and started off with a strong redistributive policy agenda, that later had to be revised due to macroeconomic circumstances. For the Austrian case, both between 1992 and 1998 and between 2009 and 2017, governments were composed of a grand coalition that steered the country out of a negative economic situation and within a few years made it fully compliant with European budgetary criteria. For both cases, the major contextual difference across time is the level of European economic integration, which during the 2010s was much more intensified than in earlier decades.

France

When in 2012 François Hollande became the first socialist president since 1995, political observers greeted the victory of the Parti socialiste at both the presidential and legislative elections as a refreshment in times when austerity was dominating the political agenda all over Europe (Clift, 2013).

The party's programme promised a more expansive socio-economic policy and more responsiveness towards social demands. Similarly, in 1981 François Mitterrand became the first socialist president of the country, with the Parti socialiste holding 57 per cent of parliamentary seats. This alternation of power brought high hopes on the left and deep concerns on the right about the direction of socio-economic policy, which the Parti socialiste promised would become more expansive and redistribution oriented. Under both presidencies, the Parti socialiste encountered substantial institutional and economic constraints to the implementation of its programmes. In the case of the Hollande presidency, the government was still confronted with the aftermath of the sovereign debt crisis and the stringent requirements of the new European economic governance. In the case of Mitterrand, under the conditions of the economic slowdown of the 1970s and 1980s, it was particularly difficult to pursue expansive policies (Hall, 1994). In addition, France was already part of the European Exchange Rate Mechanism which obliged it to reduce inflation. In both cases, in the middle of the legislative period the government took a U-turn on its policy programme. In March 1983, François Mitterrand decided on the famous *tournant de la rigueur*, which ended the expansive policy course and initiated a period of austerity policies. In the case of the Hollande presidency, after less than two years in office, the government substantially revised its policy programme, announcing substantial expenditure cuts. As can be seen from Figure 3.3, in the last year of the legislative period public spending was declining under both presidencies. In the case of Mitterrand, the government reversed the expenditure increases initiated largely by itself. In the case of Hollande, the government inherited an already high level of public spending. Its initial spending increases were relatively marginal and in the second part of the legislative term it engaged in reducing the overall level of public spending.

Another important aspect to highlight is that in the years of the Mitterrand presidency, French governments were accustomed to making five-year economic plans. The Hollande presidency, instead, operated in years in which economic policy had to be coordinated with European institutions on a yearly basis (Karremans and Damhuis, 2020, pp. 307–308). The cross-time comparison between the governments of the Mitterrand and Hollande presidencies thus offers a first tangible insight into how different levels of autonomy from international institutions may affect the criteria by which governments pursue their economic policies.

Based on a slight reorganization of the data collected and analysed in my work with Koen Damhuis (2017, 2020), Figure 3.4 reports the share of statements falling under each of the five main justification categories described

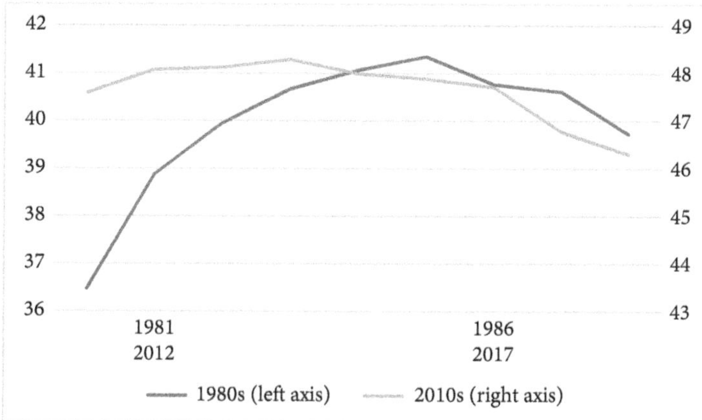

Figure 3.3 Public spending (as percentage of GDP) under the Mitterrand and Hollande presidencies

Source: World Bank data

in Chapter 2, for the budget speeches presented under the first Mitterrand (1981–1986) and the Hollande (2012–2017) presidencies.

In both cases, statements referring to the overall national economy are the largest category of policy justifications coded from the budget speeches. These are statements presenting government policy against the background of, or functional to, the country's growth levels. As was discussed in Chapter 2, in terms of responsiveness and responsibility these statements may be interpreted in both ways, as on the one hand they can be seen as improving societal well-being and at the same time they are aimed at increasing state revenues in the long term. Statements focusing on social goals, instead, are more unambiguously responsive to the demands of the Parti socialiste's voters. Under both Hollande and Mitterrand, these statements are the second largest category. Similarly, statements emphasizing the financial situation of the country are unambiguously a manifestation of responsibility. In both cases, these statements are the third largest category.

Beyond these similarities, the comparison also reveals several important differences. Firstly, the share of socially oriented statements is substantially lower under Hollande than under Mitterrand, by almost 10 per cent. To some extent, this difference results from the fact that by the 2010s the Parti socialiste had shifted parts of its attention from the needs of low-income groups to those of the middle class (Damhuis and Karremans, 2017, p. 1278). As statements referring to the middle class are associated with tax reductions, in Figure 3.4 they are counted under the category 'private economic freedom'.

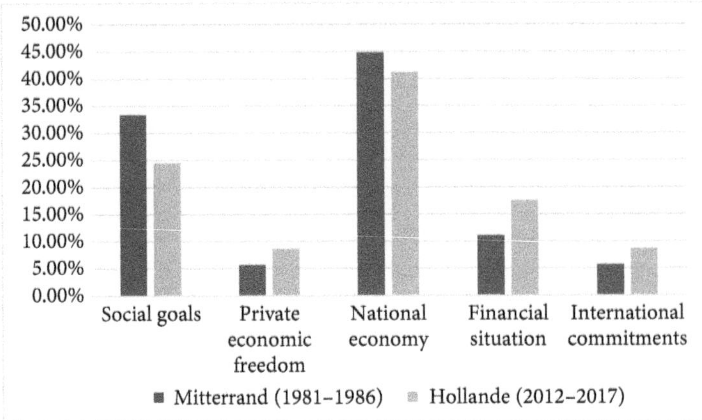

Figure 3.4 Focus of policy justifications in budget speeches delivered in France under the presidencies of Mitterrand (1981–1986) and Hollande (2012–2017)

Source: Author's calculations of the data featured in the Appendixes of Damhuis and Karremans (2017), and Karremans and Damhuis (2020)

Perhaps more importantly, the statements emphasizing financial and international commitments have a higher relative frequency of respectively 6 per cent and 3 per cent under Hollande. This indicates that in the 2010s the budgets presented by governments of the Parti socialiste were about 10 per cent less concerned with social goals and about 10 per cent more concerned with financial commitments.

In addition to these quantitative frequencies—which are based on hand-coding and therefore inevitably tied to some level of subjective interpretation—it is important to look at the qualitative contents of the discourses in the two periods. In my work with Koen Damhuis, we emphasize how the contents of the justifications that we classify as manifestations of responsiveness feature cross-time differences that are attributable respectively to the industrial and post-industrial contexts. While in the 1980s the responsiveness of the Parti socialiste was almost entirely focused on low-income groups, in the 2010s it is not only more focused on the middle classes, but it also emphasizes the party's intentions 'not to oppose social groups' (Damhuis and Karremans, 2017, pp. 1282, 1278). In parallel, the contents of the discourse that we classify as 'responsible' also feature an important difference. In the speeches delivered between 1981 and 1986, the government and the president take full responsibility for the *tournant de la rigueur*, presenting it as their autonomous decision, which they took in the country's interests after evaluating the economic situation. Under Hollande, instead, the government adopts more of a strategy of blame avoidance for justifying its policies of expenditure cuts, blaming it on the policy prescriptions of the European Commission or the World Bank (Karremans and Damhuis, 2020, pp. 313–314). In terms of contents, the Parti socialiste's socio-economic responsiveness seems to have become less ideologically laden and less anchored in specific redistributive preferences. In parallel, responsibility seems to be less motivated by the government's autonomous evaluations of the country's long-term interests and more by international commitments.

The cross-time differences are on the one hand partially in line with Mair's account of a hollowing out of democratic representation and about the increasing difficulties for governing parties to autonomously make decisions about the country's long-term interests (2013). At the same time, they are also in line with theories about the realignment between voters and parties. These cross-time differences in fact confirm that the Parti socialiste was to some extent responsive to its more diversified electorate which, beyond being composed of middle classes and sociocultural professionals, may also be in favour of a government that complies with the prescriptions of international institutions (Häusermann and Kriesi, 2015; Kitschelt and Rehm, 2015). This cross-time comparison thus indicates that the comparative study of budget speeches offers relevant insights into the balance between responsiveness and responsibility, but at the same time calls for further comparative research.

Austria

In both the 1990s and 2010s, in Austria a coalition government between Christian—and social democrats pursued a similar path of fiscal consolidation. In the 1990s this happened in the context of the Economic and Monetary Union (EMU) accession criteria under the third, fourth, and fifth Vranitzky governments, with public deficits reaching a low point of –6 per cent of national GDP in 1995 and being brought back well within the EMU threshold of –3 per cent in 1997. In the 2010s, fiscal consolidation happened in the context of the strengthening of the Stability and Growth Pact under the first two Faymann and then Kern governments, with public deficits reaching a low point of –5 per cent in 2009 and being gradually brought to less than –1 per cent in 2017 (Karremans and Kaltenleithner, 2021, pp. 3–4). In terms of economic growth, though under different dynamics, at the beginning of the 1990s Austria had emerged from an economic recession that made the reduction of public deficits a difficult endeavour. The budgetary policies of the 1992–1997 and 2009–2017 periods are thus suitable for comparison, bearing in mind, however, that in the 1990s there was an urgency to join the

EMU while the 2010s featured the aftermath of a much more severe economic crisis.

Based on a recalculation of the data analysed in my work with Johann Kaltenleithner (2021), Figure 3.5 reports the shares of justification statements for each decade among the five categories described above. Similarly to the cross-time comparison between the Hollande and Mitterrand presidencies, the first aspect that meets the eye is the overall cross-time similarity. In different decades, governments of the same ideological composition operating under similar contexts, weigh their goals and priorities in relatively similar terms. While the French socialist-led governments discussed above give relatively more importance to economic and social goals than to financial targets in their budget speeches, in the Austrian coalition governments the attention to these three broad goals is more evenly distributed in both decades. The cross-time differences are reduced to the fact that during the 1990s the policy of fiscal consolidation was relatively more justified in terms of international commitments. In the 2010s, instead, the justifications emphasizing the importance of reducing deficit and debt levels refer more to national rules, such as an agreement about a debt brake reached in spring 2012 between the central and local administrations (Karremans and Kaltenleithner, 2021, p. 5).

Furthermore, in terms of cross-time differences in the qualitative contents of budget speeches, the justification statements of the 2010s are more precise regarding the policies being pursued and the obligations being fulfilled (Karremans and Kaltenleithner, 2021, pp. 7–8). Statements from the speeches of

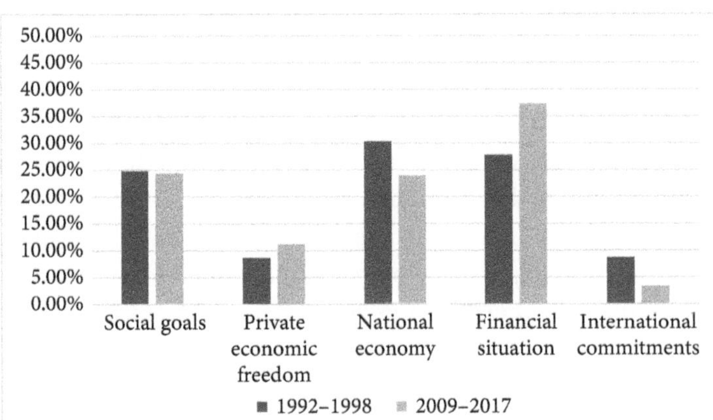

Figure 3.5 Focus of policy justifications in budget speeches delivered in Austria during the 1990s and 2010s

Source: Author's calculations based on coding of Austrian annual budget plans. See also Karremans and Kaltenleithner (2021)

the 1990s tend to be more vague as regards both the measures being introduced and the goals being pursued. In the 2010s, instead, the speeches tend to be more detailed in their references to which amounts are being spent on which purposes, and which institutional obligations are being met by specific expenditure cuts. Thus, from the perspective of democratic accountability the speeches of the 2010s offer a more positive picture than those of the 1990s, as they appear more transparent in presenting what the government does and why (Karremans and Kaltenleithner, 2021, p. 10). This can also be seen as a relatively better quality of responsiveness, as parliaments and voters are offered the possibility to better evaluate measures with which certain social goals were met.

Overall, the comparison between the Austrian budget speeches of the 1990s and 2010s does not reveal major differences in terms of their emphasis on social, macroeconomic, or financial goals. In the 1990s the financial commitments were expressed relatively more in terms of the government's overall effort to lead the country into the EMU. By the 2010s, Austrian governments were subjected to a greater amount of fiscally stringent rules, many of which, however, were part of its own national legislation (Doray-Demers and Foucault, 2017). Considering that, compared to some European countries, such as France or Italy, in general Austria and Germany are more favourable towards the European budgetary thresholds (Johnston and Regan, 2018; Matthijs, 2017; Wasserfallen et al., 2019), the Austrian government's compliance with fiscal discipline can be seen as in line with its national macroeconomic interest. This could indicate that intensified European integration is more constraining for some countries than for others.

What is there left to find out?

The descriptive inferences emerging from these cross-time comparisons reveal that European integration did not bring a sea change in the contents of budget speeches between the 1980s and 2010s. Despite the stringent fiscal framework, most EU member states continue to feature public spending levels of above 40 per cent of national GDP. As argued in this chapter, this amount could either be seen as an indication that governments continue to deliver substantial amounts of goods and services to domestic constituencies, or as a burden that governments need to keep financing and, at the same time, contain. If international economic integration does affect the balance between responsiveness and responsibility, this does not take place overnight but happens through a slow and corrosive process. In the eurozone during the 2010s, the elements potentially causing such a corrosion were strongly present, namely high international financial speculation on sovereign bonds and supranational governance structures ensuring that member states comply to the same standards of fiscal discipline. The budget speeches delivered in eurozone countries during this decade are thus a crucial case for establishing whether international economic integration slowly corrodes the room for manoeuvre that governments have to be responsive to domestic constituencies.

When analysing the budget speeches of the 2010s, though, it is important to disentangle the political consequences of the sovereign debt crisis from those of European economic integration. As argued in this chapter, policymaking during hard times features several patterns that make the decision-making processes of the 2009–2013 period relatively similar to those of other economic crises of the twentieth century. To establish whether the strengthened European economic governance altered the balance of criteria that characterizes the decision-making of democratic governments, the next chapter investigates the extent to which the pressures for fiscal discipline reached beyond the period of the crisis and kept constraining governments for the entire duration of the decade.

As the cross-time comparisons discussed in this chapter exemplify, exceptional macroeconomic circumstances and new supranational rules can create a momentum of high compliance to fiscal discipline that may only be temporary. Similarly to the early 2010s, also during the 1990s several European countries introduced intrusive fiscal stringency rules in order to be compliant with the criteria for accession to the monetary union (Doray-Demers and Foucault, 2017). In Italy, for instance, technocratic governments were appointed in both the 1990s and the 2010s in order to speed up the country's compliance with European rules (Culpepper, 2014; Dyson and Featherstone, 1996). Once the accession to the monetary union was complete, several governments became less rigorous in their compliance with European budgetary thresholds. During the 2000s there was in fact a temporary suspension of the Excessive Deficit Procedure, as the most powerful member states were not compliant with the agreed thresholds (Leblond, 2006). A similar dynamic may be expected for the 2010s. As the urgency of rule compliance withers away with time, governments may return to more generous and possibly even 'irresponsible' expenditure policies. Unless, that is, the strengthened European rules prevents them from doing so.

4

Responsiveness and responsibility under European economic governance

Introduction

On 5 July 2015, the citizens of Greece were confronted with a remarkable decision that created high suspense among citizens and governments across Europe and beyond. Since 2010 the country was under a bailout programme that allowed it to stay in the eurozone under the conditions of harsh austerity conditions which were putting social cohesion at risk. The bailout programme was needed to finance the state's most essential running expenditures. The unsustainable debt and deficit levels were preventing the government from borrowing money at affordable rates from financial markets, because there was no longer any confidence that the government was able to repay loans. In January 2015 the legislative elections were won by Syriza, a radical left party led by Alexis Tsipras that had promised a thorough renegotiation of the bailout conditions and an end to the austerity agenda. It also promised that if circumstances required it, the government would hold a referendum in which the Greek people could choose between abiding with the European Memoranda of Understanding or accepting the challenging possibility of a future outside the eurozone. On 5 July 2015 this moment arrived. After persistent disagreements with the European Council, the European Commission, and the European Central Bank about the bailout conditions, the Tsipras government called a referendum in which Greek citizens were asked if they agreed that the government should accept the austerity conditions attached to the bailout programme.

The referendum resulted in a large victory of the 'no' vote, which signified vast popular support to the government's stance of refusing to accept the European prescriptions for fiscal consolidation, even at the risk of being expelled from the eurozone. Paradoxically, a few days later Prime Minister Tsipras signed an agreement for a new European loan programme that featured possibly even harsher conditions for austerity policies, including the broadening of the tax base to increase revenue, reform of the pension system

Between Voters and Eurocrats. Johannes Karremans, Oxford University Press. © Johannes Karremans (2024).
DOI: 10.1093/oso/9780192886583.003.0004

to contain costs, and automatic cuts in public spending to generate primary surpluses. The agreement was passed through parliament on 14 August 2015, with forty-three Syriza party members voting against or abstaining, and the government needing to rely on support from opposition parties. Following internal disagreements within Syriza, the government resigned and new elections were called. These were again won by Syriza, and Alexis Tsipras proceeded to lead a new government until 2019. The second Tsipras government was much more moderate and diligently followed the European prescriptions on budgetary policy. By August 2018, the Greek government successfully completed the bailout programme and, for the first time in eight years, it could borrow money at market rates.

This Greek story is a case of extreme tension between responsiveness and responsibility (Lefkofridi and Nezi, 2020). Similar tensions, though, were present in most eurozone countries between 2009 and 2013. Governments' responses to the global financial crisis of 2008 had required substantial amounts of public resources, deepening the levels of debt and deficit. The poor state of public finances, in turn, resulted in negative assessments from rating agencies on governments' abilities to repay loans. This made borrowing money from financial markets to finance running expenditures increasingly difficult as the cost of borrowing went up. Investors would transfer their capital from the government bonds of more troubled countries like Spain or Italy to financially more secure countries like Germany (De Grauwe, 2016). This instability had to be corrected by improving the financial situation of all member states, in order to induce more positive credit ratings to reduce borrowing costs. The wave of austerity policies witnessed in Europe during the early 2010s were an effort to resolve this conundrum.

These policies generated vast popular discontent, as they involved cuts in many popular spending programmes (Alonso and Ruiz-Rufino, 2020; Bojar et al., 2021). Besides being a response to the crisis, these policies were also integral to the framework for European economic governance under the European monetary union. This framework was strengthened in a series of steps between 2009 and 2013, giving the European Commission more powers to ensure member states' compliance with European budgetary rules. This strengthening followed the institutional logic of European economic integration, namely the gradual introduction of more and more stringent rules regarding how governments can tax and spend (Doray-Demers and Foucault, 2017; Verdun, 2015). The Six-Pack (2011) and the Fiscal Compact (2013) can be seen as the most recent steps in a process that dates back to the Maastricht Treaty of 1993, which introduced the 3 per cent deficit and the 60 per cent debt thresholds. The development of this governance framework inevitably has consequences for governments' autonomy in deciding their spending and taxation policies (Laffan, 2014; Maatsch and Cooper, 2017).

Following the arguments of Mair (2013), Scharpf (2015) and Rodrik (2000), under such constraints governments are forced to increasingly pursue policies that can only be justified with responsibility rather than responsiveness. The implications of this argument would be that fiscal responsibility as a dominant criterion for socio-economic policymaking would not remain circumscribed to periods in which countries face a risk of default such as that of Greece in 2010. Instead, this argument implies that, as European rules are designed to a priori prevent countries facing such a situation, fiscal responsibility will inevitably remain a dominant criterion even after the ghost of sovereign default is gone, to ensure that public finances remain compliant to specific targets. Testing this implication is rendered more troublesome by the arrival on the scene in February 2020 of the coronavirus pandemic, which brought a new major economic downturn and also a temporary suspension of the Stability and Growth Pact. The implications of the argument therefore need to sought in the 2014–2019 period.

By the second half of the 2010s, for Austria, France, Germany, Italy, and Spain, sovereign default was only a remote possibility. Mario Draghi's statement about the ECB doing 'whatever it takes' to save the euro meant that even a country with high public debt like Italy could secure the financing of its activities by releasing government bonds on financial markets. Unlike Greece, the five countries selected for this study could finance their running expenditures relatively autonomously. Persistent high levels of responsibility during the second half of the 2010s would perhaps be necessary to meet European budgetary targets, but would at the same time be a democratic anomaly that corroborates the idea that increasing international economic integration leads to less room for responsiveness. As argued in Chapter 1, governments cannot rely exclusively on responsibility, but need to adequately alternate it with responsiveness in order to maintain citizens' trust over the long-term (Linde and Peters, 2020). This chapter therefore investigates the empirical implications of this expectation.

The analysis presented in this chapter shows that responsibility was the dominant policymaking criterion between 2009 and 2013, and progressively declined afterwards, while responsiveness visibly increased. Furthermore, the evidence reveals a positive association between levels of responsibility and centre-right governments during the years of the sovereign debt crisis. This suggests that the choice of austerity in the early 2010s was linked to the centre-right composition of the key governments in the eurozone and confirms the role that politics plays in crisis periods. The analysis also reveals that the changes over time in levels of responsiveness and responsibility also embody clear changes in policy choices. Before concluding, the chapter analyses the annual budget plans presented after the outbreak of the coronavirus pandemic, in order to assess the extent to which—under these unprecedented circumstances—the balance between responsiveness and responsibility deviates from that of previous years.

Predictors for responsiveness and responsibility

The contemporaneousness of the sovereign debt crisis and the reform of European economic governance in the early 2010s makes it difficult to assess whether the latter induced governments to be more responsible. Fortunately, political science offers us insights into how governments respond to crises and how this relates to levels of responsiveness and responsibility. The pioneering work of Peter Gourevitch (1986) on policymaking in hard times helps to develop theory-driven expectations about how the sovereign debt crisis may have affected the balance between responsiveness and responsibility. The empirical implications of these expectations can be distinguished from those related to how European economic governance may affect government's decision-making criteria. Evidence of the typical patterns of policymaking in hard times, and counter-evidence to expectations about the constraints of European rules, would imply that in the 2010s patterns of decision-making were similar to those that existed during the major crises of the twentieth century, despite deepening levels of European economic integration.

As discussed in Chapter 3, policymaking in times of crisis is characterized by the choice of a particular response strategy and the consistent pursuit of it. The choice of the austerity-based response to the sovereign debt crisis matured in several intergovernmental negotiations, and featured a contraposition between governments favouring an approach based on fiscal transfers across member states and an approach based on national fiscal discipline (Lehner and Wasserfallen, 2019; Wasserfallen and Lehner, 2017). The former approach, favoured mostly by France and southern European member states, would allow governments to pursue more fiscally expansive measures. The latter approach was advocated by Germany, Austria, and northern member states, and entailed more austerity policies. The latter were more successful in asserting their ideas in the negotiations and therefore in ensuring that the common response of the eurozone countries to the sovereign debt crisis was one based on austerity. This suggests that the unpopular austerity policies were a political choice and not structurally predetermined. Had the southern European countries been more successful or had the numerical balance between governments in the negotiations been different there could potentially have been a different policy response.

Building on the knowledge that austerity became the macroeconomic settlement in response to the eurozone crisis, we can expect budgetary discourse in the period 2009–2013 to be dominated by notions of fiscal responsibility, namely by justifications emphasizing the need to focus on the sustainability of public finances and to adhere to international (European) rules. A dominance of responsibility during this period would be in line both with the 'politics in hard times' argument that responsibility was a political choice to respond to the crisis, but also with arguments about the structural constraints of European economic governance. To establish which of the two lines of argument are more accurate, measuring the balance between responsiveness and responsibility in the following years can be highly revealing. For the analysis, therefore, time is the main predictor for the balance between responsiveness and responsibility.

The decade from autumn 2007 to 2019 can be divided into four different time periods that differ in terms of their economic and European institutional context. First, the budget speeches delivered between autumn 2007 and 2009 were concurrent with the outbreak of the global financial crisis but preceded the tightening of European economic governance rules. The second period (2009–2013) coincides with the climax of the sovereign debt crisis, during which there was widespread concern about the future of the European common currency. The third period (2014–2016) brought the first signs of economic and financial recovery, during which the potential threat of a collapse of the eurozone started to wither away. Finally, in the fourth period (2017–2019) the economic and sovereign debt crises finally seemed to have been relegated to the past. Differentiating between these periods facilitates isolating the crisis-related context from the constraints of European economic governance. As crises are also largely about perceptions, their impact should be greater when policymakers *perceive* they are in the middle of a crisis and smaller when they perceive they are on the way out. The constraints of European economic governance, instead, should be related to factual budgetary situations, and its effect should be visible regardless of the time period. While the implications of the 'politics in hard times' and the European constraints arguments coincide for the 2009–2013 period, they partially diverge for the 2014–2016 period and substantially for the 2017–2019 period.

The 'politics in hard times' explanation would indicate that the fiscal responsibility of the early 2010s was a political choice that was coordinated at the international level. Following the discussion in Chapters 1 and 2, we can add that democratic governments cannot permanently rely on notions of responsibility to justify their policies. In the sphere of taxation and spending policies, governments can to some extent legitimize their actions in the name of the long-term sustainability of public finances but they also need to have a story about what this brings back to voters. For fiscally conservative parties, for instance, the legitimation behind fiscal rigour is generally not limited to arguments about the state's current account but is connected to arguments about how this leads to lower taxes. In partisan discourse, therefore, even austerity is justified with both responsive and responsible arguments, with the former referring to what it brings to voters (lower taxes) and the latter referring to what is appropriate in the context of the state's debt and deficit levels. If, in the 2009–2013 period, policymaking was mostly portrayed in terms of state interest, we can expect that in the subsequent years governments felt a need to portray their policies more in terms of what they delivered to domestic constituencies by presenting proposals for stimulus policies, with left-oriented governments presenting social expenditure policies and right-oriented governments introducing tax reductions. Building on the insight that responsiveness is an important element in the legitimacy of and trust between governing institutions and citizens (Linde and Peters, 2020), we can expect that after a period of high levels of responsibility governments will gradually become more responsive to win back the trust of the electorate. The return to responsiveness should be more than rhetoric and substantial in the form of proposals for fiscal stimulus measures.

Following the European constraints argument, instead, we would expect the new European rules such as the Six-Pack (2011) and the Fiscal Compact (2013) to have a substantial and lasting constraining effect. From this perspective we would expect the post-2014 return to responsiveness to be limited overall and absent in cases where the European budgetary thresholds were not being met. Deficit levels can therefore be used as a proxy for European constraints, considering also that the debt levels of the five countries always exceeded the 60 per cent threshold in the time period observed (with the exception of Germany in 2019). If in the year preceding the delivery of the budget speech the country was also exceeding the European 3 per cent deficit threshold we can assume that the European pressure for fiscal responsibility was at its highest. Figure 4.1 reports the deficit levels of the five countries during the period observed.

The crisis years (2009–2013) are the years in which the five countries registered the highest levels of public deficit. In this period the European constraints coincided with the context of the sovereign debt crisis. The post-2013

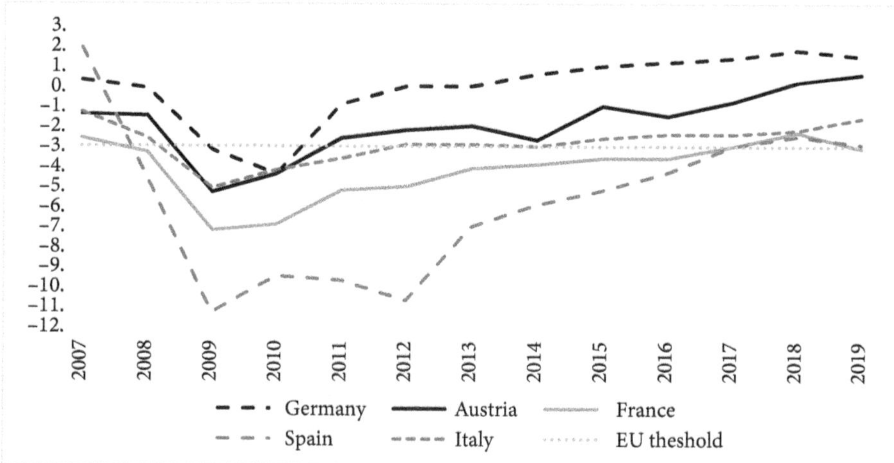

Figure 4.1 Deficit levels in Austria, France, Germany, Italy, and Spain between 2007 and 2019 (values reported as percentage of GDP)

Source: Eurostat data

financial outlook suggests a recovery from the crisis, with the fiscal balance improving in all cases. In terms of policymakers' perceptions, from 2014 onwards the crisis could increasingly be seen as a thing of the past. In terms of the European budgetary rules, however, in the second half of the decade only Austria and Germany were compliant (even though still not meeting the 60 per cent debt target). Italy began with a deficit of less than 3 per cent of GDP from 2013 onwards, but due to its large public debt (around 130 per cent of GDP during most of the decade) it remained closely observed by the Commission in the following years and was pressured to meet specific yearly budgetary targets. Spain and France continued to exceed the deficit target until 2017, while at the same time having a debt to GDP ratio of more than 90 per cent. Under these conditions, from the perspective of European budgetary rules, Italy, France, and Spain should have had too many constraints for their governments to be responsive to domestic constituencies.

The dire straits of the public finances of France, Italy, and Spain during the decade were also reflected in assessments by credit-rating agencies during this period (Figure 4.2). Credit-rating agencies assess the capacity of states to repay loans. One of the key aims of the European budgetary rules is to achieve relatively homogeneous and positive credit ratings for all the member states. Negative credit ratings would entail higher borrowing costs and are therefore a danger to the stability of public finances. Furthermore,

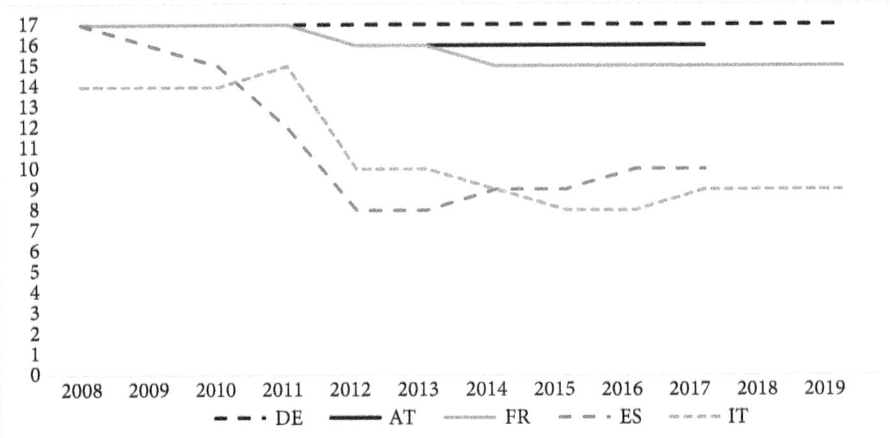

Figure 4.2 Credit ratings of Austria, France, Germany, Italy, and Spain between 2007 and 2019

Source: Author's coding of data retrieved from tradingeconomics.com

heterogeneous credit ratings within a currency union bear a risk of severe macroeconomic imbalances as, during a sovereign debt crisis, they would trigger huge capital transfers from countries with a negative rating to those with a positive rating (De Grauwe, 2016). From the perspective of institutional constraints, negative credit ratings are an additional pressure on governments to be more fiscally responsible. Figure 4.2 illustrates the credit ratings of the five countries between 2008 and 2019 measured on a 17-point scale in which 17 indicates a triple A rating—the rating that was given to most eurozone countries before the sovereign debt crisis. Considering that one of the objectives of the EU is to have high credit ratings for all its member states, the argument about the impact of European constraints would mean that the negative credit ratings of Italy and Spain—and to some extent France—would induce the governments of these countries to remain fiscally responsible after 2014.

Finally, another important factor to take into consideration is government partisanship. As shown by research on election campaigns (Hutter and Kriesi, 2019; Kriesi et al., 2012), fiscal discipline is to some extent more compatible with the ideological propositions of the right than those of the left. We may expect, then, that cabinets with a dominant composition of centre-right parties will tend to being relatively more responsible. By the same token, we can expect cabinets led by more left-oriented parties to be more inclined to increase public spending and therefore to be relatively more responsive. In cases of coalition governments in which centre-left and centre-right parties are quasi-equal partners, the partisan effect is more contingent on intra-cabinet dynamics, which cannot really be captured through the type of analysis carried out in this chapter. Table 4.1 reports how governments can be categorized depending on their partisan composition.

The aim of this categorization is to distinguish unambiguously conservative from unambiguously progressive governments in order to trace differences in the responsive–responsible balance by partisanship. The 'left' and 'right' categories only include governments that featured a dominant composition of (centre-)left or (centre-)right parties respectively. Most of the cases, however, do not have a clear position on what Kriesi et al. (2012) call the welfare–liberal dimension. These are categorized as 'centre/unspecified'. This category includes cabinets featuring large coalitions of centre-right and centre-left parties, such as the German third and fourth Merkel governments and the Italian Renzi and Gentiloni cabinets. The French government under the Macron presidency is also included because its programme contains both social-progressive and liberal values. Finally, the 'centre/unspecified' category also includes the Italian technocratic Monti government, which was supported in parliament by the centre-left and the centre-right, and the Conte I government, which was a coalition between the populist left and the populist right. The effects of technocratic and populist government compositions are investigated in Chapter 5. The analysis in this chapter, instead, tries to grasp what happens to the responsive–responsible balance when the government ideology is clearly leaning towards one side of the traditional left–right dimension.

Table 4.1 Governments categorized by left–right ideology

	Left	Centre/unspecified	Right
France	Hollande presidency (2012–2017)	Macron presidency (2017–present)	Sarkozy presidency (2007–2012)
Germany		Merkel III (2013–2017) and IV (2017–2021)	Merkel II (2009–2013)
Italy	Conte II (2019–2021)	Monti (2011–2013); Renzi (2014–2016); Gentiloni (2017–2018); Conte I (2018–2019)	Berlusconi IV (2008–2011)
Spain	Zapatero II (2008–2011)		Rajoy I (2011–2016) and II (2016–2018)
Austria		Faymann I (2008–2013) and II (2013–2016); Kern (2016–2017)	Kurz I (2018–2019) and II (2020)

Responsiveness and responsibility 2007–2019

In the budget speeches delivered in the five countries between the outbreak of the global financial crisis and 2019, the overall balance between responsiveness and responsibility clearly shifted over time, with a predominance of the latter in the budgets delivered between autumn 2009 and 2013 and a progressive increase in the former from 2014 onwards. Figure 4.3 reports the yearly share of responsive, responsible, and neutral justifications at the aggregate level for all five countries. The balance between responsiveness and responsibility evolves symmetrically. The highest shares of responsibility and the lowest shares of responsiveness are registered for the speeches delivered between autumn 2009 and 2013. In the speeches in the 2017–2019 period, instead, there is the opposite scenario. The same pattern is visible when looking at more unambiguous subcategories, with social- and market-oriented justifications for stimulus policies being almost absent between 2009 and 2013 and progressively increasing after 2014, while justifications for fiscal consolidation measures referring to financial commitments are mostly present in the period 2009–2013.

When looking at the individual cases, the same pattern is confirmed. Figure 4.4 reports the annual share of responsive justifications in each country. The pattern is the clearest in Germany, where the annual increase between 2014 and 2019 appears almost linear. A post-2014 increase in

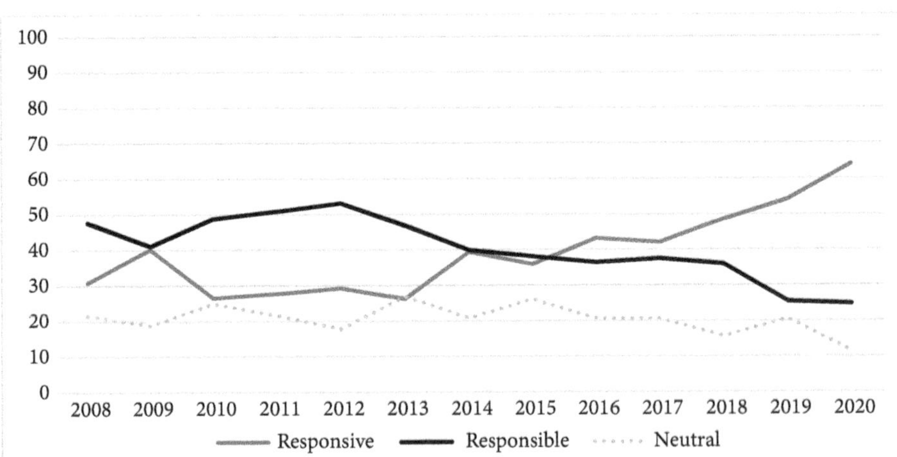

Figure 4.3 Share of annual responsive and responsible justifications in the five eurozone countries (2007–2019)

Source: Author's calculations of the data presented in Chapter 2
Note: The years are the budget years: e.g. a speech delivered on 8 October 2012 is for budget year 2013
N = 7,328 policy justifications

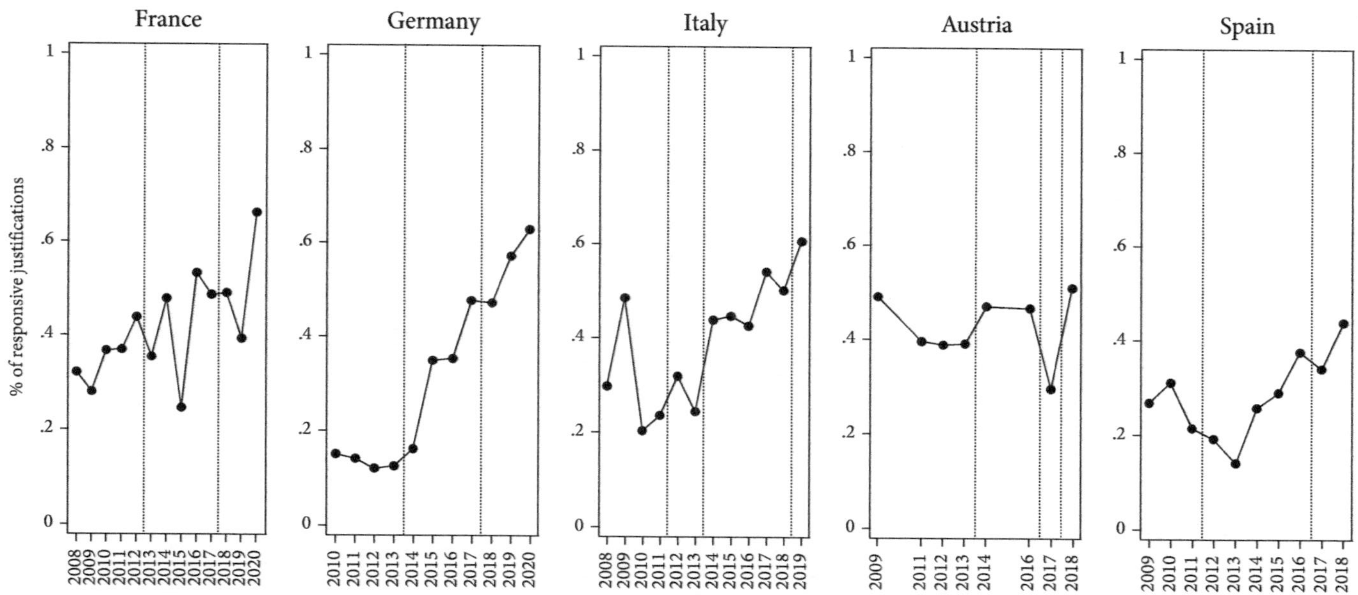

Figure 4.4 Share of responsive justifications in annual budget speeches

Source: Author's coding of budget speeches (see Chapter 2)

Note: Vertical dotted lines indicate legislative periods

responsiveness is also clearly visible in Italy and Spain, and partially in France. In the Austrian case the pattern is less evident, even though the post-2014 period still features a higher share of responsiveness than the period 2009–2013. Interestingly, besides being the case featuring the least clear pattern of difference over time, Austria is also the one where, during the years of the eurozone crisis, responsiveness did not decrease below 40 per cent in the annual policy justifications. In the German, Italian, and Spanish cases, between 2009 and 2013 responsiveness was around or below 20 per cent and increased almost linearly in subsequent years. Following the logic that responsiveness is a generator of trust between governments and citizens (Linde and Peters, 2020), this suggests that in these three cases after 2014 the governments were comparatively under stronger domestic democratic pressure to be more responsive. In all the cases, the yearly frequencies of justifications suggest that the governments were not constrained to be responsive to these pressures after 2014. The fact that the yearly increase in responsiveness is also visible in the fiscally more troubled countries—France, Italy, and Spain—suggests that European budgetary thresholds do not prevent governments from shifting their focus to the needs of domestic constituencies.

In order to verify the validity of this interpretation, Table 4.2 reports estimates of how the share of responsive justifications varies over the four time periods based on multivariate ordinary least squares regression models. The level of responsiveness is calculated against the level of responsibility—excluding observations categorized as neutral—and therefore indirectly also shows the variation of responsibility (that is, when responsiveness increases, responsibility declines and vice versa). The units of observation for the analysis presented in Table 4.2 are thus the annual shares of responsive policy justifications, calculated as a percentage of the annual total number of justifications that were coded as either responsive or responsible.

The analysis controls for countries in order to verify that the shifts over time in the shares of responsiveness and responsibility are not driven by specific cases. In Models 2 and 3, the analysis introduces controls for the political and institutional variables discussed in the previous section. In Model 4, the levels of responsiveness are weighted by their subcategories, with the more unequivocal responsive policy justifications receiving a greater weight than the more ambiguous observations. The weights are assigned following the categorization that was presented in Chapter 2. Thus social- and market-oriented justifications for fiscal stimuli receive a score of 4, macroeconomic justifications for fiscal stimuli a score of 3, social- and market-oriented justifications for the overall budget receive a score of 2, and social- and

Table 4.2 Ordinary least squares models estimating the association of responsiveness with the time period, institutional budgetary constraints, and government partisanship

	Responsive justifications			
	Model 1	Model 2	Model 3	Model 4
Time (reference: 2007–2008 [a]*)*				
2009–2013 [b]	−0.057***	−0.029	−0.058**	−0.097***
	[0.020]	[0.026]	[0.027]	[0.018]
2014–2016	0.055***	0.070***	0.022	0.011
	[0.020]	[0.026]	[0.027]	[0.019]
2017–2019	0.174***	0.182***	0.135***	0.121***
	[0.022]	[0.026]	[0.027]	[0.019]
Institutional constraints				
Surplus_lag		0.008	0.005	0.020***
		[0.005]	[0.005]	[0.004]
scale17_creditrating		0.003	0.001	−0.009***
		[0.004]	[0.004]	[0.003]
Government partisanship (reference: Left)				
Centre/unspecified			0.027	0.025
			[0.029]	[0.020]
Right			−0.058**	−0.112***
			[0.023]	[0.016]
Country (reference: France)				
Germany	−0.103***	−0.142***	−0.130***	−0.172***
	[0.018]	[0.029]	[0.032]	[0.023]
Italy	0.002	0.01	−0.021	−0.105***
	[0.017]	[0.027]	[0.028]	[0.019]
Austria	0.028	0.007	−0.02	−0.104***
	[0.018]	[0.022]	[0.027]	[0.018]
Spain	−0.109***	−0.074**	−0.070**	−0.079***
	[0.019]	[0.030]	[0.031]	[0.023]
Constant	0.387***	0.351***	0.426***	0.813***
	[0.021]	[0.073]	[0.091]	[0.064]
Observations	7,328	7,328	7,328	15,245
R-squared	0.043	0.043	0.047	0.086

Note: Time refers to the year when speeches were delivered.
[a] Includes the Austrian budget speech delivered in April 2009.
[b] Includes the German budget speech delivered in January 2014. Robust standard errors in brackets.
P-test: *** $p < 0.01$, ** $p < 0.05$, * $p < 0.1$.

market-oriented justifications for fiscal consolidation receive a score of 1. By weighting the subcategories of the responsive justifications, the analysis tests whether and to what extent governments in the post-2014 period were unconstrained in presenting fiscal stimulus measures and justifying them as beneficial to domestic redistributive goals.

The estimates in Model 1 show the association between the time period and the share of responsive policy justifications net of country differences. Compared to the policy justifications collected in the speeches delivered between autumn 2007 and spring 2009 (reference category), during the years of the eurozone crisis (2009–2013) there is a decline of 5 percentage points. In the subsequent time period there is an increase in the share of responsive justifications of 5 percentage points compared to the reference category. In the budget speeches delivered between autumn 2017 and autumn 2019 the increase is even higher, namely more than 17 percentage points. For all the time periods, the estimates are statistically significant (P value < 0.01).

Model 2 introduces two controls to account for variation over time in the institutional constraints: annual deficit/surplus levels and credit ratings. The estimates suggest that these constraints explain the decline in responsiveness in the 2009–2013 period. The increases in the 2014–2016 and 2017–2019 periods also remain significant after controlling for the countries' budgetary situations. This implies that the stark differences in the shares of responsive and responsible discourse between the different time periods are not explained by changes in the fiscally induced pressures to which the governments were exposed, except in the period 2009–2013. Model 3 introduces the partisan control variable, with left-wing governments as reference category. The model shows that a right-wing partisan government composition is negatively associated with responsiveness. However, the time period has an independent effect on the levels of responsiveness net of partisanship, especially in the eurozone crisis and the years 2017–2019. During the eurozone crisis, the level of responsiveness was lower while in 2017–2019 it was higher regardless of government partisanship. For the 2014–2016 period, by contrast, government partisanship almost entirely explains the higher level of responsiveness. In Germany, France, and Italy, in fact, between 2012 and 2014 social democratic parties entered or increased their presence in the governing coalitions.

Model 4 reproduces the same analysis but introduces weights for the different subcategories of responsive policy justifications. Assigning greater weights to the unequivocal responsive categories—those in which fiscal stimulus policies are justified with responsive arguments—does not alter the findings from the previous models. If anything, the lower levels of responsiveness during the eurozone crisis are larger in magnitude. This means that the policy justifications in these years are clearly different to those in other time periods. Furthermore, even after introducing the weights, the increase in 2017–2019 is substantial and statistically significant (P value < 0.01), meaning that the increase in responsiveness is not expressed in ambiguous terms but with proposals for actual fiscal stimulus policies. Regarding the control variables, after introducing the weights, the estimates show that a better budgetary situation seems to have a positive independent effect on the level of responsiveness. This is in line with the logic that when governments have a better budgetary situation they have more possibility to introduce fiscal stimulus measures and justify them in terms of domestic social- or market-oriented needs. Contrary to the expectation of the structural constraints argument, the estimates also show that worse credit ratings are not associated with less responsiveness. The effects of right-wing government partisanship are confirmed.

The evidence of the independent partisan effect and the weak support for the structural constraints argument suggest that government ideology matters in the balance between responsiveness and responsibility. As discussed at the beginning of the chapter, in an unconstrained world, government responses to crises are largely shaped by political processes. Therefore, government ideology should be particularly influential in crisis years as it substantially contributes to defining the framework for government policy responses. In the case of the eurozone crisis, this would entail that policy responses based on fiscal responsibility were strengthened by the ideology of the parties in government. In order to verify the validity of this interpretation, a model was run with responsibility as the outcome variable and the same controls and weights for the subcategories of responsibility as in Model 4 in Table 4.2, while introducing an interaction term between partisanship and the time period. Similarly as with Table 4.2, the analysis excludes the observations categorized as neutral and therefore indirectly also shows the variation of responsiveness (that is, when responsibility increases, responsiveness declines and vice versa). Figure 4.5 reports the model estimates plotting predictive margins for the levels of responsibility of left- and right-oriented governments. The governments categorized as 'centre/unspecified' were included in the analysis, but the results for them are not reported in the figure for clarity of visualization.

The predictive margins for left and right governments indicate that government partisanship is only relevant in the balance between responsiveness and responsibility in the peak years of the eurozone crisis, during which right-wing governments were significantly more responsible than left-wing

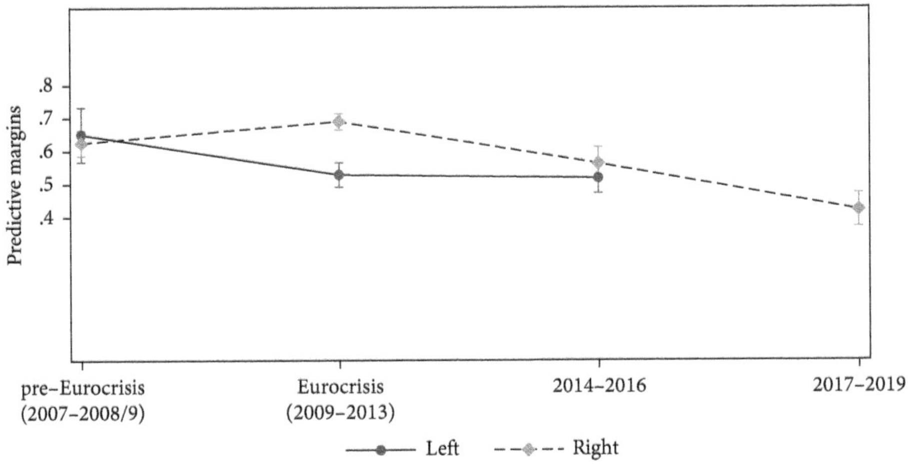

Figure 4.5 Predicted shares of responsible policy justifications in different time periods by government partisanship

Source: Author's coding (see Chapter 2)
Notes: Ordinary least squares (OLS) regression model with controls for surplus/deficit levels, credit ratings, country dummies, and an interaction term between the time period and government partisanship (three categories: left, centre, right; the figure excludes the 'centre' category for ease of visualization). The subcategories of responsibility justifications are weighted
The 2017–2019 features no 'left effect' because none of the budget speeches or documents collected during this period were delivered by a government composed of only left-oriented parties (see also Tables 4.1 and 2.1)

cabinets. Between 2007 and 2009, the years of the outbreak of the global financial crisis, both right- and left-leaning governments featured relatively high levels of fiscal responsibility, possibly induced by the concerns of the global financial crisis, which forced governments into large bank bailouts and therefore generated concerns over the sustainability of their finances. As financial markets started speculating on countries with large fiscal imbalances, thereby triggering higher borrowing costs for highly indebted countries, governments were trapped in a dilemma between adapting to market pressures for fiscal discipline or responding to social demands in a time of deep economic recession. As has been anticipated, the European intergovernmental negotiations led to a fiscal discipline policy response, which was adopted by all the member states (Wasserfallen et al., 2019). However, the predictive margins in Figure 4.5 indicate that centre-right and centre-left governments differed in the extent to which they adopted this policy approach, with centre-right governments considerably more inclined to shape their budgets towards fiscal consolidation. In the subsequent time periods, the partisan differences lose their effect on the balance between responsiveness and responsibility, as under centre-right governments the share of discourse about fiscal consolidation and deficit levels declines to the same level as that of centre and centre-left governments.

The different approaches of centre-right and centre-left governments to the responsiveness–responsibility dilemma during the eurozone crisis is also visible in qualitative terms. Spain and France had alternations of government partisan composition in 2011 and 2012 respectively. In the former case, the centre-right replaced the centre-left; in the latter, the opposite was the case. In the Spanish case, between the centre-left Zapatero and the centre-right Rajoy governments there was a clear change in how austerity policies were approached and justified. In the case of the Zapatero government, the austere budgetary policy was justified with quasi-technocratic arguments. The following passage is an example of the discourse with which Finance Minister Salgado Mendez announced the fiscal consolidation policy that the Spanish government would pursue in 2010:

> Ladies and gentlemen, the expenditure and taxation policy that I have just set out is compatible with a deficit target for the Central Administration in 2010 of 5.4 per cent of GDP, which is higher than that established in the General Budget Stability Law. Therefore, next week we will send to this Chamber an economic-financial rebalancing plan that will also be sent to the European Commission. … This document will detail the fiscal consolidation process that will allow us to comply with the Stability and Growth Pact. It will represent a process of fiscal consolidation that begins already in this budget for the year 2010 through a reduction of 7,500 million euros in terms of expenditure and a moderate tax increase that will allow us an increase of 6,500 million euros in tax revenue.
>
> **(Salgado Mendez, Spanish Congreso, 20 October 2009)**

The responsible discourse of the Zapatero government is highly defensive, profiling the fiscal consolidation policies as something it had—but did not want—to do. In the speeches of the first Rajoy government, instead, the same kind of measures are justified with a more proactive approach by Finance Minister Montoro Romero. The fast reduction of the public deficit is presented as a success, as in the following passage:

> This had never been done in Spain: down from a structural deficit of the order of 7 per cent to almost half in a single year in 2012. That is what we are doing as a country; that is what we are being valued for internationally …. Never in the history

> of Spain ... has such a budgetary effort been made, such an austerity effort made to direct our public finances towards the objective of correcting the public deficit and, therefore, containing the public debt.
>
> **(Montoro Romero, Spanish Congreso, 23 October 2012)**

While in the case of Zapatero, the austerity policies are presented as a necessary evil, in the case of the Rajoy I government, they are portrayed more as the policy course that the government is convinced to follow.

In France, where the alternation in government between centre-left and centre-right followed the opposite chronological order, there are similar partisan differences in the budget speeches. The centre-right governments under the Sarkozy presidency (2007–2012) were confronted with the outbreak and beginning of the sovereign debt crisis, while the centre-left governments of the Hollande presidency (2012–2017) were confronted with its continuation. Shortly after the outbreak of the global financial crisis, in October 2008 the centre-right Fillon government asserted the importance of fiscal discipline in tackling the crisis, with Finance Minister Éric Woerth stating the following:

> It is control of spending that guarantees the solvency of the State. ... The plan for financing the economy works mainly through loans guaranteed by the state. In a crisis, the state is the only actor that the markets still agree to lend to, the only one that the markets trust. This confidence depends on the structural recovery of our public finances, which only a determined action on spending can guarantee.
>
> **(Éric Woerth, French Assemblée Générale, 20 October 2008)**

Similarly to the justifications by the Spanish Rajoy government, fiscal responsibility is not presented as an imposition but rather as the government's choice to deal with the country's economic situation. After the victory of the Parti socialiste in the 2012 election, the governments of the Hollande presidency tried to change the policy course. However, during the term of office the government could not avoid the introduction of fiscal consolidation measures. Rather than as a self-chosen policy path these were mostly justified with the argument that they were needed in order to meet the demands of international institutions (Karremans and Damhuis, 2020, pp. 313–314). Similarly to the Spanish case, also in France during the eurozone crisis the centre-left government portrayed fiscal responsibility as a temporary necessity imposed by external circumstances.

Together with the quantitative data, these examples are indicative of how, during the decade from the global financial crisis until 2019, the extent to which governments were responsive or responsible was not structurally predetermined by the European economic governance rules. In the German case, evidence shows that the adoption and promotion of fiscal discipline ideas at the European level was at its highest when the finance ministry was led by the fiscally conservative Wolfgang Schäuble (see also Karremans, 2021b). When, after the 2017 election, Schäuble was replaced with Scholz, the focus shifted to how the German fiscal surplus should be used to finance social policy and environmental goals. These differences among governments will be examined further in Chapters 6 and 7. The quantitative and qualitative evidence corroborates the idea that during the eurozone crisis politics still mattered, and that the predominance of fiscal responsibility during the early 2010s was the result of political views that fiscal discipline was the best approach to tackle the crisis. The European structural constraints argument is further weakened by the post-2014 increase in responsiveness, which was unconstrained by European budgetary requirements. The progressive increase in responsiveness continued even further in budget speeches delivered in autumn 2020.

Responsiveness and responsibility in 2020

Soon after the outbreak of the coronavirus pandemic and the lockdown measures introduced throughout Europe, on 20 March 2020 the European Commission announced its intention to activate for the first time the general escape clause in the Stability and Growth Pact, temporarily suspending the institutional mechanisms with which the Commission could make member states implement structural adjustment programmes. In 2020, the budget speeches were therefore delivered in a less formally constrained environment. The shares of responsive and responsible justifications reflect this change, with the aggregate share of responsiveness amounting to almost 66 per cent. Table 4.3 reports the frequencies for the four countries analysed for this period—namely Austria, France, Germany, and Italy—and the aggregate level.

Most importantly, however, the shares of responsiveness observed in autumn 2020 do not seem to drastically change from the pattern of yearly increases observed in the second half of the 2010s. Against the background of the trends in budgetary discourse during the second half of the 2010s, the high shares of responsiveness in the speeches delivered in autumn 2020 appear to be independent of the relaxation of European rules. They instead reflect the urge governments had to provide assistance to businesses, families and all types of social actors that were forced to interrupt their activities during the period of the lockdown measures.

In the responsive policy justifications—which constitute the vast majority of the observations—the different governments displayed relatively similar commitments to delivering public services and meeting the demands of domestic socio-economic groups. At the same time, each government introduced typical partisan measures. In the Austrian case for example, we see the introduction of the 1-2-3 Klimaticket, which was an electoral promise of the Green party, which since 2019 has been in coalition with the Christian-democratic Österreichische Volkspartei. Similarly, the budget speech in Germany confirms a trend of increasing attention to social inequalities in public budgeting, a trend that started when the social democrat Olaf Scholz became finance minister in 2017. In the French case, in line with the ideological stance of the governing party La République En Marche (LREM), responsiveness was directed more to domestic small and medium-sized enterprises with provisions of loans guaranteed by the state and tax deferrals. The budget speeches therefore strongly suggest that also in 2020, the cycle in which political parties connect citizens' preferences to public policy was still working. The different contents of responsiveness justifications by governments of different partisan compositions will be further explored in Chapter 6.

Finally, the figures in Table 4.3 highlight another important general point: despite the pandemic, the social demand for government support, and the relaxed European rules, fiscal responsibility remained a criterion in socio-economic policymaking that governments continued to emphasize in their policy justifications. The share of around 14 per cent responsible policy justifications indicates that under these conditions too, governments followed the logic that responsiveness needs to be counterbalanced, to some extent, with

Table 4.3 Percentages of responsive and responsible policy justifications during the coronavirus pandemic

	Austria	Germany	France	Italy	Aggregate
Responsive	68.97	62.77	69.60	61.00	*65.69*
Responsible	12.93	13.14	16.80	34.00	*18.41*
Neutral	18.10	24.09	13.60	5.00	*15.90*
Total	*100*	*100*	*100*	*100*	*100*
N	*116*	*137*	*125*	*100*	*478*

Source: Author's own coding of annual budget plans presented in year 2020

a level of responsibility. The budget speeches display an overall commitment to the principle of long-term sustainability of public finances, with statements acknowledging the effects of the stimulus measures on public debt and deficit levels and asserting that they will need to be brought back in future years. As will be analysed in further detail in Chapter 7, however, the budget speeches in autumn 2020 feature a clearly more distinct logic of fiscal responsibility than during the 2010s.

Regular patterns or a sequence of imbalances?

Between 2007 and 2020, the balance between responsiveness and responsibility has not shifted towards responsibility, as was expected following pessimistic accounts about how European economic integration may affect national democracy. At the same time, the balance has been far from stable. The vast majority of the policy justifications from the annual budget plans presented between 2009 and 2013 focused on the need to reduce debts and deficits in order to regain the confidence of financial markets and to fulfil European commitments. From 2014 onwards, the policy justifications are increasingly responsive. In the budget plans that were presented from 2018 onwards, more than half of the policy justifications are about delivering resources domestically in order to serve citizens' social or private needs. The budget plans presented in the year of the outbreak of the coronavirus pandemic follow this trend, with responsive policy justifications nearing 70 per cent of the annual observations. The long decade that ranges from the global financial crisis of 2008 to 2020 is thus characterized by waves of different policymaking criteria, with responsibility being at first dominant, then being relatively in balance with responsiveness between 2014 and 2017, and finally responsiveness being dominant from 2018 onwards.

The aim of this analysis was to establish whether the strengthening of European budgetary rules in the early 2010s confirmed the theoretical argument that deepening international economic integration leads governments into a straitjacket in which they can only develop policies based on responsible criteria and they are therefore forced to neglect the preferences and needs of domestic constituencies. The gradual decline of responsibility and progressive increase of responsiveness from 2014 directly contradict this argument and confirm that the high levels of responsibility observed between 2009 and 2013 follow to a large extent the patterns of policymaking in hard times evidenced by Gourevitch (1986).

By late 2009, governments' finances featured deep deficits largely as a result of the bank bailouts that were triggered by the 2008 global financial crisis. These deficits caused great concerns about the stability of the public finances of countries that were already highly indebted and investors started transferring capital from high-debt to relatively lower-debt countries. This entailed capital flows from the European (southern) periphery to the continental northern countries, thereby threatening the stability of the common currency and triggering the sovereign debt crisis (De Grauwe, 2016, pp. 118–122). During the intergovernmental negotiations that took place between 2009 and 2013, the governments of the eurozone were initially divided on which policy approach to adopt in response to this crisis. One camp favoured a policy of fiscal solidarity in order to allow every member state to respond to domestic socio-economic demands and the other claimed that the main problem was the high debt and deficit levels of several eurozone members and that strict rules were needed to enforce fiscal discipline (Wasserfallen et al., 2019). The member states eventually settled on the latter approach and agreed on a common policy response based on fiscal consolidation. The budgetary policies of the early 2010s were therefore justified in terms of responsibility, namely ensuring the sustainability of public finances and adhering to the European budgetary rules.

As, from a democratic legitimacy perspective, governments cannot permanently rely on responsible policymaking criteria, but are also expected to deliver resources to their constituencies, responsiveness is bound to become more dominant as soon as the pressure of crisis falls into the background. The constraints of multilevel governance—and in particular the European budgetary rules—could potentially prevent such a reorientation of policy criteria, particularly in countries that failed to meet the prescribed targets. The analysis presented in this chapter, however, shows that European economic governance did not prevent the rise of responsiveness in the years following the sovereign debt crisis. As soon as the perception of a potential imminent collapse of the eurozone disappeared, governments started to increasingly shape their budgetary policies according to responsive criteria, even in countries that were still not compliant with the budgetary targets agreed on at the European level. The return to responsiveness was not only expressed in rhetorical terms but also in conjunction with concrete fiscal stimulus proposals which, as we will see in more detail in the following chapters, entailed measures such as investments in social housing in Germany and the introduction of support measures for low-income groups in Italy.

The budget speeches delivered after the outbreak of the coronavirus pandemic feature a continuation of this increase in unequivocal responsiveness, mostly introducing fiscal stimuli to support socio-economic groups facing the consequences of the lockdown measures. The fact that the response to economic recession in 2020 was radically different to that in 2009 can be seen as yet another confirmation that under European economic governance socio-economic policies are not structurally predetermined but subject to political processes that may lead to different alternatives. Compared to past episodes of 'politics in hard times' (Gourevitch, 1986), the only difference seems to be that in the context of European monetary union the policy response is coordinated at the international level. Thus, in times of crisis, governments have to agree on policy responses that may not be the ones they would themselves have chosen. The quantitative evidence in this chapter shows that, during the years of the eurozone crisis, responsibility was higher among centre-right than centre-left governments. Qualitative evidence in turn shows that, while centre-left governments presented fiscal consolidation policies more as an externally imposed and temporary necessity, centre-right governments presented them more as a choice they actively supported. This evidence suggests that different actors may have different perceptions about what responsibility means in policy terms. As will be further explored in Chapter 7, this signifies that the European consensus on fiscal responsibility is contestable and is not bound to be static.

At the same time, the sharp alternation between responsibility and responsiveness observed during the 2010s also indicates that budgetary policymaking in eurozone countries has been characterized by several years of imbalances in decision-making criteria. As argued in Chapter 1, a loss of balance between responsiveness and responsibility is a challenge to the legitimacy of democratic governments. Exclusive reliance on responsibility is the ideal recipe for policymaking in technocratic visions of public policy, while exclusive reliance on responsiveness is the utopia advocated by populist parties. The next chapter explores the extent to which the imbalances found in this chapter can be seen as deviations towards technocratic and populist forms of rule.

5

Policy justifications under technocratic and populist cabinets

Introduction

In November 2011 the Italian head of state Giorgio Napolitano gave the mandate to economist and former European Commissioner Mario Monti to form a technocratic government, with the specific aim of 'rescuing Italy' from financial speculation and possible default. The Monti government followed the fourth Berlusconi cabinet, which was labelled by most observers as populist and had lost the trust of both national and international institutions in its competences for handling the crisis (Albertazzi and McDonnell, 2015; Jones, 2012). When appearing in front of the Senate on the occasion of the vote of confidence, Mario Monti announced that his action was going to be solidly founded on a *senso dello stato*—a sense of the state (Repubblica, 2011). This sense of state was narrowly related to the responsibility towards Italy's European partners, as failure to resolve the country's economic and financial problems would be disastrous for the European monetary union. The government received support from the vast majority of parliament, with the main centre-right and centre-left parties agreeing that a year of austerity measures was needed in order to reduce deficits and regain the confidence of financial markets in Italy's ability to repay its debts. What followed was a series of broad encompassing policy packages that were entirely designed within the technocratic cabinet and with little or no involvement from parliamentary actors or representatives from civil society (Culpepper, 2014). The unpopularity of measures such as the increase of the retirement age or the increase of value-added taxes triggered a transformation of Italian political competition, with the brand new party Movimento Cinque Stelle (M5S, Five Star Movement) navigating the discontent and winning an unexpected 25 per cent of vote share at their first participation in national elections in 2013. From then on, Italian politics became characterized by a strong new demarcation between populist and mainstream political forces (Karremans et al., 2019).

Between Voters and Eurocrats. Johannes Karremans, Oxford University Press. © Johannes Karremans (2024).
DOI: 10.1093/oso/9780192886583.003.0005

In February 2021 this new contraposition led to another occasion in which a cabinet with populist tendencies was replaced by a technocratic-led government. After the 2018 general elections, the Five Star Movement had become Italy's largest party, with the promise of a universal income scheme and large investments in environmental policies. After extensive negotiations, it formed a coalition government with the Lega, a populist right-wing party that promised generous tax cuts. This coalition, led by Giuseppe Conte, brought together two of Europe's foremost examples of populist challenger parties, voicing respectively the dissent of left- and right-oriented voters (Katz and Mair, 2018). In summer 2019 the coalition fell apart due to internal disagreements, and the M5S formed a new coalition government with the more moderate centre-left Partito Democratico (PD), again under the leadership of Giuseppe Conte. This coalition was not approved by everybody within the PD. Former leader Matteo Renzi created his own new party and, albeit remaining in the governing coalition, it expressed a more critical voice to the M5S's policy agenda, calling for more long-term responsibility and less responsiveness to short-term demands. In January 2021 Matteo Renzi's new party withdrew from the coalition, causing the government to lose the parliamentary majority. Giuseppe Conte was forced to resign and, in the context of the ongoing coronavirus pandemic and upcoming new European commitments, the head of state Sergio Mattarella gave the mandate to former President of the European Central Bank Mario Draghi to form a technocratic-led cabinet and urged parties to support it until the end of the legislature (Garzia and Karremans, 2021).

After a decade marked by multiple crises, Italian political competition seems to have moved beyond the contraposition between economic liberalism and social democracy—or conservativism versus progressive cultural views—and it increasingly reflects different views on the combination of popular representation and policy expertise. Similar developments are observable in other advanced democracies. In France, the decade-long competition between the Republicans and the Parti socialiste has been mostly replaced by a contraposition between the pro-European Emmanuel Macron, who made a career in the French state apparatus, and Marine Le Pen, a key exponent of Europe's populist right (De Vries and Hobolt, 2020). Another example is the Netherlands, where parliamentary opposition parties are increasingly divided between those 'constructively' cooperating with the cabinet in meeting budgetary targets and those only concerned with voicing popular dissent (Hemerijck et al., 2022a). The new demarcation line between populist and technocratic views of governance is visible across many European party systems, and is present among both parties and citizens, with some people favouring direct representation of their interests while others favour expertise in government (Bertsou and Caramani, 2020; Caramani, 2017). The peculiarity of the Italian case is that between 2008 and 2020 the composition of government has featured a clear alternation between technocrats, populists, and traditional governing parties.

The Italian case therefore allows a comparative exploration of what happens to the balance between responsiveness and responsibility when populist and technocratic forces take power. The policy justifications of these cabinets provide empirical insights into the extent to which a technocratic composition of government indeed leads to higher levels of responsibility, and into the extent to which populism leads to more responsiveness. At the same time, they provide the empirical grounds for reflecting more substantially on whether the high levels of responsibility registered in the five eurozone countries between 2009 and 2013 are similar to those of a technocratic government. By the same token, they allow us to reflect more concretely on the extent to which the governments of the 2017–2019 period feature levels of responsiveness that are as high as those of a populist cabinet. Building on the theoretical continuum presented in Chapter 1 between the responsiveness–responsibility and the populism–technocracy dichotomies, the chapter situates the Italian governments of the 2008–2019 period on this scale and formulates expectations about how each executive should feature a different balance between responsiveness and responsibility. These expectations are tested through a combination of quantitative and qualitative methods, which are used to analyse the arguments with which each government justified its budgetary policies. The levels of responsiveness and responsibility of these Italian governments are compared to the aggregate levels of the governments of the other four countries operating contemporaneously.

The overall findings are in line with the idea that technocratic-led cabinets govern more in the name of institutional commitments and the long-term sustainability of public resources, whereas populist governments tend to place greater emphasis on the policies that reflect their political preferences. Governments run by traditional governing parties, instead, tend to produce a more balanced discourse. The technocratic Monti government features relatively higher shares of responsibility than its predecessors and successors, but these are roughly equal to the shares of fiscal responsibility registered in other countries in the same years. The share of responsive policy justifications of the populist first Conte government is comparatively higher than both the cabinet that preceded it and that of other European governments operating in the same years. At the same time, for the entire 2014–2019 period, Italian governments appear comparatively more responsive than in the other four countries. The comparisons with other cases thus suggests that populist and technocratic alternation in government changed the balance between responsiveness and responsibility only to a limited extent.

Finally, perhaps the most revealing finding is that the technocratic and populist cabinets analysed in this chapter also needed to try to strike some balance between responsiveness and responsibility. With the aid of qualitative evidence, the chapter shows that populist governments need to show a certain level of responsibility and that technocratic governments cannot solely justify their actions on the basis of institutional commitments but they need to indicate their preferences regarding how society and the economy should be governed. This latter point entails that parliaments and the public are informed about the government's political choices and so have the possibility of voting for or against it. Thus, overall, the Italian case suggests that technocratic and populist forces do indeed challenge the balance between responsiveness and responsibility, but, through comprehensive and effective accountability mechanisms, democracies have an embedded institutional resilience to such challenges.

Italy as a laboratory for political research

As was anticipated in Chapter 1, the populist and technocratic visions of democracy are in many ways extensions of critiques of the representative and governmental qualities of party governments as they oppose compromises between responsive and responsible policy criteria and give exclusive importance to the former and the latter respectively. While party governments are expected to combine political and institutional legitimation principles, populists and technocrats refute institutional constraints and political motives respectively (Caramani, 2017). In the populist conception of democracy, budgetary policy can only be justified on the basis of political preferences expressed by the people, and therefore on the basis of the preferences represented by the party winning the most votes in elections. In the technocratic conception of democracy, budgetary policy should only be justified on the basis of what should and can be done, with the sustainability of public finances being the main anchor guiding the government's action (McKenna and Graham, 2000). By respectively claiming to know the will of the people and presuming to know what is best for the country, both populists and technocrats have an aversion to the intermediary role played by political parties. At the same time, the two challenges tend to fuel one another as technocratic rule strengthens the populist appeal of representation of the people's will while ineffective populist rule may strengthen the appeal of technocratic experts. Technocracy and populism can therefore be seen as syndromes that affect the balance between responsiveness and responsibility. The more these two syndromes are active in governing institutions, the higher the risk that democracy becomes 'disfigured' (Urbinati, 2014), featuring irresponsible governments under populist rule and unresponsive executives under technocratic rule.

This claim has, however, never been put to empirical scrutiny. To validate this theoretical claim it is necessary to identify cases of alternation in office between populist, party, and technocratic governments in which several contextual factors remain constant. As responsiveness refers to societal demands and responsibility to institutional commitments, the empirical meaning of these two concepts may vary over time and between countries, as different societies have different demands and different governments have different commitments (Lefkofridi and Nezi, 2020). The fact that in Italy the experiences of the technocratic Monti government and of the populist first Conte government took place in the same decade offers a unique opportunity for comparative research. The decade is characterized by the consequences of the 2008 global financial crisis. During the period ranging from 2008 to 2019, in budgetary terms responsiveness can be broadly conceived as responding to societal demands for either more social protection or for tax reductions (Hutter and Kriesi, 2019). Responsibility, particularly in the eurozone, can be conceived as a focus on the long-term stability of public finances, emphasizing in particular the government's duty to run low public deficits and reduce public debt, which is also emphasized in various European agreements (Laffan, 2014).

The Monti and first Conte cabinets are the closest empirical resemblances of the extremes of the theoretical dimension illustrated in Chapter 1, with technocracy on one end and populism on the other. The Monti government has been identified in the literature as one of the most extreme examples of technocratic cabinets (McDonnell and Valbruzzi, 2014, p. 665). It was exclusively composed of technical experts who had no affiliation with any political party and it was appointed with the specific institutional mandate of safeguarding the long-term stability of Italy's public finances (Culpepper, 2014). The fulfilment of this mandate required policies that the previous cabinet was unwilling to pursue. The previous Berlusconi IV government was a coalition of centre-right and populist right political parties, namely the Popolo della Libertà and the Lega Nord. The two governing parties committed to 'keep their hands out of Italians' pockets' and to reduce the fiscal pressure on entrepreneurs (Ginsborg and Asquer, 2012). In 2010, these electoral commitments came into sharp contrast with the demands of Italy's European partners, which became concerned about the state of Italy's public finances. These concerns eventually led to the resignation of the Berlusconi IV government and the appointment of the Monti cabinet in November 2011.

The Conte I government, on the other hand, was composed of two populist parties which had strong electoral mandates to respectively increase social benefits (M5S) and reduce taxation (Lega) (Karremans et al., 2019; Newell, 2019). The electoral mandate came after the 2013–2018 legislature, during which Italy saw a succession of three different prime ministers—Enrico Letta, Matteo Renzi, and Paolo Gentiloni[1]—all belonging to the centre-left Partito Democratico. Despite various internal reshuffles and some party fusions and splits, the governments in the 2013–2018 legislature were composed of Italy's most centrist political parties from both the centre-left and centre-right, with the Partito Democratico being the biggest stakeholder. The coalition gave itself the mandate to distinguish itself from the populist challenger parties in opposition while at the same time bringing politics back into government after the technocratic experience (Garzia, 2013; Karremans et al., 2019).

On the basis of existing depictions and classifications in the literature, the four different government experiences can be identified as examples of populist, technocratic, and party governments featuring different degrees of populism. This makes the Italian case a perfect laboratory for political research. The different governments can be located on a scale ranging from populism to technocracy, with the expectation that they feature different balances between responsiveness and responsibility. Figure 5.1 illustrates this scale.

The party governments, which are located roughly in the centre of the figure, are expected to feature a balance between responsive and responsible criteria for decision-making. The broad coalition that governed between 2013 and 2018—under the leadership of Letta, Renzi, and Gentiloni successively—is expected to feature such a balance as it was composed of parties that on the one hand had electoral concerns and on the other wished to profile themselves as 'good' governors (Garzia, 2013). Technocratic governments, instead, with no specific group of voters to be responsive to, are expected to legitimize their actions only on the basis of responsible criteria, namely, explaining how their actions fit their institutional mandate to serve the country's long-term interests. Therefore, we should expect the Monti

[1] As discussed in Chapter 2, the analysis presented in this book does not include any budgetary plan of the Letta government because the plan for 2013 was developed by the Monti government and the 2014 plan by the Renzi government.

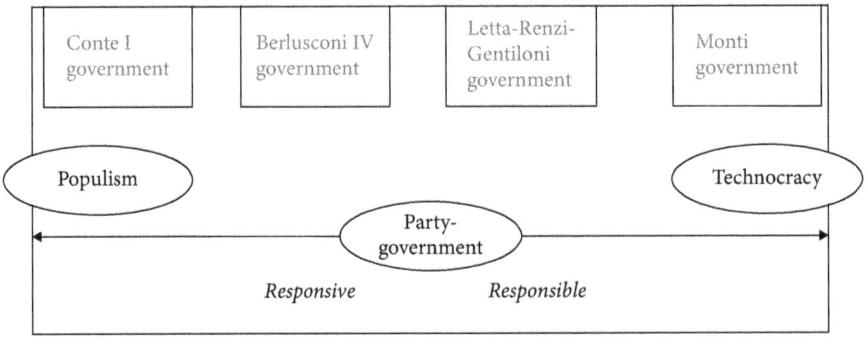

Figure 5.1 Theoretical expectations: governments on a responsive–responsible continuum
Source: Author's illustration

government to be more responsible than the coalition governments of the 2013–2018 legislature. When party governments have strong populist tendencies, as the Berlusconi IV government had, we should expect them to increasingly neglect responsibility policy criteria and increasingly legitimize their actions in terms of what is expected from them as representatives of the will of the people. The Berlusconi IV government should therefore be relatively more responsive and less responsible than the Letta-Renzi-Gentiloni governments. Finally, following the same logic, governments that are led by populist forces alone should legitimize their policies only in terms of their redistributive preferences and neglect the institutional responsibilities of the executive. The Conte I government is therefore expected to have the highest level of responsiveness and the lowest level of responsibility among the case selection.

As analysed in Chapter 4, the balance between responsiveness to societal demands and fiscal responsibility may to some extent be affected by financial and economic circumstances (Truchlewski, 2020). More precisely, in economic good times governments tend to have more room for manoeuvre to provide their voters with resources. In economic and financial hard times, instead, pressure for responsibility rises, as a growing number of institutions—international partners and debt holders—become concerned about the sustainability of public finances. In 2010, the pressure for responsibility during preparation of the government's budget was likely to be relatively higher than, for example, in 2017, as in 2010 the government needed to take into account the large loss of revenue caused by the previous year's recession and the related steep growth of the public deficit. Centre-right governments, in turn, may be relatively more inclined to respond to such crises by applying fiscal responsibility criteria. Overall, however, in the Italian case, every year from 2008 to 2020 was financially critical. As public debt remained well above 120 per cent of GDP, Italian public finance remained under the strict surveillance of European institutions during the entire decade, and governments were pressured to bring the deficit closer to zero (Codogno and Merler, 2019). While taking into consideration the shock of the 2009 recession, the governments in this case selection operated in a relatively similar context of economic and financial uncertainty in which they were pressured to consolidate their budgets.

Following the theoretical continuum presented in Figure 1.1 in Chapter 1, the expectation would be that the balance between responsiveness and responsibility would change according to the type of government and follow the pattern presented in Figure 5.1. This implies that the Conte I government should be the most preoccupied with responsiveness to societal demands and that the Monti government should be the most preoccupied with public debt and deficits. In between, the Berlusconi IV and the Letta-Renzi-Gentiloni governments should feature more balanced discourse, with the former leaning more towards responsiveness than the latter. The Berlusconi IV government may provide some exceptions to this expectation which can be explained by the shock of the 2009 recession.

Following European patterns

Coding the Italian budgetary plans in the 2008–2019 period produced a total of 1,804 observations representing policy justifications. The annual balance between responsiveness and responsibility followed the same pattern as that identified at the aggregate level in Chapter 4, namely a dominance of responsibility in the four budgets between 2010 and 2013 and a gradual increase of responsiveness and decline of responsibility between 2014 and 2019. Figure 5.2 reports the percentages of responsive, responsible, and neutral policy justifications for each yearly budgetary plan.

Beside the differences between time periods, the yearly distribution of responsive and responsible policy justifications also partially reflects the expectations illustrated in Figure 5.1, with the budgetary plans presented under the Conte I government appearing to be relatively more responsive than those of the Renzi and Gentiloni governments, which in turn appear to be less responsible than the technocratic Monti government. Another interesting observation is that, for both the Conte I and Berlusconi IV governments, the percentage of policy justifications that have been

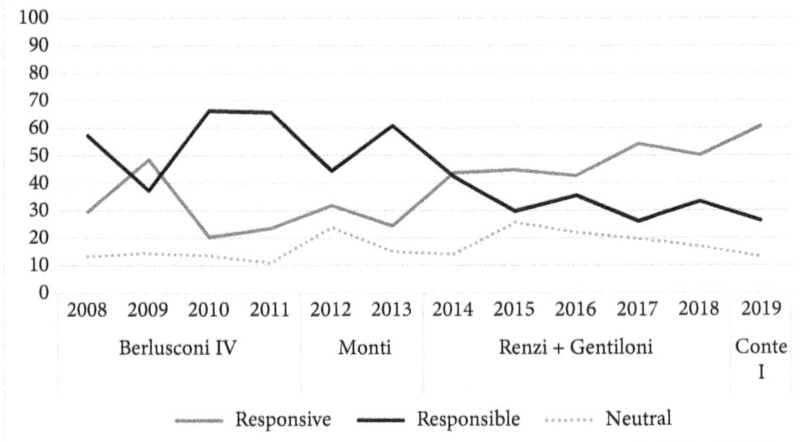

Figure 5.2 Responsiveness and responsibility in Italy (2008–2019)
Source: Author's coding of Italian annual budget plans 2008–2019 (N = 1,804 policy justifications)

classified as 'neutral' is around 13 per cent, while in the case of the Monti and Renzi/Gentiloni cabinets it is 20 per cent. This means that in the latter two cases a larger share of policy justifications make general statements about how the budgetary plans are intended to serve the country's well-being without specifying whether the decisions follow the principle of fiscal sustainability or whether they are designed to deliver resources to the domestic socio-economic sphere. In the Berlusconi IV and Conte I budgetary plans, instead, a larger share of policy justifications make clear statements in this regard.

From the perspective of the populism–technocracy scale, however, the most puzzling feature is the budgetary plans of the Berlusconi IV government (2008–2011). The shares of responsive and responsible policy justifications in these plans contradict the theoretical expectation that the budgetary discourse of a populist party government should feature high levels of responsiveness. The budgetary plans for 2008, 2010, and 2011 contain high levels of responsibility. Table 5.1 reports the shares of responsive and responsible policy justifications by the type of government while excluding the 'neutral' justifications, therefore allowing us to see the emphasis that governments give to responsiveness vis-à-vis responsibility when they make clear statements about the criteria behind their actions. The table also reports the shares of the more specific subcategories.

The theoretical expectations in Figure 5.1 are partially confirmed for the technocratic and populist governments. The Monti government has the

Table 5.1 Responsiveness and responsibility by government type

	Populist government	Populist party government	Mainstream coalition government	Technocratic government	
	Conte I	Berlusconi IV	Renzi & Gentiloni	Monti	Aggregate
			BROAD CATEGORIES		
Responsiveness	69.75	38.34	51.19	35.95	50.98
Responsibility	30.25	61.66	40.81	64.05	49.02
Total	*100*	*100*	*100*	*100*	*100*
			RESPONSIVE–RESPONSIBLE SUBCATEGORIES		
Responsive policy	34.45	11.53	26.85	8.68	20.62
Responsive economics	14.29	3.75	6.98	5.79	6.56
Responsive discourse	20.17	18.77	24.3	19.01	21.7
Responsive rhetoric	0.84	4.29	1.07	2.48	2.1
Responsible rhetoric	8.4	6.17	6.71	6.2	6.63
Responsible discourse	18.49	28.15	23.62	35.12	26.23
Responsible economics	0	2.41	0.81	1.65	1.28
Responsible policy	3.36	24.93	9.66	21.07	14.87
Total	*100*	*100*	*100*	*100*	*100*

Source: Author's coding of annual Italian budget plans (2008–2019)

highest share of responsible justifications and the lowest share of responsive ones, while for the Conte I government the opposite is the case. The same pattern also holds to a large extent for these two governments when looking at the more specific subcategories. In line with the theoretical expectations, the Conte I government has the lowest share of responsible justifications for fiscal consolidation policies and the highest share of political arguments justifying expenditure increases and/or tax reductions ('responsive stimulus'). In line with the expectations, the Monti government has the lowest share of 'responsive stimulus' arguments and, somewhat surprisingly, only the second highest share of responsible justifications for fiscal consolidation. Contrary to the theoretical expectations in Figure 5.1, the highest share of responsible justifications for consolidation policies is observed for the Berlusconi IV government. In terms of the shares of the broad categories, the Berlusconi IV government appears only slightly less responsible than the Monti government and substantially more responsible than the Renzi and Gentiloni governments.

Following the insights in Chapter 4, the potential reasons for the relatively high shares of responsibility and low shares of responsiveness in the policy justifications of the Berlusconi IV government need to be sought in its concomitance with the crisis period and its ideological composition of exclusively right-oriented parties. Of these two potential reasons, only the former is exogenous to the domestic democratic system. The context of the crisis may have reduced the potential effect of the populist composition of the Berlusconi IV government on the balance between responsiveness and responsibility. The years of the sovereign debt crisis may to some extent be considered an exceptional period during which even a populist party government was forced to show some level of fiscal responsibility. If the relatively high levels of responsibility are instead linked to the ideological composition of the government, it would mean, in this case, that the populist characteristics of the government did not have the predicted impact on the balance between responsiveness and responsibility. It would mean that the Berlusconi IV government behaved like a typical centre-right government, delivering resources to domestic constituencies when circumstances allowed and opting for fiscal responsibility in times of crisis. In order to establish which of the two interpretations is more accurate, the following two sections present first a statistical analysis of the extent to which crisis-related factors explain the differences between the government types in terms of their balance between responsiveness and responsibility, and second a more in-depth qualitative investigation into the responsible justifications by the Conte I and Berlusconi IV governments and the responsive justifications by the Monti government.

Evidence of populist and technocratic imbalances

The tenure of the Berlusconi IV cabinet was concomitant with the outbreak of both the financial and the sovereign debt crises. Compared to the Conte I, Renzi, and Gentiloni governments, it sailed into comparatively more troubled waters. At the same time, as discussed in Chapter 4, the macroeconomic and financial outlook between 2014 and 2019 was not rosy either, with the public debt reaching 130 per cent of GDP and the government barely succeeding in keeping the public deficit within the −3 per cent threshold. Unlike the governments in the post-2014 period, however, the Berlusconi IV government operated in a context in which there was widespread concern about the survival of the European common currency. Even though for a populist government the 'will of the people' is far more important than the stability of a currency, one may conjecture that the outbreak of the sovereign debt crisis, particularly in Italy, had a shock effect that may have induced the government to temporarily prioritize responsibility. Therefore, in addition to the structural factors used in the Ordinary least squares (OLS) regression models in Chapter 4, this chapter also introduces a control for the start of the crisis. In practice, this consists of excluding the budgetary plan for 2010 from the analysis. This was the first budget that was presented after Greece called for external help in early 2010 and received the EU–IMF bailout package, triggering a cascade reaction in which international lenders became increasingly anxious about excessive national debt and demanded higher interest rates from countries like Italy with higher debt levels and current account deficits. By controlling for the 2010 budgetary plan, the analysis therefore seeks to isolate any effect that may have been caused by a temporary panic reaction.

Figure 5.3 plots the coefficients for the level of responsibility in the discourse of each type of government. The darker dots report the probabilities predicted by Model 1 (M1), which has no controls. The lighter grey dots report those predicted by Model 2 (M2), which has controls for deficit/surplus levels, credit ratings and the start of the crisis. As in Chapter 4, the analysis includes weights for the subcategories of responsiveness and responsibility, and for each budgetary plan the deficit/surplus level and credit rating in the previous year are taken into consideration.

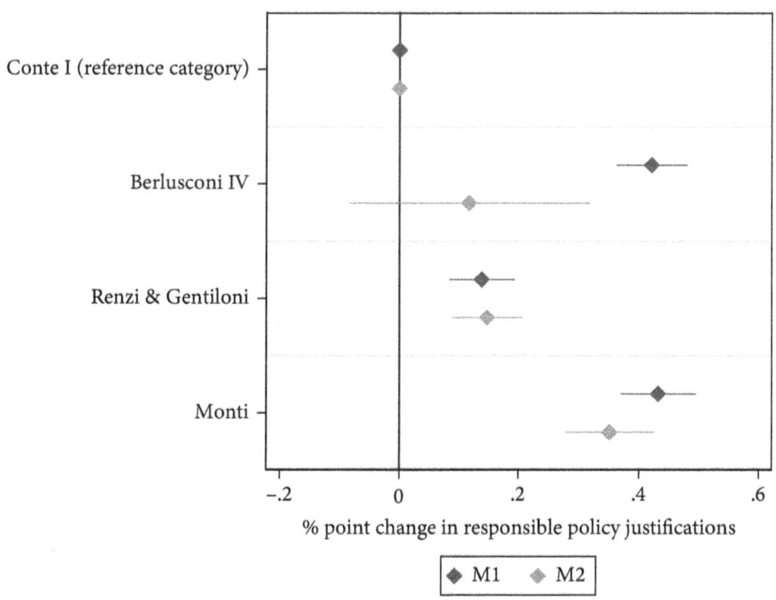

Figure 5.3 Predicted probabilities for responsible policy justifications by government type, including weights for subcategories

Source: Author's coding of Italian annual budget plans 2008–2019

The predicted probabilities in Model 1 indicate that the differences between the shares of responsible of responsible justifications for the Conte I, Renzi/Gentiloni, and Monti governments are substantial and statistically significant (P value < 0.01). At the same time, they also show that the balance between responsiveness and responsibility for the Berlusconi IV government is almost identical to that of the Monti government. The estimates from Model 1 therefore mostly reflect the difference between governments that operated in crisis and non-crisis years rather than between populist and technocratic cabinets.

Model 2 introduces controls for surplus/deficit levels, credit ratings and the start of the sovereign debt crisis. The estimates show that after controlling for these factors, the predicted probabilities of the budgetary plans of the Berlusconi IV government containing responsible policy justifications decline substantially. This suggests that if all the governments had had similar surplus/deficit levels and credit ratings—and controlling for any potential shock effect of the outbreak of the sovereign debt crisis—the Berlusconi IV government would have been considerably less responsible than the Monti government and its discourse would have contained a similar share of responsible justifications to that of the Renzi and Gentiloni cabinets. The control variables seem to have little effect on the share of responsible policy justifications by the three other governments. This suggests that the differences in levels of responsibility between the Conte I, Renzi/Gentiloni, and Monti governments are not explained by surplus/deficit levels and credit ratings and that they may be interpreted as a result of the extent to which the cabinets were composed of populist, mainstream partisan and technocratic actors. At the same time, the differences between these three cabinets follow the same pattern observed for the other countries analysed in Chapter 4, with responsibility being dominant until 2013 and gradually declining in subsequent years. This raises the question of whether the balance between responsiveness and responsibility observed for the Monti and Conte I governments would have been different if they had been party governments composed of mainstream parties.

In order to investigate this question, it is possible to compare the shares of responsible justifications made by the Italian governments with those made by the governments of the other countries analysed in the same time periods. Figure 5.4 plots the predicted probabilities of the shares of responsible policy justifications for each Italian government type and compares them with those of the contemporary governments in Austria, France, Germany, and Spain.

The estimates are in line with the main finding of Chapter 4, namely that the time period in which the governments operated is the main predictor

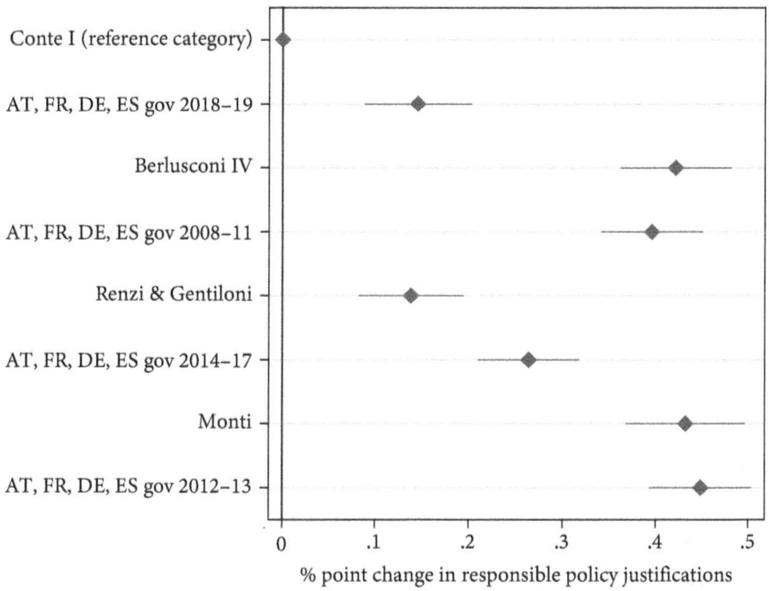

Figure 5.4 Predicted probabilities for responsible policy justifications by Italian governments and by the contemporary governments in Austria, France, Germany, and Spain

Source: Author's coding of annual budget plans

of the balance between responsiveness and responsibility, with the governments that operated between 2008 and 2013 being considerably more responsible than those that operated between 2014 and 2019. The levels of fiscal responsibility observed for the Berlusconi IV and Monti governments are comparable to those observed for the governments in Austria, Germany, France, and Spain during the same years. Similarly, the estimates for the governments that operated between 2014 and 2019 confirm that the share of responsibility declined in all cases, including one with a high public debt like Italy. At the same time, the estimates in Figure 5.3 also show that in the Italian case the share of responsible justifications declined even more than in the other countries. Under the Renzi and Gentiloni governments, the share of responsible policy justifications is substantially and significantly lower than that of the executives in the other European countries in the 2014–2017 period. The same difference is observed between the Conte I government and its contemporaries with the proportion of responsibility justifications being significantly and substantially lower for the Italian populist government.

The results in Figure 5.4 indicate that, despite its tumultuous alternations in government composition, between 2008 and 2019 Italy featured relatively similar patterns in the balance between responsiveness and responsibility as the other countries. The technocratic composition of the Monti government does not therefore seem to have made a substantial difference in terms of the balance between responsiveness and responsibility. The results also confirm that after 2014 the share of responsibility declined regardless of European constraints. Despite Italy's high public debt, its share of responsible justifications declined even more than in the other countries. The sharper decline in the Italian case suggests that the high levels of populism in the Italian party system during the 2010s may have played a role in the post-2014 decline in responsibility (see also Karremans et al., 2019). Recent studies have shown, for instance, that the Renzi government was sensitive to short-term popular demands when shaping its fiscal policies, combining technocratic expertise with responsiveness to the demands of large groups of citizens (Guasti and Buštíková, 2020). The huge electoral success of the Five Star Movement in the 2013 election and the growing electoral appeal of the Lega may therefore have induced the Renzi and Gentiloni governments to be more responsive to the demands of domestic constituencies than governments faced with relatively weaker populist opposition. Furthermore, even though the decreasing levels of responsibility in the period 2018–2019 were not particular to the Conte I government, its populist composition seems to have had an effect on the balance between responsiveness and responsibility making it even more responsive than its predecessor and its European contemporaries. This effect, however, seems to be contingent on—and therefore often reduced by—several contextual factors.

Evidence of institutional resilience

The case of the Berlusconi IV government is indicative of how in times of financial and fiscal crises a populist party government is also forced to focus on the sustainability of public finances rather than on people's short-term needs. From the perspective of the theoretical expectations in Figure 5.1, however, the shares of responsive and responsible justifications in the discourse of the Berlusconi IV government are not the only surprising finding from the analysis. Despite being composed of only technocratic experts, the Monti government justified its budgetary policy with more than 30 per cent of its political arguments being about how it would benefit society and the private sphere. A considerable number of these arguments refer to expenditure increases and tax reductions, thus measures that would not directly consolidate the budget. Similarly, in the budgetary plans of the Conte I government, responsiveness does not characterize the entirety of its justification discourse and instead responsibility is invoked in around 30 per cent of the justifications. Despite being fully composed of populist parties, the Conte I government needed to partly justify its budget also in terms of how it preserved the long-term sustainability of public finances. These figures suggest that—just as party governments are not free to entirely shape policies according to their preferences (Powell, 2004; Schmidt, 1996)— populists and technocrats also need to adapt their government activities and legitimation strategies to the long-established practices of representative democracy. In other words, despite their critiques of representative democracy, populists and technocrats cannot entirely circumvent the legitimizing principles behind representative government. These principles are embedded in the expectations of a wide range of actors and constitute the backbone of trust between citizens and governments (Linde and Peters, 2020).

The relevance of combining the two types of policy criteria is expressed in the budget documents of all the governments. The following excerpt from the Berlusconi IV government, for example, clarifies the two main drivers behind its 2008 budget.

> To begin with, our budgetary policy is developed: a) in line with the political and legal commitments made at the European level over the past few years by the Italian Republic; b) in line with the political commitments made by our coalition during the election campaign that brought it into government.
>
> **(Italian government, Documento di Economia e Finanza, 2008)**

Even before the outbreak of the crisis, the Berlusconi IV government acknowledged its duty to act in line with European commitments. These are integrated in the political commitments made during the 2008 election campaign, which in budgetary terms consisted largely of tax reforms aimed at stimulating private enterprise. The surprising feature of this passage, and the 2008 budget in general, is that a government with strong populist tendencies emphasized its institutional commitments even in the absence of a high public deficit or a sharp recession. Despite the fact that the 2008 budget was presented in June 2008 and thus three months before the outbreak of the global financial crisis, it features a similar responsive–responsible balance to that of the technocratic Monti government (Table 5.1).

Furthermore, the long-term sustainability of public finances is sometimes presented in relation to demands of the electorate. In the budget discourse of the Berlusconi IV government in 2008, fiscal responsibility is presented as a way to distinguish the government's action from the expenditure-driven policy of the preceding centre-left cabinet—its main political opponent. The following excerpt from the 2008 budget plan is an example of how the Berlusconi IV government closely linked responsibility discourse with more populist rhetoric about responding to people's demands.

> Leaving things as they are, letting them continue on their own and relying on chance, is certainly easier. But that's not what Italians are asking for and it's not what Italy needs. We know that ruling is not easy. But we also know that it is necessary and that there are no alternatives. ... In any case, we can no longer go ahead with a system in which only the deficit and the quarrels grow, not gross domestic product. It is on this basis, it is in this logic, that our action plan is developed.
>
> **(Italian government, *Documento di Economia e Finanza*, 2008)**

This passage exemplifies how fiscal responsibility can sometimes be part of the political competition between governing parties, and how some parties may try to win voters' trust by profiling themselves as the most responsible. In the competition between the centre-right and the centre-left, the former regularly accuse the latter of overspending and therefore of being fiscally irresponsible. Consequently, fiscal responsibility tends to be less costly in electoral terms for centre-right than for centre-left parties (Alonso and Ruiz-Rufino, 2020). Together with the effect of the crisis and the related high public deficit, interactions among these factors may explain why the budgetary plans of the Berlusconi IV government contain a relatively high share of responsible justifications. More importantly, it suggests that parties that have been alternating in government for many years have internalized the responsive–responsible dilemma in their electoral competition, and—as is shown by recent research (Lavezzolo et al., 2020)—that there is also an expectation among voters that governments cannot always be responsive but must sometimes be responsible.

The Conte I government's budgetary discourse also contains passages that would not be expected from a populist government that took office with the explicit aim of challenging the status quo. The following passage, for instance, describes how the government intended to respect the European Stability and Growth Pact and how it planned to introduce measures that would ensure that the public deficit would remain within the given thresholds.

> For the following years, the [government's] stability programme traces a path of public finance that gradually reduces the public deficit to 1.5 per cent in 2022 .... According to new official projections, the structural deficit would drop from 1.5 per cent of this year's GDP to 0.8 per cent in 2022, in line with a gradual

> convergence towards structural balance. The programmatic objectives outlined in the programme are in line with the [European] Stability and Growth Pact.
>
> **(Italian government, *Documento di Economia e Finanza*, 2019)**

The Conte I government's responsive measures—consisting of, for example, the introduction of a basic income for poorer families and proposals to flatten the tax rate—are also embedded in a broader framework of fiscal responsibility.

The Conte I government's responsible discourse indicates that on entering office, populist governments are also confronted with a series of institutional commitments which require them to provide information on their policy plans. This is particularly true in the framework of European economic governance, in which national governments are expected to closely cooperate with European institutions in the preparation of their national budgets in order to ensure that specific budgetary targets are met. If governments fail to do this they risk incurring infringement procedures, which can be highly costly to the country's public finances and may therefore jeopardize their future ability to deliver public goods to voters. Even though it introduced a generous basic income scheme for unemployed citizens (*reddito di cittadinanza*) and started making plans to introduce a flat tax rate, the 2019 budgetary plan was the result of extensive negotiations with the European Commission during autumn 2018 on the level of public deficit that Italy was allowed to have. While initially aiming at a discrepancy between expenditure and revenue of 2.4 per cent of GDP, the government had to agree with the Commission that the 2019 budget would generate a deficit no larger than 2.04 per cent of GDP, reducing the disparity by €6.3 billion (Carli, 2018). As also happened with similar government experiences in Greece (Lefkofridi and Nezi, 2020), being embedded in European institutional practices seems to prevent governments from acting entirely 'irresponsibly', from pursuing, that is, budgetary policies that would derail the balance between expenditure and revenue agreed at the European level.

At the other end of the populism–technocracy spectrum, the Monti government's budgetary discourse was not limited to justifying its intervention in terms of its institutional mandate but also provided an explanation of the political views behind its actions. Despite not having any partisan affiliation, the Monti government still needed the formal support of the centre-right and centre-left parties in parliament. By extension, these parties were still accountable to their voters and they openly voted their approval of the policies of the technocratic government. Even though at the moment of the government's appointment the centre-left and centre-right voted in favour of the executive agenda without a thorough debate (Culpepper, 2014), the circular dynamic with which parliament held the cabinet to account indirectly induced the government to expose the full list of criteria behind its policy decisions. Therefore, even though it had a specific institutional mandate to preserve the sustainability of public finances, the technocratic Monti government still sometimes needed to make choices that went beyond this mandate and provide appropriate justifications, which sometimes were inevitably political. The following excerpts, for instance, are taken from the introduction to the 2012 budget.

> Let's try to imagine that for a woman reconciling family and work is not an obstacle race because there is modern parental leave, childcare facilities for children and care facilities for the elderly .... Imagine opening an economic activity without asking for authorisation and, if we are under 30 years old, starting a business with one euro of capital. ... Let's imagine that for a young researcher it is worth thinking about a career in Italy because investment in research has grown to 1.53 per cent of GDP. ... Reflecting on scenarios like these and on the policy actions necessary to achieve them is not an abstract diversion. It is the essence of the exercise that every year Italy and the other Member States of the Union must carry out.
>
> **(Italian government, Documento di Economia e Finanza, 2012)**

This passage provides a justification of the government's action that goes beyond its institutional mandate to safeguard the sustainability of public finances. It illustrates a list of services that the government believes it should provide to citizens. The provision of these services inevitably involves political choices, including choices about how public resources should be redistributed. Consequently, the budgetary plans presented by the Monti government also present some budgetary choices that are not in line with the goal of fiscal consolidation and that are justified with political arguments. The following excerpt from the budgetary plan for 2012, for instance, reveals how the government redistributed part of the resources gained through its fiscal consolidation by reducing business taxation.

> Part of the major resources that have been recovered are used to finance measures to support growth, business and employment. In order to favour the recapitalisation of companies, businesses can deduct from their income the notional return from invested capital. To favour employment and in order to reduce fiscal pressure, businesses are allowed to deduct from their income the IRAP tax paid for the costs of employees and assimilated personnel.
>
> **(Italian government, *Documento di Economia e Finanza*, 2012)**

Despite relying on an institutional mandate that is strictly focused on the long-term sustainability of Italian public finances, the Monti government made use of its limited room for manoeuvre to make decisions about economic growth by introducing measures that are generally subject to political debate. Centre-right political forces would generally agree with a reduction of taxation on businesses, while centre-left parties may have a preference for using the limited room for manoeuvre to enhance families' purchasing power. The choice to stimulate growth by reducing taxation of businesses was a political decision, thus one that a government with different political preferences could have taken differently. Interestingly, this choice was transparently presented to the parliament and the public, both of which had the opportunity to express their approval or rejection of these choices in a substantive way: the parliament through votes on the budgetary proposals; the public through their votes at the subsequent election.

While technocratic cabinets tend to be clearly more responsible and populist governments clearly more responsive, the accountability mechanisms with which government activity is scrutinized by parliament, supranational institutions, and voters seem to help maintain a balance between the two decision-making criteria. Technocratic and populist governments cannot entirely escape the need to justify their policies in both responsive and responsible terms. This is because the accountability mechanisms holding governments under control scrutinize their actions from different perspectives, forcing them to provide both political and institutional justifications. By contributing to ensuring that governments think and act in both responsive and responsible terms, accountability mechanisms can provide effective institutional resilience to technocratic and populist challenges.

The importance of accountability mechanisms

The analysis presented in this chapter shows that the alternation in government between technocratic and populist forces provides some alteration to decision-making criteria, with technocrats clearly prioritizing responsibility and populists clearly prioritizing responsiveness. At the same time, the evidence also shows that between 2008 and 2011 the Berlusconi government largely followed the European trend of shaping its budgetary plans in terms of fiscal responsibility. The crisis context thus mitigated the potential effect of the populist composition of this executive, making its balance between responsiveness and responsibility largely similar to that of the technocratic Monti government (2011–2013). The findings in this chapter are thus largely in line with those in Chapter 4, showing that the high levels of responsibility observed between 2009 and 2013 were common to all countries and were strengthened by a centre-right composition of government, as in the case of the Berlusconi IV government. As will be investigated and discussed in further detail in Chapter 7, the balance between responsiveness and responsibility is also affected by the dominant economic ideas about how to guarantee the long-term sustainability of public finances.

The findings for the 2014–2019 period are in line with the pattern of declining responsibility and increasing responsiveness observed in Chapter 4, but also show that the Italian governments were considerably more responsive than their contemporaries despite Italy's high public debt. The findings from this period corroborate the idea that the high levels of populism in the Italian party system after the 2013 election had an impact on the balance between responsiveness and responsibility. Even though during the 2018–2019 period responsiveness increased in all cases, the share of responsive policy justifications under the Conte I government was substantially and significantly higher than that of its predecessor and than the aggregate level of responsiveness of the contemporary governments in Austria, France, Germany, and Spain. The idea that a higher level of populism in the government leads to lower levels of responsibility is therefore supported by the findings for the 2014–2019 period.

At the same time, the qualitative evidence suggests that both populist and technocratic governments need to take into account the institutional context in which they operate. Both responsive and responsible justification arguments remained consistently present irrespective of the type of government, entailing that populist executives cannot avoid providing responsible justifications and technocrats need to provide political explanations for their choices. The contents of the responsible justifications of the more populist governments and the responsive justifications of the technocratic Monti government suggest that the likely reason for this is that all the governments in this case selection were subject to accountability mechanisms in which their actions were scrutinized by a wide range of actors. When the institutions monitoring the country's long-term interests in a specific policy area become excluded from accountability mechanisms, the polity becomes more vulnerable to the populist challenge, as, once populist forces win government office, they are freer to neglect responsible criteria for public action. Similarly, when policymaking becomes disconnected from electoral rewards and punishments, the more the polity is vulnerable to the technocratic challenge, as policymakers have no incentive to receive the public's support for their decisions.

Just as electoral rules ensure that both governing majorities and opposition parties are represented in parliament, accountability mechanisms ensure that governments are forced to legitimize their actions both in terms of the democratic inputs they have received and in terms of the country's long-term interests. The balance between responsiveness and responsibility is consequently also dependent on the audiences involved in the accountability mechanisms and the powers that these audiences have to control the government. In Europe, the involvement and the sanctioning powers of European institutions in national budgetary policymaking seem to contribute at least to some extent to making populist governments take into account fiscal sustainability criteria. Similarly, the involvement and control powers of the parliament and the direct connection between parliamentary parties and voters ensure that the 'chain of responsiveness' (Powell, 2004) also persists under technocratic governments. The importance of accountability mechanisms in maintaining the balance between responsiveness and responsibility also seems to be indirectly confirmed by efforts of both populist forces and bureaucratic institutions to reform national polities. In Hungary, for instance, the three successive Orbán governments since 2010 have pursued and partially enacted a series of reforms that strengthen the majoritarian character of the Hungarian polity, with the explicit aim of transforming it into an illiberal democracy (Pappas, 2016). At the other end of the spectrum, the technocratic institutions of the European Union have often been blamed for trying to shelter policymaking from parliamentary and public oversight, leaving parliaments and citizens unable to judge and influence the policies pursued by governments, particularly in the sphere of European economic governance (Crum, 2013; Scharpf, 2011).

Among both technocratic and populist forces, therefore, there is an effort to alter the range of actors to which governments are accountable. The lesson from the Italian case is that the more the accountability mechanisms are effective and involve an encompassing range of actors, the more populist and technocratic challenges can be contained, pressuring governments to design their policies according to both responsive and responsible criteria. In this sense, the case of the Five Star Movement is emblematic. In the 2013 Italian election, voters had the opportunity to reward or punish the political parties that had supported the policies of the technocratic Monti government. For a large share of the electorate, resentment of such policies resulted in a vote for the newly established Five Star Movement which, just one legislature later, entered government office and introduced various expansive measures, which were in turn kept in check by the European rules on fiscal sustainability. The evidence in this chapter is therefore one more confirmation that during Europe's decade of crises the balance between responsiveness and responsibility remained largely intact, even in a country that was deeply affected by populist and technocratic challenges.

6 National variations of responsiveness

Introduction

The governing experience of the Five Star Movement in Italy under the first Conte government exemplifies how far the European pressures for stable public finances reach. It indicates that European constraints do not necessarily prevent governments pursuing policies that they promised to their electorates, even if these involve generous social assistance schemes like the Italian *reddito di cittadinanza*, which in 2019 provided a basic income to 1.1 million family units (INPS, 2020) and became an important safety net during the coronavirus pandemic (ISTAT, 2022). The introduction of this policy is illustrative of how devolving resources to the benefit of domestic constituencies is possible under the conditions of European economic governance, even in a country like Italy featuring a public debt higher than 120 per cent of national GDP. The analysis in Chapter 5 highlighted how—for the Conte government—the obligations to meet European budgetary targets did not prevent the pursuit of a policy that was responsive to the demands of a large section of the Italian electorate. Instead, they arguably helped to prevent the financial failure of the potentially unsustainable social assistance scheme. Under pressure from the European Commission, the scheme was designed in a way that would keep public deficit within the prescribed targets.

The introduction of this Italian social assistance scheme emerged in a context in which responsiveness was increasing in all the cases analysed. The findings presented in Chapters 4 and 5 indicate that from 2014 onwards, governments across the eurozone started to be increasingly more inclined to devolving resources to the benefit of domestic constituencies, rather than pursuing unpopular policies that would make them more compliant with European budgetary targets. This tendency grew gradually and was particularly acute between 2018 and 2020. This gradual increase also becomes evident when looking more deeply into the development of social assistance in Italy, as the *reddito di cittadinanza* followed the *reddito d'inclusione*

Between Voters and Eurocrats. Johannes Karremans, Oxford University Press. © Johannes Karremans (2024).
DOI: 10.1093/oso/9780192886583.003.0006

introduced by the previous Gentiloni government, which was a smaller and more targeted scheme that provided basic social assistance only to the most marginalized members of society, amounting to 500,000 thousand family units between January 2018 and March 2019 (INPS, 2019). The social policy of the Five Star Movement thus followed a pathway that had, at least partially, already been undertaken and that was in line with a more general tendency among European governments in the second half of the 2010s.

The graduality and the cross-country commonalities of the trends analysed in Chapter 4 call for a deeper exploration into whether the increases in responsiveness reflect distinct political preferences under different governments. Overall, the post-2014 increases in responsiveness align with an improved macroeconomic situation in the eurozone which, as will be discussed more extensively in Chapter 7, also made EU-level policymakers relatively more supportive of socially friendly policies (Schmidt, 2020a; Zeitlin and Vanhercke, 2018). It could therefore be that the higher shares of policy justifications focusing on 'giving' rather than 'taking' more resources domestically do not necessarily embody higher shares of responsiveness, but simply reflect a situation in which there is less urgency to speak about debts and deficits. In order to be true manifestations of responsiveness, these policy justifications also need to reflect the proposals on the basis of which the governing parties campaigned. This chapter therefore explores for each case the actual contents of the policy justifications that were classified as responsive and the policy choices they embody.

The analysis in Chapter 4 was based on a definition of responsiveness aimed at drawing a clear demarcation line from responsibility. Having once isolated the electoral from the governmental logics, though, responsiveness must be conceived as a cyclical process in which different groups of electorates express different demands, parties compete to represent these demands and try to pursue congruent policies once they are in office, in order to deliver to voters what they had demanded (Karremans and Lefkofridi, 2020a, p. 274). This process requires a certain degree of government autonomy that allows governing parties to make choices that are in line with specific political preferences. The findings in Chapter 4 indicate that European economic governance does not necessarily stop governments from devolving resources for the benefit of domestic constituencies. This chapter complements those findings with more in-depth qualitative analyses of the contents of responsive policy justifications containing clear policy commitments.

Between 2018 and 2020, during which the highest levels of responsiveness are registered, the five cases feature very diverse governments in terms of their ideological composition. In Austria, the first Kurz government was composed of the centre-right Österreichische Volkspartei (ÖVP) and the populist right Freiheitliche Partei Österreichs (FPÖ). The electoral programmes of the two parties shared a commitment to substantially reduce the size of the public sector and thus to reduce taxation to enhance private economic freedom (Karremans and Kaltenleithner, 2021). In Germany, the fourth Merkel government was a coalition between the country's largest centre-right and centre-left parties that were increasingly under pressure from sections of their electorates to divert the government's agenda from austerity to more socially friendly policies (Rixen, 2019). In France, under the Macron presidency the government was led by the party La République En Marche, which had campaigned the 2017 national elections on the basis of a social-liberal programme, featuring commitments to welfare reforms, reductions in taxation with commitments and environmentally friendly policies. In Italy, as discussed already in Chapter 5, the first Conte government featured a coalition between two parties that expressively voiced the popular discontent with the austerity policies of the previous governments and had a policy agenda promising both high social expenditures and significant tax reductions. In Spain, the second Rajoy government was composed of the country's largest centre-right party. Thus, with a diverse political composition of the cabinets, the contents of responsive policy justifications across the five countries should be substantially different particularly in the 2018–2020 period.

Austria: balancing equality and entrepreneurship

Of the five cases analysed, Austria features the least acute differences over time in terms of the balance between responsiveness and responsibility. Figure 6.1 reports shares of responsive, responsible, and neutral policy justifications, classifying the responsive statements into those targeted at the social and those targeted at the private spheres.

The peak of the sovereign debt crisis was handled by the first Faymann government, which was in power between 2008 and 2013 and was composed of a coalition between the centre-right ÖVP and the centre-left Sozialdemokratische Partei Österreichs (SPÖ). During the sovereign debt crisis, the policy of fiscal discipline was relatively well aligned with the preferences of large parts

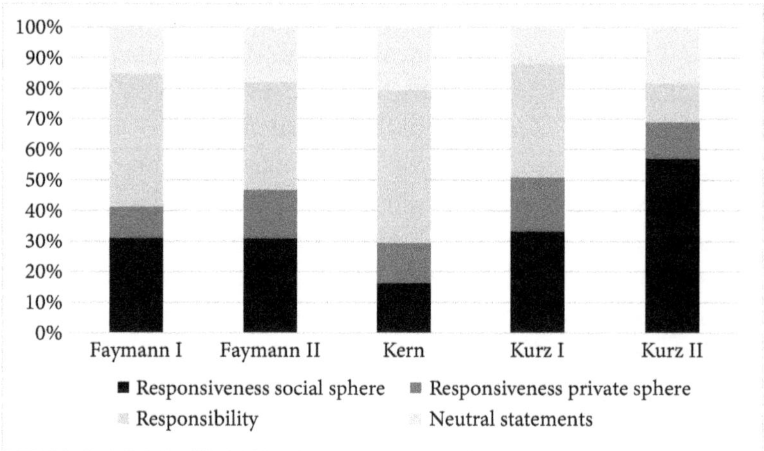

Figure 6.1 Policy justifications for each Austrian government (2009–2020)
Source: Author's coding of annual budget speeches
Note: Bars represent total of policy justifications collected for each government

of the ÖVP's electoral base, but this was also compensated with redistributive measures such as the introduction of a solidarity tax, by which wealthier households were asked to contribute substantially more to the policy of austerity than low income groups. In justifying the solidarity tax, the government highlighted the government's commitment at maintaining social peace in the country, for example in the following passage:

> Despite the necessary austerity, we always keep an eye on the social peace that makes this country so worth living in.
>
> **(Maria Fekter, 16 October 2012)**

Compared to other cases, in Austria the government thus remained relatively responsive to domestic redistributive concerns also during the peak of the sovereign debt crisis.

The second Faymann government featured the same coalition and operated between December 2013 and May 2016. It delivered two budget speeches of which the first, 29 April 2014, had to address primarily the financial consequences of the Hypo Alpe Bank scandal. The bank had been nationalized in 2009 and was dismantled in 2014 in relation to criminal activities. Referring to the scandal, in the budget speech of April 2014, Finance Minister Michael Spindelegger announced that public debt would rise by €17.8 billion. Consequently, the finance minister announced several measures to ensure that public finances would remain within the Maastricht criteria. In these efforts, the government reassured the audience that no one would be 'suffocated' by these measures. The following passage is an example of how the responsible discourse about debts and deficits flows into a responsive statement about citizens' needs and demands:

> The Maastricht deficit will rise, but remain below the 3 per cent mark despite the Hypo Alpe Bank issue. Despite all these burdens, we will remain at 2.7 per cent Maastricht deficit. Despite Hypo Alpe, we will be going into the future with these budgets with a large package of burdens as far as government debt is concerned—over 79 per cent—but with this one-time increase in government debt, we will also be reducing it year after year, and it is important to really signal a trend reversal. In order to bring about this turnaround, everyone must make a contribution, there is no question about it—and I, as Minister of Finance, must ask all Austrians for their understanding. We are tightening a lot of screws here—with the citizens, with the administration, with everyone in this country who makes their contribution—but we are not suffocating anyone, ladies and gentlemen, to speak clearly.
>
> **(Michael Spindelegger, Nationalrat, 29 April 2014)**

Following the idea of not letting citizens 'suffocate' under the government's fiscal policies, the responsiveness of the second Faymann government is to a considerable extent oriented towards increasing the level of private economic freedom through a reduction of taxation rates. The following passage from the budget speech of 14 October 2015 is illustrative of the political preferences and consequent commitments of the government:

> As an experienced entrepreneur, I can tell you honestly: I would have wished for much more far-reaching and faster reforms, but here too a first step must always be taken. As a federal government, we have therefore agreed on a clear reform plan.
>
> **(Hans Jörg Schelling, Nationalrat, 14 October 2015)**

The reform plan consisted of a redesign of the tax rates, mainly in the form of reductions at various income levels. The success of this reform was also highlighted in the only budget speech delivered by the subsequent Kern government (2016–2017), which was again composed of a coalition between ÖVP and SPÖ. Even though the main focus was on responsibility and the importance of a balance, the budget speech of the Kern government announced several fiscal stimulus measures targeted at domestic social groups. These included tax reductions aimed at enhancing companies' investment possibilities, the allocation of €83 million to support tackling the migration crisis, €350 million to support the employment chances of vulnerable groups, and an increase of €210 million in the budget for universities and research.

When Sebastian Kurz became leader of the ÖVP in May 2017, he dissolved the coalition with the social-democrats. After the legislative elections of December 2017, the ÖVP formed a decisively more right-wing oriented coalition with the FPÖ. In economic terms, the two parties shared the objective of reducing the domestic fiscal pressure, and the coalition programme also partially took over the FPÖ's stance that welfare benefits should reach deserving Austrians first (Rathgeb and Gruber-Risak, 2021). In the budget speech of 21 March 2018, this commitment was expressed in these terms:

> We stand by the fact that those who finance our system, our state through their commitment in this area, also have the right to a reasonable form of duties and taxes. Therefore, our clear goal is to reduce the tax ratio to 40 per cent by 2022, and we will achieve that with the steps we have taken. This is what we will achieve! And because our tax policy means relief, we have already started with the first measures. First and foremost, we have provided significant relief for tax-paying families with children. We reach 950,000 families with around 1.6 million children.
>
> **(Hartwig Löger, Nationalrat, 21 March 2018)**

While asserting the commitment to this policy direction, in the speech the finance minister also addressed concerns from the centre-left opposition about how the reduction of taxation would eventually lead to cuts in welfare provisions due to less revenue. In addressing this concern, the finance minister highlighted that in 2019 the funds earmarked for social security would increase rather than decrease, and thus that the government would continue to finance support and solidarity-based social services. The attention towards socially oriented issues thus was substantial also in the budget speech of this centre-right coalition government.

The tenure of the first Kurz government came to an early end due to a corruption scandal within the FPÖ, known as the Ibiza affair. In January 2020 an unprecedented alliance between the ÖVP and the Greens formed the second Kurz government. In the budget speech delivered in October 2020, after the outbreak of the coronavirus pandemic, the Finance Minister Gernot Blümel (ÖVP) illustrated the government's support package against the economic downturn induced by the lockdown measures. To a large extent, the policy illustrated reflected the policy course undertaken by the previous cabinet, namely that of a reduction of the tax burden.

> If the external framework conditions become difficult, then we have to make it easier for citizens and companies. That is why, as of 1 July 2020, we lowered value-added tax for certain sectors to 5 per cent and, when implementing this in practice,

> relied on as much goodwill as possible and as little bureaucracy as possible. Due to the continuing tense situation, we will extend this measure until the end of 2021, as long as the European Commission approves it. Especially now there is a need for special support for families, for employees, for the unemployed and for pensioners. Above all, people with low incomes should now have more money in their wallets—we are implementing this with this budget, ladies and gentlemen! (Applause from the ÖVP and the Greens.) With the corona-bonus, we are relieving Austrians with a total volume of around €2.7 billion.
>
> **(Gernot Blümel, Nationalrat, 14 October 2020)**

Besides the tax reductions, the government also introduced financial incentives for the use of public transport, which was an election promise made by the Greens. In parallel, and in line with the political preferences of the ÖVP and its electorate, the speech also announced aid for companies and an increase in the police budget.

In sum, in Austria, responsiveness largely took the form of a balancing act between commitments towards a balanced budget, the centre-left's concerns about social justice, and the centre-right's political objectives regarding taxation levels. The latter became increasingly prominent from 2016 onwards, first under the Kern government and then under the two cabinets led by Sebastian Kurz.

Germany: administration of a fiscal surplus

From a fiscal balance perspective, in the second half of the 2010s Germany was arguably one of the member states better placed to start a policy of domestic expenditures. From 2013 onwards, it ran annual fiscal surpluses, producing surplus revenue that could be spent domestically. Even though, overall, the third Merkel government remained cautious on the use of its surplus (Rixen, 2019), compared to the preceding cabinet the focus of its budget plans was substantially more directed at social issues. Figure 6.2 reports the share of responsive, responsible, and neutral policy justifications for each German government between 2009 and 2020, distinguishing between the responsive justification targeted at the social sphere and those targeted at the private sphere.

The share of responsive and responsible policy justifications reflect the pattern discussed in Chapter 4, with responsibility being dominant between 2009 and 2013 under the second Merkel government, and then a gradual increase of responsiveness in subsequent years. Across all three governments,

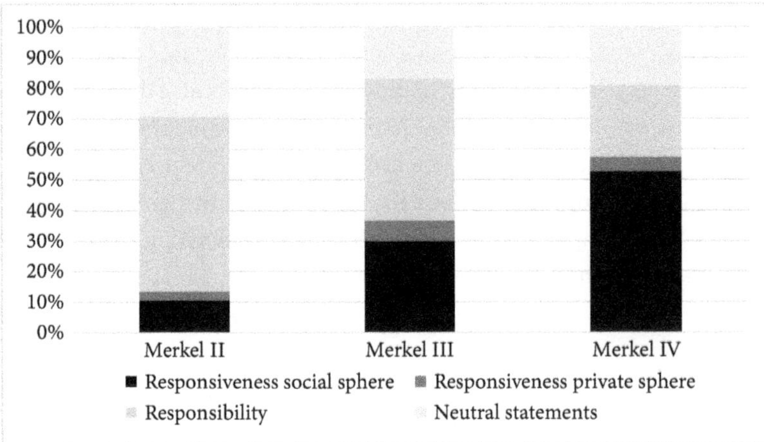

Figure 6.2 Policy justifications for each German government (2010–2020)

Source: Author's coding of annual budget speeches
Note: Bars represent total policy justifications collected for each government

responsiveness is almost entirely about socially oriented issues, whereas the statements emphasizing private economic freedom are only a minor part of the discourse. In the case of the second Merkel government, which featured an entirely centre-right-oriented coalition between the Christian Democratic Union parties (CDU/CSU[1]) and the liberal Freie Demokratische Partei (FDP), most part of the discourse is about fiscal discipline, which to a large extent aligned with the preferences of the voters of the governing parties (Rixen, 2014; van Riet, 2021). While in those years the lack of responsiveness was common to most, if not all, eurozone countries, for a centre-right cabinet, fiscal responsibility somehow compensated for the lack of emphasis on tax reductions for private entrepreneurship. In the case of the third and fourth Merkel governments, there was arguably more autonomy to choose the preferred policy path and therefore to tailor the discourse more explicitly to the expectations of the governing parties' voters. As these two cabinets were a coalition between the CDU/CSU and the centre-left Sozialdemokratische Partei Deutschlands (SPD), there were relatively more electoral pressures regarding the quality and quantity of welfare benefits and services. The increase of socially oriented justifications can thus be seen as a reflection of the political composition of the cabinets (see also Karremans, 2021b).

[1] CDU stands for Christlich Demokratische Union Deutschlands; CSU stands for Christlich-Soziale Union in Bayern.

An important element of the increased attention to social issues under the third Merkel government, is constituted by an exogenous shock, namely the Syrian refugee crisis that hit Europe in 2015. The budget speeches delivered between 2015 and 2017 reflect the government's policy of welcoming asylum seekers. The budget speech of September 2015, for instance, opens with the following statement:

> This budget debate is also characterized by the current refugee situation. It is a test for Germany and for Europe, and it presents us all, state and society, with the greatest challenge for a long time. That is why mastering this demanding task has absolute priority. The task is now, and we will do it now, and we must finance it now, if possible without new debt.
>
> **(Wolfgang Schäuble, 8 September 2015)**

The budget speeches delivered in these years underline the government's commitment to a welcoming policy towards refugees, while at the same time ensuring that this does not create imbalances in the public budget.

Beyond the exogenous shock of the 2015 migration, the increased attention to social issues in the budget speeches of the third Merkel government mostly reflect some socio-economic commitments that had characterized the tenure of the first Merkel government between 2005 and 2009, which was composed of the same coalition between CDU/CSU and SPD. These socio-economic commitments regard the work–life balance concerns of families and human capital development, which since the 2000s had become important concerns among the constituencies of both the centre-left and the centre-right (Seeleib-Kaiser, 2016). The following passages are illustrative of how the cabinet was committed to deliver resources in this area.

> The most important and first focus is the area of education, science and research. The federal government takes over all of the payments for BAföG[2] benefits from the federal states—we decided and implemented this recently. More pupils and students have access to BAföG. We adapt the standard rates to the cost of living. We continue to finance the university pact and thus ensure additional university places. We are also topping up the 'Childcare expansion' special fund once again. It has also been agreed with the federal states that the relief from taking over the BAföG will be used for additional investments in schools and universities. We are continuously increasing spending on science and research, by €1 billion in 2015.
>
> **(Wolfgang Schäuble, Bundestag, 9 September 2014)**

[2] This abbreviation stands for Bundesausbildungsförderungsgesetz, which is Germany's Federal Training Assistance Act for students who attend secondary schools and universities.

> We have massively increased spending, especially in research, education and transport infrastructure, we have relieved states and municipalities more than ever before, and we will continue to do so. This is why states and municipalities can reliably finance their tasks, especially in the areas of infrastructure, education and childcare.
>
> **(Wolfgang Schäuble, Bundestag, 6 September 2016)**

The spending commitments announced are not only justified in terms of their social purpose, but also in terms of the contribution to the country's overall economic performance. The following passage is an example of how the investments in education and infrastructure are part of the government's macroeconomic strategy.

> The German Institute for Economic Research in Berlin has determined that the research expenditures, which have been increasing since 2007, are mainly due to increased public investments. But of course, in addition to investments in education, investments in basic infrastructure are also necessary to secure Germany's economic strength. Consequently, the expenditure in the individual plan of the Federal Ministry of Transport and Digital Infrastructure in the budget for 2016 is around €24.4 billion, which is €1.1 billion more than in the previous year. This increase in spending primarily reflects the expansion of transport investment.
>
> **(Wolfgang Schäuble, 8 September 2015)**

Under the third Merkel government, there is thus an increase in attention and commitment towards social issues. Such statements, however, are regularly accompanied by justifications either reassuring the audience about the continuation of a fiscally responsible policy, or how the investments in the social sphere are part of a strategy that ensures economic growth. To some extent, the socially oriented responsiveness observed under the third Merkel government is subordinated to the persistent commitment to fiscal discipline. This blend of policy justifications can be seen as a result of compromises within the governing coalition, with the Christian democrats remaining committed to the fiscal consolidation policy path and the social democrats wishing to prove that their entry into government marks a breakaway from the austerity policies of the previous executive.

After the elections of September 2017, the CDU/CSU and SPD suffered important electoral losses. Despite these drawbacks, due to a lack of coalition alternatives, they again formed a government, still under the leadership of Angela Merkel (CDU/CSU) but with a social democratic finance minister, namely Olaf Scholz (SPD). In the meantime, the electoral losses for the governing parties continued in subnational elections, particularly for the SPD. Seemingly, growing numbers of left-oriented voters were increasingly disappointed in the SPD's lack of determination in prioritizing social policy commitments over budgetary targets (Barber, 2019). The increase of attention towards social issues under the fourth Merkel government is congruent with these electoral pressures on the SPD, and is also aligned with the welfare expectations of parts of the electoral base of the CDU/CSU (Karremans, 2021b; Rixen, 2019, 2014; van Riet, 2021).

In Olaf Scholz's budget speeches, furthermore, the socially oriented policy justifications are more unequivocally targeted at reducing gaps in life chances between richer and poorer social groups. In his first budget speech on 15 May 2018, Olaf Scholz expressed the government's commitment to take more action targeted at equalizing life opportunities for all citizens, with—for example—the following statement:

> Our citizens must be able to live where they work. This includes affordable housing. We are seeing more and more people moving to cities. A natural consequence of the move to the metropolitan areas is increasing pressure on housing and rental costs. But we don't want a situation like London, Paris or New York, where only the wealthy can afford decent housing in the city centre. That's why we're investing €2 billion in social housing over the next few years and using the same amount for other funding instruments, such as child benefit.
>
> **(Olaf Scholz, Bundestag, 15 May 2018)**

Following this reasoning, the fourth Merkel government started to increase the resources allocated to social housing. In the budget for 2020, the government committed €40 billion to this purpose (Karremans, 2021b). In addition, it committed to more investments in renewable energies. In the wake of the coronavirus pandemic, the government continued—and possibly reinforced—the socially and environmentally oriented policy course. In the budget speech of 29 September 2020, the finance minister also underlined how public investments were a strategy for economic growth.

> If you look at the numbers, they're impressive too. For example, for the period from 2021 to 2024—we are now discussing next year's budget and financial planning up to 2024—we have earmarked a total of almost €200 billion, or €199.2 billion, in investments. That is considerably more than, for example, in the four-year period of the last legislative period—over €80 billion—and it will have a positive effect on work and employment and the future viability of our country, because all these public investments also mean that we have many new additional private

investments at the same time. They trigger investment costs for the future, and they contribute to our economy being able to grow again quickly.

(Olaf Scholz, Bundestag, 29 September 2020)

After the 2009–2013 period in which fiscal responsibility was the dominant criterion for budgetary policymaking across Europe, German governments started gradually shaping their budgets according to domestic social needs. Under the third Merkel government, the CDU/CSU and SPD continued the policy course initiated during the coalition government of the 2005–2009 period, before the global financial and sovereign debt crises. Under the fourth Merkel government, with growing electoral pressures on the SPD for more socially oriented policies, budgetary policy became even more shaped according to domestic social and environmental concerns.

France: attempts to reduce the tax burden

With its semi-presidential system, France is arguably the most majoritarian form of democracy in Continental Europe. When the party of the president also has a parliamentary majority, the president has a far-reaching influence on the government, as it appoints and can ask for the resignation of the prime minister. For this reason, in this study, French executives are named after the presidencies under which they served. Under the presidency of Nicolas Sarkozy, the centre-right Union pour un Mouvement Populaire (UMP) was the dominant party in both the legislative and executive branches. In the 2012 elections, the Parti socialiste won both the presidential and the legislative elections, and was therefore the dominant party in the 2012–2017 legislative period, with François Hollande as president. The 2017 presidential and legislative elections, instead, were won by the new LREM, which under the leadership of Emmanuel Macron presented itself as a liberal and progressive party.

A strong alternation in government is also likely to have tangible implications for the contents of responsiveness, determining whether it is oriented more to the social or the private sphere. As can be seen in Figure 6.3, the shares of policy justifications oriented to either sphere do not reveal such a stark contrast, particularly between the Sarkozy and Hollande presidencies.

The differences between the different presidencies in terms of the share of responsive and responsible justifications are in line with the patterns identified in Chapter 4. The share of policy justifications that are responsive to domestic demands increases gradually across the presidencies and thus over

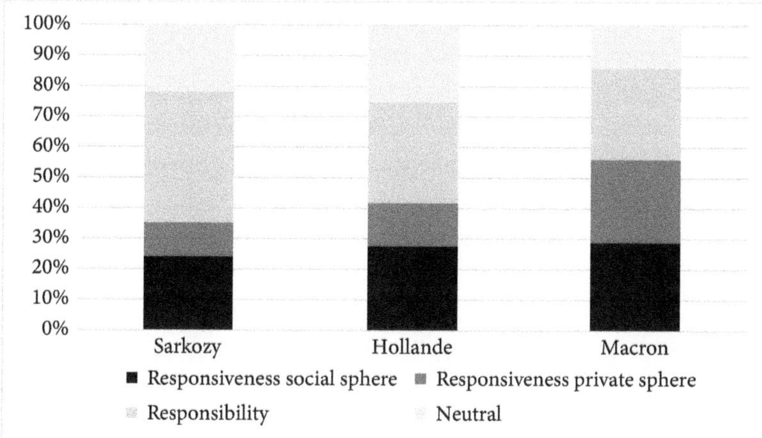

Figure 6.3 Policy justifications in budget speeches under each French presidency (2007–2020)

Source: Author's coding of annual budget speeches
Note: Bars represent total of policy justifications collected for each presidency

time. In terms of the contents of responsiveness, the French policy justifications feature a relatively high share of statements targeted at private economic freedom, such as stimulating entrepreneurship, rewarding talent or preserving the value of private property. Despite the alternation between centre-right and centre-left, in the budget speeches delivered under both the Sarkozy and the Hollande presidencies responsiveness is divided in relatively similar ways presenting fiscal stimuli measures targeted at the private sphere and provisions directed at social policy.

Even though the main focus was on the commitment to reduce public debt and deficit and on the need to abandon a spending culture, the budget speeches delivered between 2009 and 2011 also announced several measures to relaunch the French economy after the Great Recession, including both tax reductions and expenditure increases. As exemplified in the following passages, expenditure increases are intended to support employment and tax reductions are mostly tailored for enterprises:

> The budget provides—in particular—for the appropriations necessary for continuation of the exceptional measures in favour of employment implemented within the framework of the FISO, the social intervention fund, €1.4 billion, but also the exemption from charges for new hires in small businesses, €410 million. ... In addition to the FISO and the exemption for new hires in small businesses, credits relating to employment will be increased by €700 million compared to the sum

> provided in the three-year budget. Corporations, for their part, will benefit from the extension of the possibility of immediate reimbursement of the research tax credit of €2.5 billion, and they will benefit above all from the abolition of business tax in one year's time. Due to the phenomena of time lags in the mechanics of taxes, this one-off abolition will provide companies with additional cash of €7 billion in 2010 compared to a normal year.
>
> **(Éric Woerth, Assemblée Nationale, 10 October 2009)**

Besides employment support and tax credits for companies, among the responsive policy justifications in the budget speeches of the Sarkozy presidency, there are also statements announcing budgetary allocations for research and education.

In the budget speeches delivered under the Hollande presidency, the support to domestic enterprises in the form of tax reductions continued to constitute a substantial share of the responsive policy justifications. In parallel, socially oriented justifications focused relatively more on issues related to social justice and the needs of low-income groups. In more concrete terms, the attention towards socially oriented issues took the form of supporting citizens' purchasing power, with special attention to low-income groups (see also Damhuis and Karremans, 2017). The following excerpts from the budget speech of Pierre Moscovici given on 15 October 2013 illustrate how responsiveness under the Hollande presidency is directed towards supporting employment and improving households' purchasing power, with particular attention to low-income groups.

> The finance bill for 2014 therefore vigorously deploys our proactive policies in favour of employment. It finances the creation by the end of 2014 of 150,000 jobs for the future .... Indeed, as we all know here, restarting employment is an essential condition—the main one, even—for restoring purchasing power, which results firstly from earned income and wages. ... If I had to summarize our action in favour of the purchasing power of the French in the context of this budget, I would say that it covers four fronts at once. ... I have already mentioned the employment front .... The other three fronts are those of action on fixed expenditures, control of compulsory levies and the fight against inequalities through progressive taxation. What are fixed expenses? These are expenses—which primarily concern housing and energy—weighing more and more on the purchasing power of the French. ... Control of compulsory levies means refusing a general tax increase, beyond the reform of VAT rates already voted, while the budgetary constraint remains strong. At the same time—as the Minister for the Budget said earlier—the income tax scale will be reindexed on the cost of living, after two years of being frozen—a decision

of the previous government: this action will make it possible to reduce the taxation of French people whose income has not increased and to preserve the income of the most modest.

(Pierre Moscovici, Assemblée Nationale, 15 October 2013)

In these excerpts where mostly responsive policies are presented, it is significant to note the finance minister's reference to the fact that 'budgetary constraint remains strong'. In a context where public spending and revenue levels hovered above 50 per cent of national GDP,[3] and where debt and deficit levels needed to be brought back within the Maastricht criteria, French governments tried to enhance domestic resources mostly in the form of tax credits, which would improve households' purchasing power. Consequently, the distinguishing feature of the post-2013 increase of responsiveness in France is that the justifications refer mostly to tax reductions.

The budget speeches delivered under the Hollande and Macron presidencies are the only ones in the entire case selection where the frequency of the references to tax reductions is almost double the references to expenditure increases. In the budget speeches delivered under the Macron presidencies, 25 per cent of all policy justifications explicitly refer to tax reductions. Compared to the speeches under the Hollande presidency, the accent is decisively more on the creation of a favourable environment for entrepreneurship, investment, and innovation. The following passage is an example of the political goals expressed in the budget speeches delivered under the Macron presidency.

It is by seizing the opportunities of the technological revolutions in progress, and those of the contemporary world, that the French will succeed and that France will remain the great economic nation that it has always been. For this, the first requirement is to put in place a tax system that encourages activity, and that allows our companies to invest in order to innovate, an essential condition for staying in the race, moving upmarket and creating the jobs of tomorrow. … We have marginal capital tax rates that penalize us compared to our neighbours: 62 per cent for interest and 44 per cent for dividends. Compare these rates with the 26 per cent practiced in Germany: you will understand why Germany invests more than France and why it creates more jobs than us. We therefore want to reduce taxation on capital to reward risk, facilitate the financing of our companies and develop innovation.

(Bruno Le Maire, Assemblée Nationale, 17 October 2017)

[3] Source: Eurostat data.

Responsiveness under the Macron presidency was thus clearly targeted at entrepreneurs and based on an idea that job opportunities for citizens needed to be provided through private investments. Besides these liberal-oriented policy justifications, the budget speeches delivered between 2017 and 2020 also reflect LREM's commitment towards environmentally friendly policies. These policies involve investments in renewable energies and several tax incentives, for example to facilitate the sales of electric vehicles. The following statement is an example of such commitment:

> We are also choosing the ecological transition. In 2020, €6.3 billion will be invested to develop renewable energies. The envelope dedicated to the car bonus and the conversion bonus will increase by 50 per cent. The tax credit for the ecological transition will be transformed into direct aid and concentrated on the most modest households. The ecological transition must not be reserved for a few: it must be accessible to all.
>
> **(Bruno Le Maire, Assemblée Nationale, 14 October 2019)**

Even though these policies were in line with LREM's electoral commitments, they also triggered public protests, including the *gilets jaunes* movement, as the other side of these tax credits were higher taxes on fossil fuels (Reuters, 2018). The widespread public protests that occurred under Macron were thus against policies that were highly responsive to a part of French society, arguably the part with relatively higher income levels.

After the outbreak of the coronavirus pandemic, the budget speech delivered in October 2020 referred substantially more to expenditure increases, targeted at supporting the national economy during and after the lockdown measures. Nonetheless, the justifications emphasized how these were both targeted at preserving citizens' purchasing power, and at providing adequate fiscal support to enterprises. As a social-liberal party that brought together various exponents from both the French centre-right and centre-left, the LREM-led government thus pursued policies that were responsive to both social democratic and liberal preferences.

Italy: making use of flexibility clauses

The Italian case was analysed in the previous chapter and therefore does not require further contextual descriptions here. The main aspect to highlight here is the extent to which there is continuity and change in the contents of the responsive policy justifications of the different governments. Figure 6.4

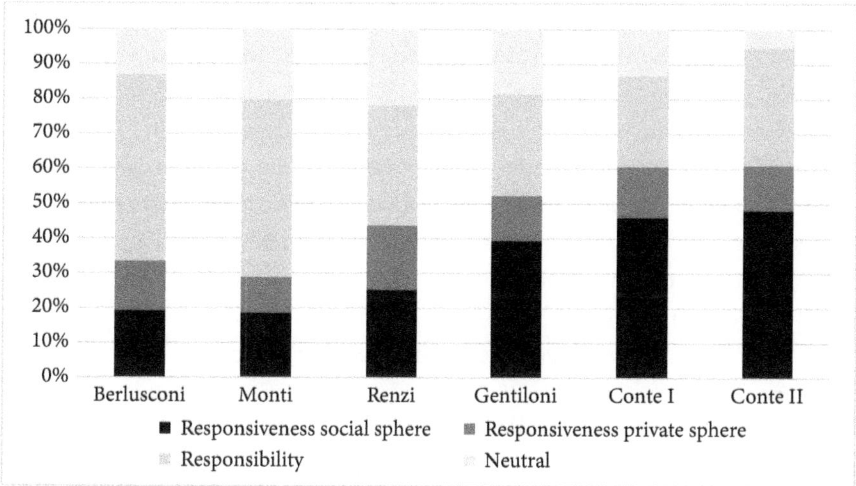

Figure 6.4 Policy justifications for each Italian government (2008–2020)

Source: Author's coding of annual budget documents (*Documento di Economia e Finanza*)
Note: Bars represent total policy justifications collected for each government

provides a first overview, by reporting for each government the share of responsive, responsible, and neutral policy justifications, and defining the responsive statements as either more socially oriented or relative to private economic freedom.

As with the German case, the Italian budget speeches resemble most closely the trend identified in Chapter 4, with responsibility being dominant between 2009 and 2013, and a gradual increase of responsiveness between 2014 and 2019. Besides this main trend, in Figure 6.4 it is also possible to observe how in the budget speeches of the Renzi and Berlusconi IV governments almost half of the responsive policy justifications are oriented towards enhancing private economic freedom. Under the Gentiloni and the two Conte governments, instead, responsiveness is predominantly socially oriented.

These differences reflect—at least partially—the different ideological compositions of the cabinets. The Berlusconi IV government was fully oriented to centre-right and thus committed to a policy of tax reductions. The Renzi government was a coalition between the PD and the more moderate components of the Italian centre-right, with Prime Minister Matteo Renzi representing the part of the Italian centre-left electorate that favoured a socially fair reduction of taxation and liberalization measures to stimulate employment (Karremans et al., 2019). As is the case in for many social democratic parties in Europe (see for example Hertner, 2018), this turn towards liberalization policies alienated a part of the PD's electoral base. The following passage is an example of how the Renzi government combined liberal economic ideas and social policy objectives:

> The revision of taxation primarily through the reduction of the tax wedge, is a measure that will intervene both on the taxes imposed on households and on the charges borne by businesses. The reduction of taxes on the lowest income brackets of employees may have the structural effect of stimulating the supply of work and the reduction of poverty.
>
> **(Italian government, *Documento di Economia e Finanza*, 2013)**

In December 2016, Matteo Renzi resigned as prime minister and was replaced by Paolo Gentiloni. In the subsequent two budget speeches, the PD-led government focused substantially more attention on social issues with, for example, the introduction of the *reddito d'inclusione*, arguably to win back the support of the alienated left-oriented voter base. Despite these efforts, the big winner of the 2018 elections was the Five Star Movement (M5S), thanks also to the radical promise of the introduction of the *reddito di cittadinanza*. The budget documents delivered by the two Conte governments reflect several electoral commitments of the M5S, particular in the fields of social assistance, pensions and environmental conservation. In the budget documents of the Conte governments, it is also important to note how the changing contents of responsiveness are also integrated with different ideas about how economic growth shall be pursued. The following passage is an example of the Conte government's macroeconomic discourse.

> With this document the Government confirms the fundamental objectives of its action: to gradually reduce the growth gap with the European average that has characterized the Italian economy especially in the last decade .... To this end, the Executive's strategy reaffirms the role of public investment as a fundamental factor for growth, innovation, social infrastructure and increased competitiveness of the production system; the tax reform action in the progressive implementation of a flat tax system as an important component of a more balanced growth model; support for companies engaged in technological innovation; and the contextual strengthening of the network of protection and social inclusion.
>
> **(Italian government, *Documento di Economia e Finanza*, 2019)**

The passage lists most of the electoral commitments of the governing parties, with the flat tax being an electoral promise of the coalition partner, the Lega, and environmental and social protection being key themes in the

M5S electoral programme. In April 2020, a few weeks after the outbreak of the coronavirus pandemic, the Conte II government—by then composed of the M5S and the PD after the exit of the Lega from the governing majority—presented a budgetary document that asserted its views about how supporting the Italian economy also required generous social policies.

Beyond these differences between the different cabinets, however, there is also one element of continuity in the responsive justifications delivered during the entire period. The budget documents of the Monti, Renzi, Gentiloni, and Conte governments all feature an explicit commitment to proactively support the Italian economy and—to this end—to make full use of the flexibility clauses contained in the European Stability and Growth Pact. The following passage from the 2013 budget document delivered by the Monti government also reflects how the most austerity-oriented Italian government was very active at the European level in seeking consensus and the fiscal space for domestic stimulus policies.

> To reap the benefits of the reforms and the sacrifices it is necessary ... to be able to exploit a European environment that is today more favourable towards investments for growth and employment. Thanks to the pressure exercised by the government in agreement with the parliament, in March 2013 the European Council recognized the need to make full use of the flexibility granted in the existing Stability and Growth Pact to stimulate public investments.
>
> **(Italian government, *Documento di Economia e Finanza*, 2013)**

The persistent references to the need to support the Italian economy, even in the budget documents of the technocratic Monti government, are in line with the idea that in southern European countries economic growth is dependent on governments' stimulus policies, and that therefore in these countries there is more tension between responsiveness and European budgetary rules (Johnston and Regan, 2018).

Spain: rewarding state officials

The tension between European budgetary rules and responsiveness towards national redistributive demands was particularly acute in Spain. As can be seen from Figure 6.5, socially oriented responsiveness was expressed only in around 21 per cent of the policy justifications of the Zapatero government, and in less than 17 per cent of the Rajoy government. Responsiveness oriented to the private sphere was less than 5 per cent for the former and

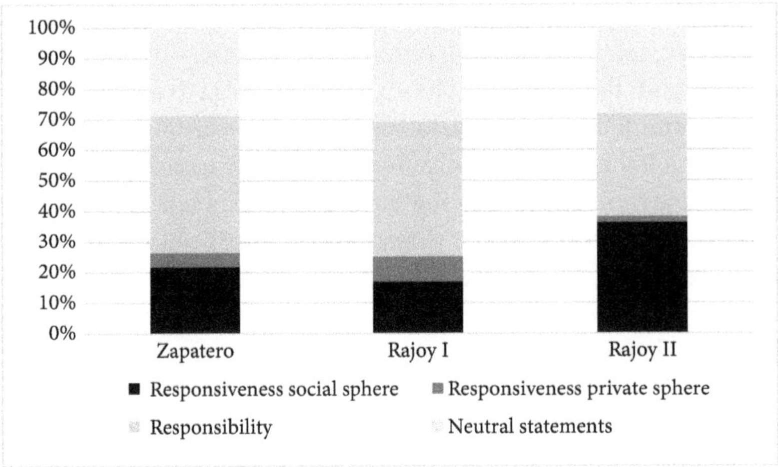

Figure 6.5 Policy justifications for each Spanish government (2008–2018)
Source: Author's coding of annual budget speeches
Note: Bars represent total policy justifications collected for each government

around 8 per cent for the latter. The low levels of responsiveness under the Zapatero and first Rajoy government are comparable to those of the second Merkel government in Germany and the technocratic Monti government in Italy, both of which were ideationally predisposed to pursue austerity.

An important difference in the responsive policy justifications of the Zapatero and Rajoy governments is that the former highlights how the necessary austerity measures are designed in a way that they have the least possible impact on families, while the latter puts greater emphasis on how businesses that are important for growth had been sheltered from the austerity measures as much as possible. The Rajoy I government was thus ideologically more predisposed to pursue austerity than the Zapatero government. Nonetheless, for both governments the overall share of responsive policy justifications was not more than 25 per cent.

As shown in Chapter 4, though, in Spain too, responsiveness starts increasing gradually from 2014 onwards, already in the last budget speeches of the first Rajoy government, and then even more so in 2017 and 2018. Remarkably, a substantial proportion of these statements are about rewarding the efforts and the sacrifices of state officials during the austerity years. The following passage is an example of this commitment.

> On the other hand, this is a budget that returns to officials a good part of the effort they have made over the years. Spain has an excellent Civil Service, and now, when we already have the economic recovery underway, it is time for civil servants to

> recover what they have ceded over these years so that the country as a whole could keep going. That is why this budget foresees a full refund of the 2012 pay, which—as I have already had occasion to explain—will be fully refunded next year, bearing in mind that a quarter has already been refunded in 2015.
>
> **(Montoro Romero, *Congreso*, 25 August 2015)**

From 2014 onwards, the two Rajoy governments also committed the devolvement of more resources to the areas of pensions, security, and national defence. These policy choices were congruent with the policy preferences of the Partido Popular (Hutter et al., 2018) but were arguably also the root of social unrest, particularly in Catalunya where separatist movements opposed how the government redistributed resources within the country. On the wave of this discontent, in 2017 the Catalonian regional government organized a referendum for regional self-determination, which was halted by the security forces of the national administration. The Spanish case is another example of how responsiveness is not necessarily a guarantee for social peace, as it often entails redistribution of resources in line with the preferences of only a part of the population.

Partisan choices and national path dependency

The responsive policy justifications of the post-2014 period in the five countries indicate that the political preferences of the governing parties were at the heart of key policy decisions. At the same time, they also indicate that these policy decisions did not occur in a vacuum, but were rather embedded in the policy legacies inherited from previous governments. These insights indicate that in non-crisis times socio-economic policies follow national trajectories that to some extent are path-dependent, and to some extent are shaped by the preferences of the political forces that are temporarily in office. The evidence emerging from this analysis aligns largely with the 'constrained partisanship' model theorized by Beramendi et. al (2015), and thus confirms that also under the conditions of intensified European economic integration, governing parties still have a considerable degree of autonomy in pursuing their preferred policies, but that their range of choices is limited to a great extent by the policy legacies they inherit.

Another insight that emerges from reflecting on the policy justifications during the post-2014 period is that responsiveness is not a guarantee for social peace nor for electoral satisfaction. The (re)distribution of resources domestically is likely to involve choices about which groups to favour and which not, and the latter may protest vehemently. This occurred in France under the Macron presidency and in Spain under the second Rajoy government, the two democracies that among the five cases are the most majoritarian. A majoritarian electoral system means that the governing party is likely to have greater control over parliament and thus to have more possibilities of being responsive to the demands of its electorate which, however, constitutes only a part of the population. In times of electoral polarization, as occurred in most European countries during the 2010s (Hutter and Kriesi, 2019), responsiveness towards a part of society involves pursuing policies that are diametrically opposed to the preferences of other social groups. This confirms that, as argued in Chapter 1, responsiveness alone is not sufficient as a legitimizing principle.

Finally, the contents of the responsive policy justifications also reveal that responsiveness is likely to be affected by the prevailing ideas about how economic growth shall be achieved. This aspect clearly emerges from the policy justifications of the two Conte governments and the fourth Merkel government. In the case of Conte, the assertion that the government is pursuing a radically different strategy for achieving growth is at the heart of the rationale by which the fiscal stimulus policies were presented. In the case of Merkel, there is a gradual change in macroeconomic ideas between 2015 and 2019 that is also at the heart of the growing share of socially oriented policy justifications. As we will see in the next chapter, this change of ideas also took place within the broader European policy community and is likely to alter the ways in which responsiveness and responsibility can be combined in coming years.

7

Fiscal responsibility between the Fiscal Compact and the Recovery Fund

Introduction

The last budget speech analysed in the present study dates from October 2020. As anticipated in Chapter 5, a few months later, in February 2021, the technocratic-led Draghi government was appointed in Italy. Besides the completion of the vaccination campaign, the institutional mandate was to develop a recovery plan that would satisfy the European criteria for the allocation of the newly created recovery package, Next Generation EU. Preliminary analyses of the announced objectives of the Draghi government suggest that it was arguably more responsible than the Conte II government, but at the same time it was likely to be considerably more inclined than the Monti government to pursue fiscal stimulus policies (Garzia and Karremans, 2021). The Monti and Draghi cabinets embody two cases of technocratic policymaking in which fiscal responsibility entailed different policies. In 2011, fiscal responsibility required the reduction of short-term deficits. In 2021, instead, as will be explored in this chapter, it was more about designing investments for future fiscal returns.

The differences in the institutional mandates of the Monti and Draghi governments are indicative of how the policy implications of fiscal responsibility are not fixed. Just as the more concrete aspects of responsiveness change from party to party and from election to election, different governments may have different notions of how to keep their responsibility commitments. In post-war history, governments in OECD countries have alternated between Keynesian and neoliberal notions of fiscal responsibility, with the former more inclined to favour expenditure that produces future fiscal returns and the latter to favour reducing the size of the public sector and therefore closing the gap between expenditure and revenue in the short term through austerity policies (Helgason, 2019). In the (neo)liberal conception, economies are believed to tend towards a natural equilibrium. Governments should interfere as little as possible with market mechanisms. This implies fiscal

Between Voters and Eurocrats. Johannes Karremans, Oxford University Press. © Johannes Karremans (2024).
DOI: 10.1093/oso/9780192886583.003.0007

caution because fiscal imbalances can cause market distortions and lead to economic crashes. In the Keynesian conception, instead, the economy may have multiple equilibria and the function of fiscal policy is to ensure that the overall direction steers towards an equilibrium with growth and high employment.

The differences between the Keynesian and the (neo)liberal conceptions of fiscal responsibility entail different ontological views of fiscal sustainability. In the here and now, the sustainability of public finances can be portrayed as the difference between revenue and expenditure, which has to be kept to a minimum. This conception is at the heart of the liberal notion of responsibility and is accompanied by the idea that if the size of the public sector remains contained, markets will do their work in triggering economic growth. With a longer term perspective, however, the balance between expenditure and revenue can also be conceived as contingent on macroeconomic and socio-economic developments. Higher employment levels mean a broader tax base and therefore higher state revenue. Higher unemployment, by contrast, means higher numbers of individuals entitled to social protection. Cutting unemployment benefits in the face of rising unemployment may therefore not be effective to reduce state expenditure. As an alternative to the liberal view, therefore, the recipe for a better long-term fiscal balance can also be conceived in terms of investment in services that facilitate the transition from unemployment to employment. This both reduces social dependency on unemployment benefits and at the same time may increase the level of employment, triggering a broadening of the tax base. This, for example, is the logic behind the so-called social investment approach, which is not only a policy strategy designed to meet new social demands (Gingrich and Häusermann, 2015) but—building on Keynesian macroeconomic theories—is also designed to guarantee the long-term sustainability of the welfare state (Hemerijck, 2012).

Despite the diverse views on how to achieve fiscal sustainability, the different notions of responsibility remain distinct from responsiveness in their focus on the financial needs of the state rather than on the demands and preferences of domestic socio-economic groups. Nonetheless, consensus around adoption of a specific notion of responsibility can have far-reaching consequences on the extent to which fiscal stimulus policies can be considered as economically appropriate. In the Keynesian conception of fiscal responsibility, stimulus policies need to be justified as investments that improve macroeconomic performance and therefore generate new state revenues. In the (neo)liberal conception, they need to be justified in terms of how they remain within certain budgetary thresholds. For example, if a government introduces a new social security scheme—like the *reddito di cittadinanza* introduced in Italy under the first Conte government—in order to fulfil (neo)liberal notions of responsibility it needs to ensure that the scheme will not make public expenditure grow beyond the prescribed budgetary threshold. To fulfil Keynesian notions of responsibility, instead, the government has to make sure that the scheme triggers additional levels of consumption and therefore higher tax returns, or at least ensure that the scheme is accompanied by active labour market policies that will generate a broadening of the tax base. Reliance on one of the notions of responsibility can therefore have substantial consequences in terms of the size and scope of social expenditure, triggering austerity in one case and social investment in the other. The dominance of the notion of responsibility adopted is also contingent on the consensus reigning at the international level. This is even more true for governments that operate in a supranational economic governance framework, as is the case of the eurozone countries.

This chapter engages with the questions of whether and how the European consensus on fiscal responsibility mutated between 2007 and 2020, and how this affected the arguments with which governments portrayed their fiscal policies as sustainable. According to various EU scholars, the responses of EU institutions to the coronavirus pandemic signal a change in their perceptions about which policy mixes ensure long-term fiscal sustainability (Schmidt, 2020b). This chapter thus first explores the dominant notions of responsibility at the EU level during the decade from the sovereign debt crisis to the year of the outbreak of the coronavirus pandemic. It theorizes the mechanisms by which the ideational frameworks that define what is fiscally responsible can change over time, and how these mechanisms should have repercussions in how governments justify their budgets. Subsequently, the chapter tests these expectations by looking in-depth at the contents of the policy justifications that are categorized as responsible. The analysis finds evidence of a dominance of the (neo)liberal notion of responsibility between 2009 and 2013, a slow—albeit limited—decline in the 2014–2019 period, and a paradigmatic change towards the Keynesian notion in 2020. Unlike the overall balance between responsiveness and responsibility, the dominance of one notion of responsibility over another seems to be independent of the partisan composition of government. The chapter ends with a reflection on the policy implications of changing notions of fiscal responsibility and the scope for democratic influence on the European consensus on fiscal policy.

European institutions changing their minds?

As discussed in Chapter 1, since the establishment of the monetary union, among EU institutions the dominant understanding of fiscal responsibility has been one centred on low debt and deficit levels (Doray-Demers and Foucault, 2017; Verdun, 2015). In the wake of the sovereign debt crisis in 2009, austerity ideas became even more dominant in prescribing the rules on fiscal responsibility (Schmidt, 2020a). Between 2009 and 2013, the motto became 'you cannot spend your way out of a crisis' and keeping deficits low was seen as the best way to reassure financial markets of the state's ability to repay its debts (Blyth, 2013). Throughout the reforms of European economic governance that occurred in these years, 'austerity ideas remained resilient and were enshrined in one agreement after another' (Schmidt, 2020a, p. 111).

In compliance with European prescriptions, southern European member states made severe cuts to their public budgets, but economic recovery remained a mirage and youth unemployment continued to grow, bringing a risk of a 'lost generation' consisting of young people with little prospect of stably entering the labour market (Tsatsanis et al., 2021). From the perspective of the long-term sustainability of public finances, the prospect of a 'lost generation' is a threat to the breadth of future tax bases and also to economic productivity. By the mid-2010s, therefore, the negative macroeconomic outlook of countries that had implemented far-reaching austerity reforms was challenging the legitimacy of austerity ideas in both input- and output-oriented terms (Scharpf, 2015). The European Commission did not remain blind to the shortcomings of its prescribed policy recipes.

Empirical research has documented a slow retreat of austerity ideas among European policymakers from 2014 onwards. From at least 2013, among the key European economic governance institutions there was a 'tacit recognition' that the austerity-based rules had to be reinterpreted (Schmidt, 2020a, pp. 111–113). This recognition also became gradually visible in public discourse. From 2014 onwards, the words 'flexibility', 'investment', and 'growth' increasingly featured in the titles of European Council and Commission policy documents. This redirection was facilitated and possibly strengthened by the new monetary approach of the European Central Bank, which from 2012 committed to doing 'whatever it takes' to save the common currency (Randow and Speciale, 2018) and which in 2014 started injecting large sums of money into the economy through a quantitative easing programme. In January 2015, the freshly appointed Juncker Commission formalized the reinterpretation of some of the rules in the Stability and Growth Pact by allowing more fiscal flexibility for specific stimulus programmes (Schmidt, 2020a, p. 113). Additional room for flexibility had been forcefully advocated by southern European member states during various Council meetings (Dijsselbloem, 2018). As was shown in Chapter 6, even the technocratic Italian Monti government was in favour of more flexibility to allow for public investment in the Italian economy.

The slow retreat of austerity in the EU's macroeconomic policy prescriptions is particularly well documented in research on the European Semester process through which the Commission reviews national reform programmes and drafts country-specific recommendations that are subsequently ratified by the European Council (Verdun and Zeitlin, 2018). From 2014 onwards, the Semester underwent a 'socialisation' (Zeitlin and Vanhercke, 2018), in the sense that actors from the Commission's Directorate-General of Employment and Social Affairs—as well as national social actors—started to become more involved in the drafting of the recommendations. The retreat of austerity appears most evidently in the recommendations to Germany which, until 2014, were expressively supportive of the German debt-brake rule and prescribed preserving 'a sound fiscal position'. From 2015 onwards, however, the government was urged to use its surplus to finance investments in infrastructure, education, and social protection (Karremans, 2021b). Between 2014 and 2019, austerity ideas remained resilient to the extent that countries with high debts and deficits were still advised to take action to meet the thresholds in the Stability and Growth Pact. In the recommendations to high debt or deficit countries, like France, Italy, and Spain, there is a double focus on the need to limit growth in public expenditure and on the need for measures to improve the performance of labour markets, social protection schemes, and educational outcomes (D'Erman et al., 2019; Haas et al., 2020). In spring 2020, after the outbreak of the coronavirus pandemic, the recommendations urged all the governments to 'take all necessary measures, in line with the general escape clause of the Stability and Growth Pact, to effectively address the coronavirus pandemic, sustain the economy and support the ensuing recovery' (European Council, 2020). In 2020, therefore, fiscal consolidation policies were no longer at the heart of country-specific recommendations.

A similar change from more restrictive to more expansive fiscal ideas over time is also visible in the discourse of another key European economic governance actor, namely the European Central Bank (ECB). Until 2011 the ECB remained firm in its view that unsustainable national fiscal policies were 'the root cause of the sovereign debt crisis' and therefore urged national governments to commit to fiscal consolidation (Starken, 2011). The ECB's ideas were anchored in the belief that monetary policy had to remain independent from governments' fiscal policies. From the point of view of a central bank, fiscal discipline reduces the risk that monetary policy becomes a function of financing government spending programmes, allowing the central bank to focus entirely on its institutional mandate to maintain long-term price stability. The ideational link between central bank independence and fiscal discipline is evident in the discourse with which the ECB justified one of its most controversial policy innovations, the Outright Monetary Transactions (OMT) programme,[1] in which the ECB would purchase sovereign bonds of countries asking for financial assistance. The programme was criticized by the German central bank and the German government for being a potential incentive for deficit spending as it would constitute a source of finance for governments. The response to the critique was fully centred on how the independence of monetary policy was guaranteed by the conditionality of fiscal consolidation policies:

> We take all our monetary policy decisions in full independence. And we have designed the OMTs [Outright Monetary Transactions] so that these decisions could never be dominated by fiscal policies. This is why a pre-condition for access to the OMTs is a strong economic adjustment programme. It ensures that we would only ever intervene in situations where fiscal discipline is firmly ensured.
>
> **(Draghi, 2013)**

The macroeconomic consequences of austerity policies in southern European member states were, however, also a concern for the executive board of the ECB (Schmidt, 2020a, pp. 111–113). As a response, in 2015 the ECB started the quantitative easing programme through which between 2015 and 2018 it injected around €2.6 trillion into the economy, bringing interest rates down to 0 per cent (Fromage et al., 2019). The programme reduced financial speculation on sovereign bonds, and the reduction in interest rates meant that governments had to pay less interest on their debts, therefore easing the financial stress on southern European member states in particular. In parallel with the gradual change of policy, the ECB's view on the appropriate recipe for national fiscal policy also changed. While maintaining the emphasis on the need for structural reforms to correct fiscal imbalances and on the importance of fiscal discipline for central bank independence, in its public speeches

[1] In the end the OMT programme was never used. However, just its announcement is considered to have played an important role in the stabilization of interest rates in the euro area (De Grauwe and Ji, 2013).

the ECB also increasingly started to encourage governments to accompany these reforms with investment in training and active labour market policies to secure jobs for the low-skilled (e.g. Draghi, 2017).

After the outbreak of the coronavirus pandemic, the retreat of austerity ideas among the members of the ECB board was even more evident. When in spring 2020 the eurozone countries suddenly entered severe recession, the ECB expanded its bond-purchasing programme, injecting liquidity into the economy with relatively loose conditions. When justifying its policies, the ECB employed a different understanding of the link between central bank independence and national fiscal policy:

> Fiscal expansion is indispensable at the current juncture to sustain demand and mitigate the long-term costs of the crisis. Monetary policy can complement these efforts. ... In such times, it would be wrong to constrain fiscal policies today to protect monetary dominance tomorrow. Quite on the contrary, using fiscal and structural policies more actively in the current environment may foster central bank independence. The reason is that such policies may boost potential growth and thereby increase monetary policy space in the future. Moreover, a counter-cyclical fiscal expansion may result in lower rather than higher government debt in the longer run.
>
> **(Schnabel, 2020)**

Despite the rigidity of the EU's fiscal rules and the complexity of supranational decision-making processes, austerity became less influential in shaping macroeconomic policymaking in the EU. Furthermore, the coronavirus pandemic may well have been the window of opportunity for a change of paradigm. The response of European governments to the economic recession caused by the pandemic in 2020 is a case in point of how the international consensus on fiscal responsibility is not static but is subject to change. In spring 2020, after intensive negotiations and tensions between the northern 'frugal' countries and southern member states, the European Council and the Commission agreed on an unprecedented stimulus package known as the Recovery Fund, or Next Generation EU, consisting of €750 billion of investment. The package is de facto the first substantive common European debt, as its funding is ensured largely by bonds issued by the Commission on behalf of the European Union. In addition, since the outbreak of the pandemic, governments have been allowed to break the rules in the Stability and Growth Pact, and negotiations remain ongoing as to whether the current form of the Pact will remain in place or whether it will be reformed. Also among the institutions that are tasked to guard—or even have a stake in the fulfilment of—European budgetary targets, the ideas about fiscal responsibility have at least partially changed between 2010 and 2020.

Theorizing changing notions of responsibility

The framework of ideas and standards that define the nature of the problems addressed by policymakers, and that shape the strategies by which solutions are pursued, is the scholarly definition of a policy paradigm (Hall, 1993, p. 279). As argued and shown throughout this book and in the literature, the framework of ideas that defined the problems and policy strategies during the years of the sovereign debt crisis was centred on a (neo)liberal conception of responsibility that involved a strong reliance on austerity policies (Bremer and McDaniel, 2020; Cavalieri and Karremans, 2022). This framework of ideas was shared among the key actors in European economic governance, including the European Council, the Commission, and the European Central Bank. In the early 2010s, the key macroeconomic problem identified was governments' public accounts. Because of the magnitude of the bailouts that many European governments paid to rescue their national banks after the global financial crisis of 2008, national public sectors were still acting as shock absorbers for failures of the banking system. Under these circumstances, if countries had a public debt that was higher than 90 per cent of GDP, it would become impossible for the state to act as shock absorber because its bond yields would become unsustainable (Blyth, 2013, pp. 6–7). Debt and deficit levels were therefore perceived as the main systemic problems to be addressed, and fiscal consolidation became the main policy strategy to pursue this aim.

Both quantitative and qualitative research traditions in public policy agree that policy paradigms shape long periods of policymaking (Baumgartner, 2013). Once a policy paradigm is established, policy change remains confined to small adaptive changes that do not jeopardize the objectives established. The resilience of a policy paradigm resides in the fact that its founding ideas are shared by an entire policy community (Hall, 1993). These ideas tend to be 'sticky' because the actors involved tend to be attached to the existing definition of the status quo (Baumgartner, 2013). This entails that policy objectives and instruments remain constant, because they are defined by ideas that are shared within the community. In the case of European economic governance, the policy community in charge of national macroeconomic policies is constituted primarily of national governments, the European Council and the Commission, which frequently interact through the

European Semester. In addition, the policies and opinions of the European Central Bank constitute a relevant background to the definition of how public finances should be kept sustainable. Once, in the early 2010s, these actors agreed on a coordinated macroeconomic policy based on fiscal discipline, the strategy of fiscal consolidation, and the objective of low public deficits and debts constituted the backbone of European macroeconomic policy coordination (Bremer and McDaniel, 2020; Laffan, 2014; Lehner and Wasserfallen, 2019; Schmidt, 2020a).

When these policy strategies start to fail or produce negative outcomes, the policy community is increasingly under pressure to find better solutions. The rise and gradual decline of austerity ideas among the key European economic governance actors parallels the three levels of policy change that first characterize and then trigger the break-up of a paradigm (Cavalieri and Karremans, 2022; Hall, 1993). The more flexible interpretation of fiscal rules observed in the second half of the 2010s can be seen as a change of policy instruments but not of objectives, as meeting the prescribed budgetary targets remained the red line in the European macroeconomic consensus. At the same time, the process by which economic growth gradually substituted deficit reduction as a policy priority can be seen as a gradual change in the hierarchy of policy goals. Finally, in 2020 we observe a potential break-up of the paradigm, namely a redefinition of both instruments and objectives, with public investment being the main tool to trigger growth and therefore the anchor for long-term fiscal stability. This only occurred after the outbreak of the coronavirus crisis, which offered a window of opportunity to rediscuss the desirability of the fiscal discipline predicated in the Stability and Growth Pact, opening up space for new ideas about how public investment is a responsible strategy to generate fiscal returns and therefore to ensure the long-term sustainability of public finances.

The gradual change of policy ideas among the key actors of European economic governance raises the question whether this influenced the changing contents of national policy justifications or, on the contrary, whether national governments—under pressure from their voters—were a driving factor behind this change over time. The flow of policy ideas between the national and supranational levels seems to be working in two directions. On the one hand, the rise of austerity ideas across all levels of European economic governance in the early 2010s suggests that an international consensus creates a 'logic of appropriateness' (March and Olsen, 2009) to which all key actors subscribe. In this sense, European economic governance first tightened and then loosened its constraints on national governments by changing its consensus on the macroeconomic priorities. On the other hand, there are clear indications of upward streams from the national to the European level, with governments bringing their preferences and concerns to the supranational level through intergovernmental processes (Karremans, 2021b; Lehner and Wasserfallen, 2019; Maricut and Puetter, 2018). The adoption of the fiscal discipline approach was largely the result of intergovernmental negotiations in the early 2010s on reforming the framework of European economic governance, in which the German-led coalition was successful in ensuring that the reform would be based on principles of fiscal discipline (Wasserfallen et al., 2019).

The definition of European macroeconomic policy priorities developed through the European Semester, is, in fact, a process that is open to national political inputs. Despite the formal centrality of the Commission in the European Semester (Verdun and Zeitlin, 2018), the drafting of country-specific recommendations has a strong intergovernmental component with power residing largely in the Economic and Financial Affairs Council (ECOFIN). As is also recognized by Commission Officials, the country-specific recommendations are mostly those of the Council (Maricut and Puetter, 2018, p. 206). From this it follows that the political forces sitting at Council—particularly on the seats of the larger member states—can have a substantial impact on the contents of these recommendations. The document exchanges between the national and European levels in the context of the European Semester often reveal how country-specific recommendations regularly find their chronological origin in the political programmes of governing parties (Karremans, 2021b, pp. 523–526; Karremans and Kaltenleithner, 2021, pp. 8–10). During the years of the eurozone crisis, the EU's intergovernmental process and the macroeconomic policy agenda thus seem to have been influenced by the inputs of fiscally conservative governments. In the second half of the 2010s, instead, the agenda was influenced by governments that were challenged by rising levels of popular discontent over the consequences of austerity policies. If democratic policymaking requires a balance between responsiveness and responsibility—and if periods of high levels of responsibility need to be followed by responsiveness (Linde and Peters, 2020)—the same logic may also apply to EU-level policymaking. In fact, the decline of austerity ideas within the European consensus on responsibility went hand in hand with a return to higher levels of responsiveness at the national level, as was shown in Chapter 4, with governments more committed to delivering resources to domestic socio-economic groups than being focused on the sustainability of public finances.

If, from a democratic legitimacy perspective, periods of excessive reliance on responsibility should be followed by responsiveness (Linde and Peters, 2020), pressures for a paradigmatic change can be expected to come from the bottom up. After several successive years of 'taking' resources from domestic socio-economic sources in order to consolidate public finances, by the mid-2010s national governments were increasingly confronted with popular discontent and a rise of challenger parties (Alonso and Ruiz-Rufino, 2020). The European elections of 2014 showed that for the first time in post-war history the joint vote share of the traditional governing parties from both the centre-right and centre-left amounted to less than 50 per cent of the total, with new challenger parties increasingly winning consent (Hobolt and Tilley, 2016). Under these conditions, governments were under pressure to again start 'giving' resources to domestic socio-economic groups, in the form of either expenditure increases or tax reductions. The paradigm for fiscal responsibility agreed at the European level may have worked as a constraint on the responses to this pressure, as the shared objective agreed by the European policy community had been to reduce deficits. The outbreak of the coronavirus pandemic and its socio-economic consequences shifted attention to different problems which demanded not only the use of different policy approaches but also created the conditions—or the necessity—to reset the main policy priorities.

Integrating the theories about changing policy paradigms with the predicaments about the cyclical alternation between responsiveness and responsibility, one would expect a gradual change in the contents of responsible policy justifications. More precisely, the dominance of unequivocal responsible policy justifications in the 2009–2013 period reflects how austerity ideas were defining both the problems to be addressed, namely public debts and deficits, and the policy strategy, namely fiscal consolidation. By the same token, the growing tendency to introduce fiscal stimulus policies in the 2014–2019 period can be seen as an effort to find alternative policy solutions, but still within the austerity framework. The first expectation is therefore that the responsible policy justifications of the 2014–2019 period refer increasingly to fiscal stimulus policies, but feature an argumentation that does not undermine or challenge the importance of meeting the debt and deficit levels prescribed by European rules. The change of ideas within the EU policy community in 2020, in turn, should trigger a change in the policy justifications of subsequent budget speeches, in which austerity ideas no longer play a role, and fiscal sustainability is pursued through stimulus policies rather than through public spending reductions and tax increases. The next two sections explore these expectations.

Responsibility under the spell of austerity

As was shown in the previous chapters, after a few years of budgetary policy dominated by fiscal responsibility, after 2014 governments started becoming more inclined to pursue fiscal stimulus policies and tailor them to the demands and preferences of domestic socio-economic groups. In the immediate aftermath of the 2008 global financial crisis, governments had to reassure their audiences that their large bank bailouts were financially responsible. Subsequently, in the budget speeches delivered between autumn 2009 and 2013 more than 46 per cent of the policy justifications were framed in terms of fiscal responsibility, with peaks of more than 50 per cent between 2011 and 2012. In the budget speeches delivered between autumn 2014 and 2017 this percentage declined to 35 per cent, and in those delivered in 2018 and 2019 it amounted to around 25 per cent on average. Figure 7.1 illustrates this trend in budget speeches delivered between autumn 2007 and autumn 2019—just before the outbreak of the coronavirus pandemic—and also shows the percentages of the different fiscal responsibility subcategories that were described in Chapter 2.

As described more fully in Chapter 2, the responsibility subcategories indicate first whether the policy justifications refer to fiscal consolidation policies, to the overall budget, or to fiscal stimulus policies. In addition, they are divided by the theme they refer to. The 'financial' category gathers justifications referring to the country's financial situation, namely the balance between expenditure and revenue or the national rules regarding debts and deficits. The 'international' category gathers justifications that portray budgetary policy as being in line with international commitments, such as those related to the Stability and Growth Pact. Fiscal responsibility also includes justifications for fiscal consolidation that are based on macroeconomic arguments (here grouped under 'responsible economics'), because they are in line with the framework of ideas on fiscal sustainability in European economic governance in the 2010s (Laffan, 2014). In addition, Figure 7.1 features a dotted line indicating the percentage of macroeconomic justifications for fiscal stimuli (responsive economics). Even though in the framework presented in Chapter 2 these justifications fall under the umbrella of responsiveness because they signal the government's autonomy in making choices according to its political preferences, they are reported here because

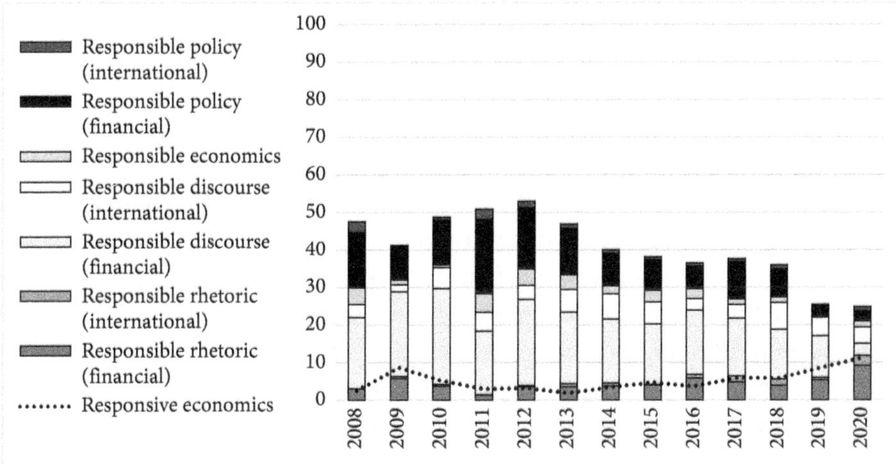

Figure 7.1 Shares of fiscal responsibility in national budgetary discourse, including subcategories (2007–2019)

Source: Author's coding of annual budget speeches in the five selected countries (see Table 2.1 in Chapter 2 for more detail)
Note: The years reported are the budget years to which the speeches refer (e.g. a speech given in October refers to the year starting from the subsequent January). Graphs are based on speeches and documents delivered between October 2007 and October 2019

they are informative of the gradual paradigm change in the notion of fiscal responsibility.

The bars indicating the yearly share of responsibility justifications, the shares of their subcategories, and the dotted line in Figure 7.1 are illustrative of the change in focus from fiscal consolidation to fiscal stimulus evident in speeches delivered between the early and late 2010s. As was anticipated in Chapter 4, the variation of fiscal responsibility over time is common to all five countries analysed, regardless of whether their public deficits exceeded European budgetary thresholds. In 2011 and 2012—the years that saw reform of European economic governance—in addition to more than 50 per cent of the government policy justifications being framed in terms of fiscal responsibility, around half of them also explicitly referred to fiscal consolidation policies. The high levels of fiscal responsibility in the early 2010s were therefore not only a matter of rhetoric to reassure audiences that governments were taking into account the sustainability of public finances but they also involved the introduction of measures explicitly designed to reduce public deficits in the short term. With a quarter of the overall budgetary discourse centred on fiscal consolidation policies and arguments about the balance between expenditure and revenue, and more than half of the overall discourse framed in terms of fiscal responsibility, in 2011 and 2012 we observe the peak of the austerity policy paradigm. In these years, austerity ideas not only defined the principles with which governments aimed to keep their public finances sustainable but also structured governments' budgetary policies in their entirety. Government expenditure and taxation policies were mostly designed to reduce debts and deficits, with relatively little consideration of the (short-term) preferences and needs of domestic socio-economic groups. Instead, government decision-making was dictated by the logic that deficit reduction would boost the confidence of financial markets and therefore guarantee state solvency in the long run. This idea also spread to the southern European countries that had advocated for more fiscally expansive policies during European intergovernmental negotiations. In France, for instance, the fiscal consolidation policy was justified as follows:

> Here is the reality, ladies and gentlemen, however blunt it may be: we are spending too much and we will never be able to match our revenues with our expenses. We just have to save money, yes, save money, a word that every household knows but too often the state tends to forget. It is not a question of ideology, it is not a theoretical debate, it is a fact, a raw fact, an indisputable fact: the only way to de-leverage the country is to reduce our public spending.
>
> **(Valérie Pécresse, Assemblee Generale, 18 October 2011)**

With its strong emphasis on the need for deficit and debt reduction, the budgetary discourse of 2009–2013 strongly evoked the idea that there was 'no alternative' to austerity policies (Alonso, 2014). Under this policy framework, there seemed to be little or no space for delivering resources to domestic socio-economic groups, and the spread of ideas from one government to another seemed to dictate that voters could not vote for alternative policy programmes.

In the budget speeches delivered from October 2013 onwards, both the overall shares of fiscal responsibility and the shares of policy statements referring to fiscal consolidation register a decline. As the shaded parts of the bars in Figure 7.1 show, the frequency of responsibility justifications for fiscal consolidation decreases, while the frequency of justifications for fiscal stimulus policies increases. In addition, the dotted line shows that fiscal stimuli were increasingly presented as beneficial for macroeconomic performance, with statements on how the government intended to actively support economic growth. The gradual decline in justifications for fiscal consolidation measures and the increase in references to stimulus policies seem to reflect the first-

and second-order changes described by Hall (1993), namely a change of policy instruments and a reordering of policy goals. Within these levels of change, the pre-existing paradigm—austerity—was expected to continue to play a structuring role. In order to establish whether austerity ideas still played a paradigmatic role in defining fiscal responsibility, a more fine-grained analysis is needed to capture the extent to which austerity ideas were substituted with arguments about fiscal stimulus in the responsible justifications.

Figure 7.2 reports the predictive margins of the percentage of responsibility justifications for fiscal consolidation and fiscal stimulus in the four time periods, with the percentages calculated as the shares of justifications that are categorized as 'responsible' rather than those of the total number of policy justifications. This allows a better grasp of the extent to which the proportion of budget speeches dedicated to the democratic principle of responsibility is dominated by a particular notion of responsibility. Following the argument developed above, the expectation is that the budget speeches delivered from autumn 2009 onwards will feature higher levels of responsible justifications for consolidation policies than those in any other time period. At the same time, the expectation is that in the speeches delivered in the 2014–2016 and 2017–2019 periods, the emphasis of fiscal responsibility is more on fiscal stimuli. To the extent that responsible justifications for consolidation measures remained significantly present until the budget speeches delivered in autumn 2019, these changes can be considered to be first and second order.

The evidence shows a symmetric development in the extent to which fiscal responsibility takes the form of financial justifications for either consolidation or stimulus policies. The analysis controls for countries in order to establish whether the patterns over time are valid across the case selection and are not driven by specific national contexts. The predictive margins indicate that in the 2009–2013 period responsibility justifications for fiscal consolidation policies were significantly more frequent while justifications for fiscal stimuli were significantly less present than in the subsequent time period. At the same time, Figure 7.2 shows that, despite the decline, responsible justifications for consolidation policies remained significantly present in the 2014–2016 and 2017–2019 periods, therefore suggesting a certain resilience of austerity ideas.

In fact, the introductions of budget speeches continued to feature statements about persistent commitments to the existing debt and deficit targets. The financial justifications for fiscal stimuli, in turn, were mostly framed in terms of how they did not represent a breaking away from these targets. For

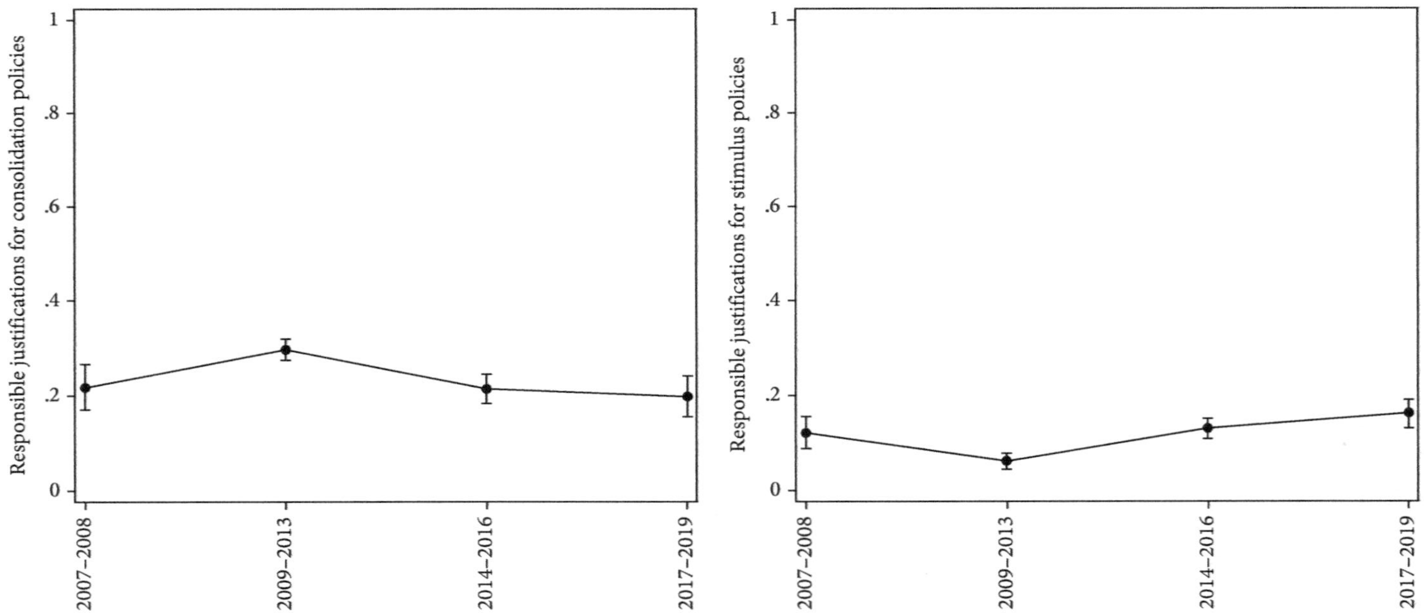

Figure 7.2 Salience of different notions of fiscal sustainability in national budget speeches (2007–2019)

Source: Author's coding of annual budget speeches in the five selected countries

example, when in 2018 the German social democratic Finance Minister Olaf Scholz announced a relatively more expansive fiscal policy course than in previous years, the justification was framed in the following terms:

> It is very possible in times of economic prosperity to increase investments significantly and at the same time not burden the budget with additional debts. … Therefore, it makes little sense to have abstract debates about whether more investment or more debt makes sense. Both are possible: more investment without new debt.
>
> **(Olaf Scholz, German Bundestag, 15 May 2018)**

Similarly, in May 2017 in a context with relatively less economic prosperity, the Spanish government announced that in 2018 pension expenditure would be increased by €30 billion, adding the socially responsive justification that this increase was fundamental for social protection. At the same time, the finance minister also emphasized that in deciding on this increase the government took into account the long-term sustainability of the pension system.

> This does not mean that we are not concerned about the future of pensions, and that does not mean that we do not appeal once again to all political groups in this Chamber so that, through the Toledo Pact Commission, we reach agreements that really guarantee the sustainability of our pension system. But I insist that this sustainability is based on employment, it is based on the increase in the social security contribution, and therefore obviously on those solutions, those measures, that we will all have to cooperate in agreeing to.
>
> **(Montoro Romero, Congreso, 3 May 2018)**

As seen in Chapter 6, between 2017 and 2018 the Rajoy II government started to restitute resources to specific social groups, in particular state employees and pensioners, to compensate for the economic losses that these groups had suffered during the previous austerity years. Also in the Spanish case, towards the end of the decade, the budgetary plans contain a growing share of expenditure increases and tax reductions designed to meet specific socio-economic needs. These measures still needed to be justified in terms of fiscal sustainability. The passage above is an example of how the idea of immediate deficit and debt reduction started losing influence as an argument for justifying the growing amount of fiscal stimulus policies in terms of fiscal responsibility. The fiscal stimulus policies would certainly not contribute to a short-term fiscal consolidation, and therefore the balance between responsiveness and responsibility had to be found through different combinations of policies and ideas. In this statement, the idea emerges that sustainability cannot be guaranteed solely by reducing the immediate gap between expenditure and revenue, but can also result from future tax returns that can be triggered by higher employment levels.

It is important to highlight that this statement in the Spanish budget speech of May 2018 came from a conservative government, indicating how the changing ideas for fiscal responsibility were common to governments of different partisan compositions. Unlike for the overall balance between responsiveness and responsibility, for the different frames of fiscal responsibility there is no interaction effect between government partisanship and the time period. Once established, in the early 2010s the austerity paradigm structured the arguments of fiscal responsibility for both centre-left and centre-right governments, with the only difference that the former would express it more as a temporary necessity and the latter as a policy choice that was actively supported. In the second half of the decade, in all five cases governments gradually started introducing fiscal stimulus policies that, however, still needed to be justified according to the existing framework for fiscal responsibility. The more fiscal stimulus policies were introduced, the less appropriate the austerity paradigm was. As we shall see below, when after the outbreak of the coronavirus pandemic government expenditures increased drastically, the frame for fiscal responsibility changed completely, with governments of different partisan compositions justifying expenditures as investments for future returns.

Fiscal responsibility in 2020

As was anticipated in Chapters 4 and 6, in the budget speeches delivered after the outbreak of the coronavirus pandemic, governments' main concern was to deliver resources to domestic socio-economic groups in order to assist them through the economic and health crisis. In budget plans delivered between April and October 2020, less than 18 per cent of the policy justifications framed budgetary policy in terms of fiscal responsibility. Figure 7.3 compares the levels of fiscal responsibility and its subcategories in the budgetary plans delivered in the 2017–2019 period with those delivered during the year 2020, showing that fiscal consolidation does not appear in governments' post-pandemic budgetary discourse. As represented by the subcategory 'responsible rhetoric', fiscal responsibility was mostly about justifying financial socio-economic support measures, which in 2020 made all governments across the eurozone exceed the European budgetary thresholds. The main differences in the budgetary plans presented during the first

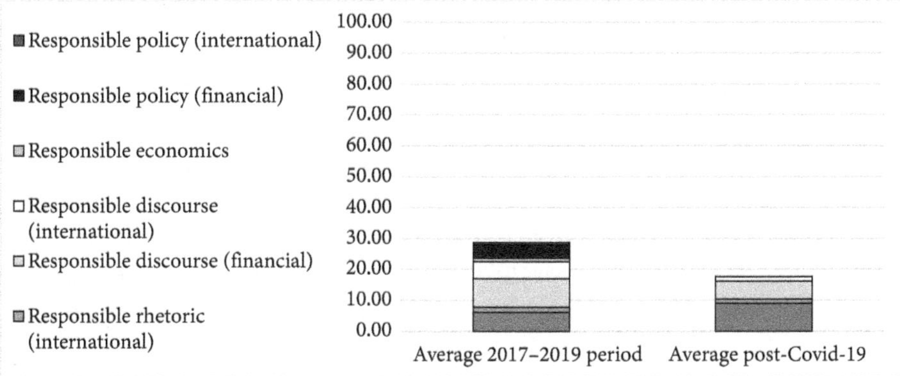

Figure 7.3 Fiscal responsibility before and after the outbreak of the coronavirus pandemic

Source: Author's coding of annual budget speeches

pandemic year are thus the complete disappearance of references to fiscal consolidation and, as discussed in Chapter 6, the explicit commitment to support domestic socio-economic groups.

In more qualitative terms, fiscal responsibility during 2020 was to a large extent expressed in terms of how the increases in public debt and deficit levels caused by the support measures would need to be brought back in future years. The Austrian finance minister, for instance, reassured parliament that the increases in the deficit and debt were only temporary:

> For us, it was always clear: a budget surplus is not an end in itself, it is a precaution for the crises of the future, and we got it right. The magic word for the debts we incur now is 'temporarily'.
>
> **(Gernot Blümel, Österreich Nationalrat, 14 October 2020)**

Similar arguments were present across the various cases, suggesting that austerity ideas had not entirely exited the policy realm. Unlike during the 2010s, debt and deficit reduction was presented as an objective to be postponed. In the Italian case, for instance, when presenting its pandemic response package in spring 2020, the government highlighted that the debt/GDP ratio would be brought back to the eurozone average within a decade, and that this return strategy was going to be 'fully compatible with the objectives of innovation and environmental and social sustainability that Europe and Italy have set themselves' (Italian government, *Documento di Economia e Finanza*, 24 April 2020). The need to bring debts and deficits down and to stick to common European budgetary standards therefore still seemed to be present in government agendas.

At the same time, compared to the budgetary discourse in the 2010s, post-pandemic fiscal responsibility features a rather novel idea, namely that temporary increases in deficit levels can be considered fiscally 'responsible'. This certainly contrasts with the ideas of fiscal responsibility that emerged in the aftermath of the eurozone crisis and that were the basis for strengthening the Stability and Growth Pact. The change is particularly striking in Germany, which during the 2010s was one of the main supporters of austerity policies in the eurozone. In September 2020, instead, the German finance minister justified the high deficit foreseen for the 2021 budget in the following terms:

> Because if we didn't act now, we would have to invest a lot more money as a result, and at the same time we would gamble away the future of our country.
>
> **(Olaf Scholz, Bundestag, 29 September 2020)**

In both the Austrian and German cases—both countries advocating fiscal discipline during the 2010s—the finance ministers emphasized that the fiscal surpluses achieved during the second half of the 2010s were 'kein Selbstzweck' (not ends in themselves) but rather buffers to finance expenditure during less fortunate times. In the German case, Olaf Scholz even added that higher deficits today would mean lower deficits tomorrow. The redefinition of the purpose of balanced public finances from a goal per se to having the function of achieving other aims resembles in many ways what Hall (1993) identifies as third-order change, namely a redefinition of the objectives governments need to pursue, and therefore also a redefinition of policy instruments.

Unsurprisingly, the same new conception of fiscal responsibility was also observable in the Mediterranean member states, which throughout the 2010s had been struggling to reconcile austerity ideas with their national economic interests. In the French case too, for instance, there is recognition that the expenditure in 2020 would cause a debt increase that would require repayment. At the same time, the government announced a fiscal stimulus as the way to ensure debt reduction, and presented the control of public finances as a secondary goal that comes after support for economic growth.

> As for the means of repayment, we first choose growth, which is the most effective and the most sustainable instrument. By launching the stimulus now, we are supporting the growth that will be used to repay the debt tomorrow. Then comes the control of our public finances, to which I know the general rapporteur of the finance committee is particularly attached. The principle of accountability must remain at the heart of public finances. We need to maintain operating expenses and support investment expenses.
>
> **(Bruno Le Maire, Assemblée Generale, 12 October 2020)**

The budget speeches thus signal a change in the approach to fiscal responsibility, featuring many characteristics of third-order change, including redefinitions of policy goals, priorities, and instruments.

To conclude

The evidence presented in this chapter shows that also under the conditions of European economic governance, fiscal responsibility is not static but is instead a contested object and is therefore subject to change. Unlike responsiveness, however, notions of responsibility do not change from one electoral cycle to another or with different parties rotating in government. Instead, notions of responsibility remain sticky also when policymakers realize that the related policies do not produce the desired effects. Against the ineffectiveness of the austerity paradigm in leading to economic growth and reducing public debt in southern European countries, governments started introducing fiscal stimulus policies in agreement with European institutions, but still within the limits of the prescribed budgetary targets. The enshrinement of austerity ideas in European budgetary agreement meant that this particular notion of fiscal responsibility remained in force for well beyond the period of the sovereign debt crisis, until at least 2019. This suggests that, while still being subject to political influences, the establishment and endurance of a particular notion of responsibility partially escapes (direct) partisan influence.

The outbreak of the coronavirus pandemic offered the occasion for European policymakers to redefine the priorities and aims of budgetary policy, therefore creating the conditions for third-order change to occur. In October 2020, governments in different countries and of different partisan compositions presented debt reduction as something to be postponed to a future time, and as an aim that did not necessarily have to be pursued through fiscal consolidation but that could be achieved through fiscally expansive policies. This notion of responsibility was not only expressed in government discourse but was also shared by the key European economic governance institutions including the ECB. The extent to which a new Keynesian-based notion of fiscal responsibility has been established needs to pass the test of time. If the new paradigm is established, in future years we should continue to observe fiscal responsibility being framed in terms of investments generating future returns.

8 Explaining the balance between responsiveness and responsibility in the eurozone

Introduction

Following the metaphor used in Chapter 1, the analysis of how the governments of five eurozone countries justified their budgets between 2007 and 2020 reveals that there was a period between 2009 and 2013 in which they were more concerned about 'taking', and that this was followed by a period in which they became gradually more and more concerned about 'giving'. The theoretical starting point for this research was that democratic governments are on the one hand pressured to be responsive to domestic constituencies, and on the other are pressured to act responsibly to keep public finances sustainable in the long term. For their legitimacy, it is important that governments maintain a balance between these two pressures: a lack of responsiveness may undermine the democratic linkage between citizens' demands and public policy, while a shortage of responsibility may undermine the long-term effectiveness of government action (Mair, 2013; Sartori, 1976).

The findings presented in this book show that during the years of the eurozone crisis the balance shifted decisively towards financial responsibility, but that from 2014 onwards it started leaning gradually more and more towards responsiveness. Together with the cross-time comparisons illustrated in Chapter 3, which show that no major changes occurred between the 1980s and 2010s in the balance between responsive and responsible policy criteria, this finding disconfirms theories about international economic integration leading necessarily to a permanent restriction of policy space and of the possibilities for governments to be responsive to their constituencies (Mair, 2013; Rodrik, 2000; Scharpf, 2011).

The analysis presented in this book shows that while economic crises may temporarily make governments' policy efforts be less focused on electoral responsiveness, international economic integration and European economic

Between Voters and Eurocrats. Johannes Karremans, Oxford University Press. © Johannes Karremans (2024).
DOI: 10.1093/oso/9780192886583.003.0008

governance (EEG) per se do not produce the expected effect of making governments focus increasingly on fiscal sustainability. If such theoretical conjecture were true, after the strengthening of the Stability and Growth Pact that occurred between 2009 and 2013, responsibility should have become a lasting dominant criterion for budgetary policymaking, particularly in countries featuring deficit and debt levels that exceed the prescribed thresholds. The empirical evidence shows almost the contrary, namely that responsibility was the dominant criterion for decision-making only between 2009 and 2013 and that responsiveness started increasing progressively from 2014 onwards.

The distinct national and partisan characteristics of responsiveness shown in Chapter 6 are a further confirmation that the preferences of domestic constituencies keep being channelled into the policymaking process. In Italy, for instance, when the Five Star Movement gained government office in 2018, it introduced the *Reddito di cittadinanza*, a social assistance scheme that the party had been campaigning for since 2013. In Spain, to maintain the support of an important part of the constituency of the Partido Popular, the Second Rajoy government raised the pay of civil servants. In France, under the Macron presidency, the governing party *En Marche* pursued several of its major electoral commitments through tax credits. In Germany, faced with discontent among left-oriented voters, the German social-democratic party contributed to giving a more redistributive-oriented character to the budgetary policy of the fourth Merkel government. In Austria, the right-oriented first Kurz government worked to reduce the tax burden below 40 per cent of GDP. In all these cases, governments have been delivering resources to domestic constituencies, largely in line with the redistributive commitments on which the governing parties appealed to voters during electoral campaigns.

The distinct ways in which different governments started delivering resources to their constituencies from 2014 onwards corroborate the predicament that a model of 'constrained partisanship' keeps structuring policymaking in post-industrial countries (Beramendi et al., 2015). The rules of European economic governance did not prevent a return to responsiveness after several years of fiscal responsibility, and the related delivery of resources to domestic constituencies took different shapes according to the political composition of each government. At the same time, the relatively homogeneous trend in the overall responsive–responsible balance observed in the five countries must not be ignored. While on the one hand responsiveness took different characteristics according to government partisanship and national contextual factors, on the other hand, all governments analysed follow certain common supranational trends, particularly in terms of the principles by which they pursue long-term fiscal sustainability.

Despite their deep social, economic, political and institutional diversity, the five country-cases not only feature the same over-time trend in the overall balance between responsive and responsible policy justifications, but also feature the same gradual change in the understanding of how long-term fiscal sustainability should be maintained. While until the early 2010s the understanding was that reducing annual deficits was the best way for gaining confidence in financial markets and fostering growth, by 2020 the rationale had shifted towards Keynesian ideas about public investments generating future fiscal returns. The analysis in Chapter 7 shows that this was a gradual shift in policy ideas common to national governments and European institutions, that fully materialized after the Covid-19 pandemic. This shift went hand in hand with the post-2014 increases of responsiveness and was parallel to declining levels of responsible policy justifications.

These cross-country trends ask for a deeper understanding. After having discussed how the measurement of responsiveness and responsibility adopted in this book allows making inferences about what governments perceive they can and cannot do, this chapter investigates the potential causes behind the common trends identified in this study. To do so, it first summarizes the preliminary answers resulting from the previous chapters, and then reflects on plausible explanations. The chapter develops the argument that, in similar ways to democratically elected governments, also supranational institutions are to some extent pressured to alternate decision-making criteria that are more oriented at the rebalancing of public accounts with criteria that are more oriented at the delivery of public goods. Under conditions of international economic integration and supranational governance, the criteria that are more dominantly present in supranational institutions subsequently have deep implications for the balance between responsiveness and responsibility at the national level. The chapter concludes with a few reflections for a research agenda on how data on policy justifications can be integrated with other data sources in a broader scholarly effort to understand the democratic cycle in the context of supranational governance.

The room for manoeuvre that governments perceive to have

This book started from the theoretical observation that democratic choices are to some extent constrained by what governing institutions can and cannot do (Bardi et al., 2014; Bühlmann and Kriesi, 2013; Powell, 2004; Schmidt, 1996). To capture this characteristic of democracies as we know them, this book used the conceptual distinction between responsiveness and responsibility, which is essentially about the institutional constraints to electoral mandates (Mair, 2013; Sartori, 1976).

Particularly with regards to their budgets, governments of advanced industrial countries are committed to multiple institutional arrangements to ensure the long-term functioning of the market economy and to prevent it from being undermined by short-term electoral commitments (Genschel and Zangl, 2014; Majone, 1994). When socializing into governing institutions, political parties and their leaders become committed into ensuring continuity of major institutional arrangements. At the same time, governments need to have some level of autonomous policy space, to give political parties and their leaders the possibility to offer a diversified range of options that are responsive to the demands of a heterogeneous electorate (Riker, 1982; Sartori, 1976). If such options were not there, the relevance of democratic elections would be substantially reduced, with the potential risk of undermining the trust between citizens and governing institutions (Linde and Peters, 2020; Mair, 2014; Ruiz-Rufino and Alonso, 2017). The analysis of this book has documented how the two criteria for decision-making coexist side by side when governments design their expenditure and taxation policies. Hence, the analysis also offers a glimpse into the room for manoeuvre that governments perceive to have.

Despite recurrent efforts of enquiry (Beramendi et al., 2015; Kitschelt et al., 1999; Schäfer and Streeck, 2013), previous empirical research has struggled to identify variation in the limits to democratic choice posed by international economic governance arrangements. Research on how democracy works in the context of the capitalist market economy has mostly settled on identifying a 'model of constrained partisanship' (Beramendi et al., 2015). In this model, political parties are responsive to different societal preferences but, at the same time, democratic choice is constrained by several factors, including existing rules and conventions about the modalities and extent to which public institutions can intervene in the market economy. The reach and variation of such constraints, though, generally remains unclear. The reason for this is arguably that theories about structural constraints on government action are difficult to either confirm or falsify, on the one hand because variation in these structures is hardly ever clear-cut, and on the other because the limits posed to democratic choices are often not directly observable (Culpepper, 2015, p. 394; Schmitter, 2009).

The method used in this book for measuring the balance between responsiveness and responsibility offers an important innovation in this regard. The empirical focus on the policy justifications that governments provide when presenting their annual budget plans allows us to identify and differentiate governments' decision-making criteria. This study thus measured responsiveness as the percentage of policy justifications that portray budgetary policy as an effort to deliver resources to domestic socio-economic groups. Responsibility, by contrast, was measured as the percentage of policy justifications portraying budgetary policy as an effort to maintain the government's institutional commitments regarding public debt and deficit levels. In addition to confirming that institutional discourse is a valuable proxy for actual policy decisions (Veen, 2011), the analysis of policy justifications makes it possible to go further than tracing governments' overall policy commitments, and to understand more deeply the purpose of their action and the extent to which they are committed to a certain policy course.

More precisely, while responsive policy justifications indicate a commitment to deliver resources domestically, responsible policy justifications indicate the boundaries within which a government perceives it can do so. The more the presentation of an annual budget plan is characterized by responsive justifications, the more this indicates that the government is focused on making full use of its policy space, with the objective of committing greater financial resources for the benefit of domestic socio-economic groups. Annual budget plans featuring high shares of responsible policy justifications, by contrast, indicate that there is not much space to finance new social services or provide tax benefits, and that the policy effort needs to be directed at balancing public accounts. Variations in the relative shares of responsive and responsible policy justifications are thus informative about the extent to which governments are engaged in pushing the boundaries of their policy space in order to meet domestic demands, vis-à-vis the extent to which they are more engaged in policies that are functional to meeting institutional commitments.

The findings of this book indicate that between 2009 and 2013 the governments of the five countries analysed were all deeply engaged in meeting the requirements of the Stability and Growth Pact, and that in subsequent years they were more and more engaged with pursuing relatively less 'responsible' policies to meet the demands of their constituencies. This trend culminated in 2020, when in response to the Covid-19 pandemic governments went beyond their means to meet the needs of their populations, who were confronted with the consequences of the lockdown measures. On the wave of these policy responses, a renewed discussion of the rules of the Stability and Growth Pact was initiated. While at the time of writing it is too premature to know the final outcome, the fact that this renewed discussion *is* taking place shows that in European economic governance, governments have the power to challenge the rules to which they are expected to abide. The post-2014 increases in responsiveness shown in this book suggest that when governments are faced with popular discontent over existing policies, they will push their institutional boundaries to meet citizens' demands. This observation runs counter to deterministic arguments about international economic integration forcing governments into a fiscal straitjacket.

At the same time, the persistence of relatively high levels of responsibility for multiple years between 2009 and 2013—and to some extent also beyond—raises questions about why the levels of responsiveness remained low for more than four years, and what made governments perceive themselves to be less constrained in subsequent years. The analysis presented in this book offers some partial answers to such questions. The next section summarizes the evidence gathered in relation to what determines variation in the balance between responsiveness and responsibility.

Who defines what governments can and cannot do?

The statistical analyses of Chapter 4 indicate that governments' political orientations are a relevant factor in explaining the high levels of responsibility of the 2009–2013 period. During the climax of the eurozone crisis, left-leaning governments were relatively less responsible (and more responsive) than right-wing governments. The analyses in Chapter 5 show that, under similar economic circumstances, technocratic executives are relatively more responsible while populist executives are relatively more responsive than governments composed of mainstream political parties. These differences between governments of different composition indicate that the political motivations matter for the extent to which policymakers push the boundaries of their room for manoeuvre. For example, if the economic and institutional context requires governments to pursue austerity policies, left-wing and populist cabinets will be more likely to carve out some policy space to deliver some resources to their constituencies.

At the same time, though, none of the political factors explain the post-2014 decline of responsibility and the growing focus on fiscal stimulus policies. This trend takes place under both progressive and conservative cabinets and, as shown in Chapter 5, remains also relatively unaffected by the rotation in government between populist and technocratic leaderships. Interestingly, the post-2014 decline of responsible policy justifications is also not explained by deficit levels or credit ratings. Even though, overall, governments inheriting high deficits and bad credit ratings tend to feature higher shares of responsible policy justifications in the presentation of their annual budget plans, the statistical analyses presented in Chapter 4 show that these two factors do not account for the post-2014 reversal of the balance between responsiveness and responsibility. As shown in greater detail in Chapter 6, the post-2014 increases in responsiveness also start taking place in countries that were exceeding the EU debt and deficit thresholds and were still subject to poor credit ratings. The over-time trend is strikingly similar in countries as different as, for example, Italy and Germany, indicating thus that it is not driven by a country's macro-economic situation.

The over-time variation in the levels of responsiveness and responsibility is more narrowly associated with a common understanding between national governments and European institutions about how to ensure long-term financial sustainability. From 2014 onwards, the Commission and national governments start giving more emphasis to the flexibility clauses of the Stability and Growth Pact to allow for more national fiscal stimulus policies. This more favourable attitude towards fiscal stimulus seems to precede rather than follow improvements in a country's economic and financial situation. As argued in Chapter 7, the gradual increasing permissiveness for fiscal stimulus that is observed from 2014 onwards is narrowly linked to a growing awareness among EU and national governing institutions about the negative effects of austerity policies. The best documented explanation for this change in policy approach consists in an ideational change that took place within the top institutions of European economic governance. Within the Commission, already in 2013 there was a growing realization about the negative repercussions of austerity policy (Matthijs, 2020; Mérand, 2021; Schmidt, 2016). Within the ECB, as shown in Chapter 7, the adoption of quantitative easing policies also led to a slow end to the idea that expansive fiscal policy is necessarily a threat to the independence of monetary policy. This change in policy ideas also seems to account for the EU-level responses to the Covid-19 pandemic, which represented a radical departure from austerity ideas (Schmidt, 2020b).

Supranational institutions are not immune from electoral pressures

This ideational-based explanation begs a deeper understanding of what provoked, allowed, or stimulated such an ideational change, and more importantly of what prevented it from occurring earlier. For more than four years, between autumn 2009 until at least autumn 2013, austerity ideas dominated the criteria for shaping national budgets and seemed to be the only alternative. Under this macro-economic paradigm, governments had to downplay many of their electoral commitments and, largely as a consequence of this, during the 2010s mainstream governing parties lost unprecedented amounts of votes (Alonso and Ruiz-Rufino, 2020; Hobolt and Tilley, 2016). From 2014 onwards, austerity ideas started gradually becoming less dominant and, consequently, governments started gradually having more room for manoeuvre to be responsive to domestic constituencies. This shift was supported, and perhaps even steered, by supranational institutions like the European Commission and the ECB.

The explanation emerging from Chapter 4 for the over-time variation between responsiveness and responsibility is that, when in contexts of an economic crisis governments see the need to pursue unpopular policies to rebalance their accounts, in subsequent years they will be under strong electoral pressure to meet popular expectations for more expansive policies. As shown in the pioneering research by Linde and Peters (2020), when governments deliver public goods and services, citizens develop a 'reservoir of trust' towards governing institutions. Based on this trust, citizens may accept that governments sometimes need to pursue more austere policies for long-term financial considerations. When governments fail to meet citizens' expectations for a prolonged period of time, the reservoir of trust may start to empty out. As suggested in the conclusion of Chapter 4, this was perhaps the situation that governments in the eurozone were facing from 2014 onwards: austerity was largely unpopular among citizens (Bojar et al., 2022) and governing parties pursuing such policies were punished severely at subsequent elections (Alonso and Ruiz-Rufino, 2020). But why would supranational institutions like the ECB and the Commission, which are largely sheltered from electoral dynamics, be preoccupied with such developments?

The answer to this question resides perhaps in the organizational entrenchment between Europe's mainstream political parties and EU institutions. The electoral growth of anti-system parties like the Five Star Movement in Italy, Podemos in Spain, or the AFD in Germany was arguably the biggest existential threat during the 2010s to the political parties that had traditionally governed European public institutions, namely Christian democrats, social democrats, and liberals. These are the political parties that since the post-war period have been the most deeply entrenched in governing institutions at both the national and European level (Bardi et al., 2020; Hertner, 2018; Katz and Mair, 2018). Given the deep organizational entrenchment between these parties and governing institutions, the prospect of having a complete turnover of political leadership was an existential threat not only for traditional governing parties but also for the key structures of European economic governance. The wave of popular discontent that followed the sovereign debt crisis led to the unprecedented scenario that the joint vote share of the traditional European governing party families was shrinking below 50 per cent. Faced with this existential threat, both mainstream political parties and European institutions had a stake in allowing national budgets to feature more fiscal stimulus policies.

In similar ways as partisan-based democratic theories predict that elections work as a corrective to unpopular or unsuccessful policies, in the eurozone during the 2010s there was a gradual move away from an austerity-based policy approach to public finance. The governing parties of the 2009–2013 period suffered substantial electoral losses, while distrust towards EU institutions grew. Faced with this public discontent, the European Commission, particularly under the leadership of Jean-Claude Juncker, became more supportive of governments seeking to correct the unsuccessful austerity-based policy course. The ECB, in parallel, started a monetary policy that reduced the borrowing costs for governments on financial markets, and in its discourse became more supportive of governments actively stimulating their economies. The response to popular discontent thus did not only come from democratically elected governments, but also from supranational institutions that are formally sheltered from electoral dynamics.

As the discontent towards austerity policies was fuelling the growth of anti-establishment parties all around Europe, it is plausible to hypothesize that democratic pressures triggered the over-time change in policy approach documented in this book, both at the national and at the European level. From this perspective, the democratic principle by which governments are evaluated by their electorates and change their policies according to such evaluations has been met, at least when assessing the entire decade. The channels, though, have become more complex, in the sense that there is now a European dimension on top of the traditional linkage between citizens and governments. This European dimension possibly explains the common trends between the five countries, and why it took more than four years to change the paradigm from austerity to a more stimulus-oriented approach. While in the 1980s, for example, the French Mitterrand presidency autonomously decided on a paradigmatic change in the government's economic policy (Karremans and Damhuis, 2020), under the conditions of European economic governance ideational change has to occur within a complex multilevel governance structure, involving multiple negotiations (Karremans, 2021b).

One effect that the strengthening of European economic governance seems have had, thus, is that it has reduced the flexibility with which governments can adapt their ideas about what is economically feasible. This reduced flexibility for national governments can be seen as a major achievement of the European integration process. To have all member states aligned in understanding what is irresponsible and what not is an important precondition for any effort to coordinate policies at a supranational level. At the same time, the experience of the 2010s also shows that delays in adapting paradigms that generate negative economic and social outcomes also have democratic spillovers. In this regard, it is important to emphasize that the high levels of responsiveness registered in the annual budget plans presented between 2014 and 2020 have not succeeded in compensating for the democratic dissatisfaction of large parts of national electorates. At the time of writing, the trends of declining electoral turnout have not reversed, electoral volatility is still high, and the persisting high vote shares of anti-establishment parties continues to pose a threat to the stability of European democracies. The underlying causes for this persisting discontent need to be researched further.

Future research avenues

The study presented in this book offers a window into a previously underexplored stage of the democratic cycle. Despite a growing richness in data, a persisting challenge for political science is to grasp this cycle in its fullness. Analytical research generally induces scholars to focus on single stages or parts of the democratic cycle, or to test the strength of associations between them, as for example between electoral behaviour and direction of policy change. The stage at which governments provide justifications towards the parliament for their policies has the function of connecting the world of policymaking institutions with the world political competition. It provides insights into how democratic commitments have survived the institutional and economic intricacies of the policy process. Integrating these insights with those generated from analyses of public opinion and policy outputs can help to achieve a more complete comparative understanding of how domestic political competition relates to actual policy change. For future research, there is great potential to integrate data on policy justifications with other data sources, for a broader scholarly effort to better understand policy change in the complex web of democratic policymaking under the conditions of international economic integration and supranational governance.

In terms of future research questions, considering that—as shown in Chapter 7—different notions of fiscal responsibility can have substantial consequences for the extent to which governments are responsive to domestic constituencies, understanding who defines such notions becomes crucial for achieving a more nuanced understanding of the relative influence of democratic dynamics or technocratic considerations for economic policymaking under EEG. To this end, it is important to grasp whether the European consensus on what constitutes responsible economic policies is shaped by entities like governments that are exposed to electoral judgement, or instead by institutions like the ECB that are entirely sheltered from it. A question emerging from Chapter 7, for example, is whether there is a causal linkage between on the one hand the ideas dominating within the ECB about the boundaries of fiscal policy and, on the other, the room for manoeuvre that governments (perceive to) have. The temporal coincidence between the shift from responsibility to responsiveness and the introduction of quantitative easing policies from 2014 onwards is a hunch that a causal linkage might indeed be present. More precisely, what seems to have been preventing fiscal stimulus during the early 2010s was the idea that excessive fiscal expansion would undermine financial markets' trust, creating thus pressures for Central Bank intervention, which would in turn undermine the independence of monetary policy. When this idea started changing and the ECB de facto started supporting government spending, governments also began to have greater room for manoeuvre to be responsive.

To explore this potential causal linkage further, the data on governments' policy justifications can be integrated with data derived from the statements on monetary and fiscal policy by the ECB's Executive Board. This would allow us to see the extent to which the room for manoeuvre that governments perceive themselves to have varies following ideational changes within the ECB. Confirming such a causal link would not only be academically relevant, but may also have important societal implications. For example, it could form the basis for the normative argument that monetary policy is not purely a matter for economic experts but that it may have important social and democratic consequences, and that therefore it may require the involvement of different sources of expertise.

A parallel important avenue for future research is to better understand how different levels of balance between responsiveness and responsibility affect electoral behaviour. The pioneering work by Linde and Peters (2020) and the electoral results of the early 2010s (Alonso and Ruiz-Rufino, 2020; Hobolt and Tilley, 2016) indicate that responsiveness fuels trust in governing parties and that excessive levels of responsibility turn voters towards anti-system parties. Yet, glancing at the electoral results of the past decade, the gradual increases in responsiveness from 2014 onwards do not seem to have been accompanied by a decrease in vote shares of the political parties that challenge the political mainstream. Despite budgetary policy becoming increasingly socially oriented, for instance, during the second half of the 2010s and early 2020s, social democrats continued losing substantial vote shares across Europe. Future research is thus needed to understand why the post-2014 responsive policy approach was not rewarded at subsequent elections. To do so, data on policy justifications could be integrated with data on how these messages reach the broader public through the media and whether such messages generate positive or negative reactions among different social groups.

To conclude, policy justifications contain information on the relative weight that different criteria have in shaping governments' policies. These criteria can be distinguished according to their origin or purpose. For example, they can be distinguished according to whether they are more related to the representation of societal preferences or to the technical advice of financial experts. As discussed in Chapters 1 and 2, democracy is to a large extent a representative process that happens through discourse. Even public spending and taxation cannot be reduced to numbers, but need to be explained in terms of which goals are being served and why policies are designed in a certain way. Policy justifications thus feature the narrative through which public policy relates back to the general public. Linking this information with other data sources may thus contribute to a better understanding of which—and perhaps *whose*—narratives are more successful in shaping the democratic cycle.

Bibliography

Afonso, A., Gomes, P., Rother, P., 2007. What 'Hides' Behind Sovereign Debt Ratings?. *Working Paper* No. 711. Frankfurt a. M.: European Central Bank.

Albertazzi, D., McDonnell, D., 2015. *Populists in Power*. Routledge.

Allan, J.P., Scruggs, L., 2004. Political Partisanship and Welfare State Reform in Advanced Industrial Societies. *American Journal of Political Science* 48, 496–512. https://doi.org/10.1111/j.0092-5853.2004.00083.x

Alonso, S., 2014. 'You Can Vote But You Cannot Choose': Democracy and the Sovereign Debt Crisis in the Eurozone. *Working Paper*, Instituto Carlos III—Juan March de Ciencias Sociales.

Alonso, S., Ruiz-Rufino, R., 2020. The Costs of Responsibility for the Political Establishment of the Eurozone (1999–2015). *Party Politics* 26, 317–333. https://doi.org/10.1177/1354068818766182

Baccaro, L., Benassi, C., 2014. Softening Industrial Relations Institutions, Hardening Growth Model: The transformation of the German political economy. *Stato e Mercato*, 3. https://doi.org/10.1425/78528

Bansak, K., Bechtel, M.M., Margalit, Y., 2021. Why Austerity? The Mass Politics of a Contested Policy. *American Political Science Review* 115, 486–505. https://doi.org/10.1017/S0003055420001136

Barber, T., 2019. SPD Result Heralds the End of Germany's 'Grand Coalition'. *Financial Times*. https://www.ft.com/content/f97f1bac-1397-11ea-9ee4-11f260415385

Bardi, L., Bartolini, S., Trechsel, A.H., 2014. Responsive and Responsible? The Role of Parties in Twenty-First Century Politics. *West European Politics* 37, 235–252. https://doi.org/10.1080/01402382.2014.887871

Bardi, L., Gagatek, W., Germond, C., Johansson, K.M., Kaiser, W., Sassano, S., 2020. *The European Ambition: The Group of the European People's Party and European Integration*. Nomos Verlag.

Bartolini, S., 2005. *Restructuring Europe: Centre Formation, System Building, and Political Structuring between the Nation State and the European Union*. Oxford: Oxford University Press.

Baumgartner, F.R., 2013. Ideas and Policy Change. *Governance* 26, 239–258. https://doi.org/10.1111/gove.12007

Bekker, S., 2016. Is There Flexibility in the European Semester Process? Exploring interactions between the EU and Member States within post-crisis socio-economic governance, SSRN *Scholarly Paper* No. ID 2743238. Rochester, NY: Social Science Research Network.

Beramendi, P., Häusermann, S., Kitschelt, H., Kriesi, H. (eds.), 2015. *The Politics of Advanced Capitalism*. Cambridge: Cambridge University Press.

Bertsou, E., Caramani, D., 2020. People Haven't Had Enough of Experts: Technocratic Attitudes among Citizens in Nine European Democracies. *American Journal of Political Science* Online First. https://doi.org/10.1111/ajps.12554

Bickerton, C.J, Accetti, C.I., 2017. Populism and Technocracy, in: Kaltwasser, C. R., Taggart, P. A., Espejo, P. O., Ostiguy, P. (eds.), *The Oxford Handbook of Populism*. Oxford: Oxford University Press, pp. 326–337. https://doi.org/10.1093/oxfordhb/9780198803560.013.24

Bickerton, C.J., Accetti, C.I., 2018. 'Techno-populism' As a New Party Family: The Case of the Five Star Movement and Podemos. *Contemporary Italian Politics* 10, 132–150. https://doi.org/10.1080/23248823.2018.1472919

Blyth, M., 2013. *Austerity: The History of a Dangerous Idea*. Oxford: Oxford University Press.

Bohle, D., 2014. Responsible Government and Capitalism's Cycles. *West European Politics* 37, 288–308. https://doi.org/10.1080/01402382.2014.887876

Bojar, A., Bremer, B., Kriesi, H., Wang, C., 2022. The Effect of Austerity Packages on Government Popularity During the Great Recession. *British Journal of Political Science* Online First, 1–19. https://doi.org/10.1017/S0007123420000472

Bovens, M., Wille, A., 2017. *Diploma Democracy: The Rise of Political Meritocracy*. Oxford: Oxford University Press.

Bremer, B., McDaniel, S., 2020. The Ideational Foundations of Social Democratic Austerity in the Context of the Great Recession. *Socio-Economic Review* 18, 439–463. https://doi.org/10.1093/ser/mwz001

Bühlmann, M., Kriesi, H., 2013. Models for Democracy, in: Kriesi, H., Lavenex, S., Esser, F., Matthes, J., Bühlmann, M., Bochsler, D. (eds.), *Democracy in the Age of Globalization and Mediatization, Challenges to Democracy in the 21st Century Series*. London: Palgrave Macmillan UK, pp. 44–68. https://doi.org/10.1057/9781137299871_3

Callaghan, J., 1976. Leader's Speech, Blackpool 1976.

Caramani, D., 2017. Will vs. Reason: The Populist and Technocratic Forms of Political Representation and Their Critique to Party Government. *American Political Science Review* 111, 54–67. https://doi.org/10.1017/S0003055416000538

Carli, A., 2018. Dal 2,4 al 2,04%: così Conte ha tagliato il deficit di 6,5 miliardi. Il Sole 24 ORE. https://www.ilsole24ore.com/art/dal-24-204percento-cosi-conte-ha-tagliato-deficit-65-miliardi-AECP2IzG

Cavalieri, A., Karremans, J., 2022. Paradigm Change in Socio-Economic Policy-Making in the Eurozone: From austerity to social investment? Paper presented at the Conference of the Council for European Studies, University of Lisbon, 1st July 2022.

Clift, B., 2013. Le Changement? French Socialism, the 2012 Presidential Election and the Politics of Economic Credibility amidst the Eurozone Crisis. *Parliamentary Affairs* 66, 106–123. https://doi.org/10.1093/pa/gss066

Codogno, L., Merler, S., 2019. The Willing Suspension of Disbelief: The contract for government and the budget. *Contemporary Italian Politics* 11, 294–309. https://doi.org/10.1080/23248823.2019.1645997

Crum, B., 2013. Saving the Euro at the Cost of Democracy? *Journal of Common Market Studies* 51, 614–630. https://doi.org/10.1111/jcms.12019

Culpepper, P.D., 2014. The Political Economy of Unmediated Democracy: Italian susterity under Mario Monti. *West European Politics* 37, 1264–1281. https://doi.org/10.1080/01402382.2014.929334

Culpepper, P.D., 2015. Structural Power and Political Science in the Post-crisis Era. *Business and Politics* 17, 391–409. https://doi.org/10.1515/bap-2015-0031

Dalton, R.J., 2018. *Political Realignment: Economics, culture, and electoral change*. Oxford: Oxford University Press.

Dalton, R.J., Farrell, D.M., McAllister, I., 2011. *Political Parties and Democratic Linkage: How parties organize democracy*. Oxford: Oxford University Press.

Dalton, R.J., Wattenberg, M.P., 2002. *Parties without Partisans: Political change in advanced industrial democracies*. Oxford: Oxford University Press.

Damhuis, K., Karremans, J., 2017. Responsive to Whom? A comparison of the Mitterrand and Hollande presidencies. *West European Politics* 40, 1267–1287. https://doi.org/10.1080/01402382.2017.1300472

Denver, D., Garnett, M., 2014. *British General Elections Since 1964: Diversity, dealignment, and disillusion*. Oxford: Oxford University Press. https://doi.org/10.1093/acprof:osobl/9780199673322.001.0001

De Grauwe, P., 2016. *The Limits of the Market: The pendulum between government and market*. Oxford: Oxford University Press.

De Grauwe, P., Ji, Y., 2013. From Panic-Driven Austerity to Symmetric Macroeconomic Policies in the Eurozone. *Journal of Common Market Studies* 51, 31–41.

D'Erman, V., Haas, J., Schulz, D.F., Verdun, A., 2019. Measuring Economic Reform Recommendations under the European Semester: 'One size fits all' or tailoring to member states? *Journal of Contemporary European Research* 15, 194–211. https://doi.org/10.30950/jcer.v15i2.999

D'Erman, V., Verdun, A., 2022. 'Macroeconomic Policy Coordination and Domestic Politics: Policy coordination in the EU from the European Semester to the Covid-19 crisis'. *Journal of Common Market Studies* 60, 3–20. https://doi.org/10.1111/jcms.13276

De Vries, C.E., Hobolt, S.B., 2020. *Political Entrepreneurs: The rise of challenger parties in Europe*. Princeton University Press.

De Vries, C.E., Bakker, B.N., Hobolt, S.B., Arceneaux, K., 2021. Crisis Signaling: How Italy's coronavirus lockdown affected incumbent support in other European countries. *Political Science Research and Methods* 9, 451–467. https://doi.org/10.1017/psrm.2021.6

Dijsselbloem, J., 2018. *The Euro Crisis: The inside story*. Prometheus.

Doray-Demers, P., Foucault, M., 2017. The Politics of Fiscal Rules within the European Union: A dynamic analysis of fiscal rules stringency. *Journal of European Public Policy* 24, 852–870. https://doi.org/10.1080/13501763.2017.1296883

Draghi, M., 2013. The Policy and the Role of the European Central Bank during the Crisis in the Euro Area. European Central Bank, 27 February 2013.

Draghi, M., 2017. Structural Reforms in the Euro Area. European Central Bank, 18 October 2017.

Dyson, K., Featherstone, K., 1996. Italy and EMU as a 'Vincolo Esterno': Empowering the technocrats, transforming the state. *South European Society and Politics* 1, 272–299. https://doi.org/10.1080/13608749608539475

Enroth, H., 2017. Cartelization versus Representation? On a misconception in contemporary party theory. *Party Politics* 23, 124–134. https://doi.org/10.1177/1354068815576293

European Council, 2020. European Semester 2020: Country-specific Recommendations Adopted. https://www.consilium.europa.eu/en/press/press-releases/2020/07/20/european-semester-2020-country-specific-recommendations-adopted/

Ferragina, E., 2019. The Political Economy of Family Policy Expansion. *Review of International Political Economy* 26, 1238–1265. https://doi.org/10.1080/09692290.2019.1627568

Flyvbjerg, B., 2001. *Making Social Science Matter: Why social inquiry fails and how it can succeed again*. Cambridge: Cambridge University Press.

Fromage, D., Dermine, P., Nicolaides, P., Tuori, K., 2019. ECB Independence and Accountability Today: Towards a (necessary) redefinition? *Maastricht Journal of European and Comparative Law* 26, 3–16. https://doi.org/10.1177/1023263X19827819

Garzia, D., 2013. The 2013 Italian Parliamentary Election: Changing Things So Everything Stays the Same. *West European Politics* 36, 1095–1105. https://doi.org/10.1080/01402382.2013.815483

Garzia, D., Karremans, J., 2021. Super Mario 2: Comparing the technocrat-led Monti and Draghi governments in Italy. *Contemporary Italian Politics* 13, 105–115. https://doi.org/10.1080/23248823.2021.1903175

Genschel, P., Schwarz, P., 2013. 'Tax Competition and Fiscal Democracy', in: Streeck, W., Schäfer, A. (eds.), *Politics in the Age of Austerity*. Cambridge: Polity Press, pp. 59–83.

Genschel, P., Zangl, B., 2014. State Transformations in OECD Countries. *Annual Review of Political Science* 17, 337–354. https://doi.org/10.1146/annurev-polisci-061312-113943

Gingrich, J., Häusermann, S., 2015. The Decline of the Working-class Vote, the Reconfiguration of the Welfare Support Coalition and Consequences for the Welfare State. *Journal of European Social Policy* 25, 50–75. https://doi.org/10.1177/0958928714556970

Ginsborg, P., Asquer, E., 2012. *Berlusconismo: Analisi di un sistema di potere.* Gius.Laterza & Figli.

Gourevitch, P.A., 1986. *Politics in Hard Times: Comparative responses to international economic crises.* Cornell University Press.

Guasti, P., Buštíková, L., 2020. A Marriage of Convenience: Responsive populists and responsible experts. *Politics and Governance* 8, 468–472. https://doi.org/10.17645/pag.v8i4.3876

Gygli, S., Haelg, F., Potrafke, N., Sturm, J.-E., 2019. The KOF Globalisation Index—revisited. *Review of International Organizations* 14, 543–574. https://doi.org/10.1007/s11558-019-09344-2

Haas, J.S., D'Erman, V.J., Schulz, D.F., Verdun, A., 2020. Economic and Fiscal Policy Coordination after the Crisis: Is the European Semester promoting more or less state intervention? *Journal of European Integration* 42, 327–344. https://doi.org/10.1080/07036337.2020.1730356

Hall, P.A., 1993. Policy Paradigms, Social Learning, and the State: The case of economic policymaking in Britain. *Comparative Politics* 25, 275–296. https://doi.org/10.2307/422246

Hall, P.A., 1994. The State and the Market, in: Hall, P.A., Hayward, J., Machin, H. (eds.), *Developments in French Politics.* London: Palgrave Macmillan, pp. 171–187. https://doi.org/10.1007/978-1-349-08873-7_10

Harmon, M.D., 1997. The 1976 UK-IMF crisis: The markets, the Americans, and the IMF. *Contemporary British History* 11, 1–17. https://doi.org/10.1080/13619469708581446

Häusermann, S., Kriesi, H., 2015. 'What Do Voters Want? Dimensions and configurations in individual-level preferences and party-choice', in: Beramendi, P., Häusermann, S., Kitschelt, H., Kriesi, H. (eds.), *The Politics of Advanced Capitalism.* New York: Cambridge University Press, pp. 202–230.

Heinisch, R., 2003. Success in Opposition—Failure in Government: Explaining the performance of right-wing populist parties in public office. *West European Politics* 26, 91–130. https://doi.org/10.1080/01402380312331280608

Helgason, A.F., 2019. The Political Economy of Crisis Responses, in: Ólafsson, S., Daly, M., Kangas, O., Palme, J. (eds.), *Welfare and the Great Recession: A comparative study.* Oxford: Oxford University Press. https://doi.org/10.1093/oso/9780198830962.003.0003

Hemerijck, A., 2012. *Changing Welfare States.* Oxford: Oxford University Press.

Hemerijck, A., Karremans, J., van der Meer, M., 2022a. Responsive Corporatism without Political Credit: Social concertation, constructive opposition and the long tenure of the Rutte II cabinet in the Netherlands (2012–2017). *Acta Politica.* https://doi.org/10.1057/s41269-022-00239-6

Hemerijck, A., Matsaganis, M., forthcoming. *Who's Afraid of the Welfare State Now?* Oxford: Oxford University Press.

Hemerijck, A., Ronchi, S., Plavgo, I., 2022b. Social Investment as a Conceptual Framework for Analysing Well-Being Returns and Reforms in 21st-Century Welfare States. *Socio-Economic Review.* https://doi.org/10.1093/ser/mwac035

Hertner, I., 2018. *Centre-Left Parties and the European Union.* Manchester University Press.

Hobolt, S.B., Tilley, J., 2016. Fleeing the Centre: The rise of challenger parties in the aftermath of the euro crisis. *West European Politics* 39, 971–991. https://doi.org/10.1080/01402382.2016.1181871

Howell, C., 2019. Neoliberalism, Capitalist Growth Models, and the State: An agenda for industrial relations theory. *Journal of Industrial Relations* 61, 457–474. https://doi.org/10.1177/0022185619834047

Hutter, S., Kriesi, H., 2019. *European Party Politics in Times of Crisis.* Cambridge: Cambridge University Press.

Hutter, S., Kriesi, H., Vidal, G., 2018. Old Versus New Politics: The political spaces in Southern Europe in times of crises. *Party Politics* 24, 10–22. https://doi.org/10.1177/1354068817694503

Inglehart, R.F., 2008. Changing Values among Western Publics from 1970 to 2006. *West European Politics* 31, 130–146. https://doi.org/10.1080/01402380701834747

INPS, 2019. Reddito di Inclusione (ReI): i dati fino a marzo 2019. INPS. https://www.inps.it/news/reddito-di-inclusione-rei-i-dati-fino-a-marzo-2019

INPS, 2020. Dati cartacei. INPS. https://www.inps.it/dati-ricerche-e-bilanci/osservatori-statistici-e-altre-statistiche/dati-cartacei-rdc

ISTAT, 2022. Rapporto Annuale 2022. Estratto della sintesi letto dal Presidente dell'Istat Gian Carlo Blangiardo alla Camera dei Deputati.

Johnston, A., Regan, A., 2016. European Monetary Integration and the Incompatibility of National Varieties of Capitalism. *Journal of Common Market Studies* 54, 318–336. https://doi.org/10.1111/jcms.12289

Johnston, A., Regan, A., 2018. Introduction: Is the European Union Capable of Integrating Diverse Models of Capitalism? *New Political Economy* 23, 145–159. https://doi.org/10.1080/13563467.2017.1370442

Jones, E., 2012. The Berlusconi Government and the Sovereign Debt Crisis. *Italian Politics* 27, 172–191.

Jones, E., Matthijs, M., 2019. Rethinking Central Bank Independence. *Journal of Democracy* 30, 127–141. https://doi.org/10.1353/jod.2019.0030

Karremans, J., 2017. State Interests vs Citizens' Preferences: On which side do (Labour) parties stand? (Thesis). https://doi.org/10.2870/862710

Karremans, J., 2021a. This Time Wasn't Different: Responsiveness and responsibility in the eurozone between 2007 and 2019. *Journal of Common Market Studies* 59, 1536–1554. https://doi.org/10.1111/jcms.13202

Karremans, J., 2021b. Political Alternatives under European Economic Governance: Evidence from German budget speeches (2009–2019). *Journal of European Public Policy* 28, 510–531. https://doi.org/10.1080/13501763.2020.1748096

Karremans, J., 2023. How do governments justify their budgets? A comparative dataset. EUI Research Data, Department of Political and Social Sciences. https://cadmus.eui.eu/handle/1814/75958

Karremans, J., Damhuis, K., 2020. The Changing Face of Responsibility: A cross-time comparison of French social democratic governments. *Party Politics* 26, 305–316. https://doi.org/10.1177/1354068818761197

Karremans, J., Kaltenleithner, J., 2021. Is Austrian Budgetary Policy Still 'Political'? A cross-time comparison of budget speeches. *Österreichische Zeitschrift für Politikwissenschaft* 50, 1–14. https://doi.org/10.15203/ozp.3440.vol50iss1

Karremans, J., Lefkofridi, Z., 2020a. Responsive versus Responsible? Party democracy in times of crisis. *Party Politics* 26, 271–279. https://doi.org/10.1177/1354068818761199

Karremans, J., Lefkofridi, Z., 2020b. The Political Economy of the European Union: Between national and supranational politics, in: Vivares, E. (ed.), *The Routledge Handbook to Global Political Economy*. New York: Routledge, pp. 472–487.

Karremans, J., Malet, G., Morisi, D., 2019. Italy—The End of Bipolarism: Restructuration in an unstable party system, in: Hutter, S., Kriesi, H. (eds.), *European Party Politics in Times of Crisis*. Cambridge: Cambridge University Press, pp. 118–138.

Katz, R.S., Mair, P., 2009. The Cartel Party Thesis: A restatement. *Perspectives on Politics* 7, 753–766. https://doi.org/10.1017/S1537592709991782

Katz, R.S., Mair, P., 2018. *Democracy and the Cartelization of Political Parties*. Oxford: Oxford University Press.

Keman, H., Woldendorp, J.J., 2020. *Transportation and the State: Governing the public domain*. Edward Elgar Publishing.

Kitschelt, H., 1994. *The Transformation of European Social Democracy*, Cambridge Studies in Comparative Politics. Cambridge: Cambridge University Press. https://doi.org/10.1017/CBO9780511622014

Kitschelt, H., Lange, P., Marks, G., Stephens, J.D. (eds.), 1999. *Continuity and Change in Contemporary Capitalism*. Cambridge: Cambridge University Press.

Kitschelt, H., Rehm, P., 2015. 'Party Alignments: Change and continuity', in: Beramendi, P., Häusermann, S., Kitschelt, H., Kriesi, H. (eds.), *The Politics of Advanced Capitalism*. New York: Cambridge University Press, pp. 179–201. https://doi.org/10.1017/CBO9781316163245.008

Kriesi, H., 2014. The Populist Challenge. *West European Politics* 37, 361–378. https://doi.org/10.1080/01402382.2014.887879

Kriesi, H., Grande, E., Dolezal, M., Helbling, M., Höglinger, D., Hutter, S., Wüest, B., 2012. *Political Conflict in Western Europe*. Cambridge: Cambridge University Press.

Kriesi, H., Grande, E., Lachat, R., Dolezal, M., Bornschier, S., Frey, T., 2008. *West European Politics in the Age of Globalization*. Cambridge: Cambridge University Press. https://doi.org/10.1017/CBO9780511790720

Laffan, B., 2014. Testing Times: The growing primacy of responsibility in the euro area. *West European Politics* 37, 270–287. https://doi.org/10.1080/01402382.2014.887875

Lagna, A., 2016. Derivatives and the Financialisation of the Italian State. *New Political Economy* 21, 167–186. https://doi.org/10.1080/13563467.2015.1079168

Lavezzolo, S., Ramiro, L., Fernández-Vázquez, P., 2020. The Will for Reason: Voter demand for experts in office. *West European Politics* 0, 1–26. https://doi.org/10.1080/01402382.2020.1778917

Leblond, P., 2006. The Political Stability and Growth Pact Is Dead: Long live the economic stability and growth pact. *Journal of Common Market Studies* 44, 969–990. https://doi.org/10.1111/j.1468-5965.2006.00670.x

Lefkofridi, Z., Nezi, R., 2020. Responsibility versus Responsiveness ... to whom? A theory of party behavior. *Party Politics* 26, 334–346. https://doi.org/10.1177/1354068819866076

Lehner, T., Wasserfallen, F., 2019. Political Conflict in the Reform of the Eurozone. *European Union Politics* 20, 45–64. https://doi.org/10.1177/1465116518814338

Lijphart, A., 2012. *Patterns of Democracy*. Yale University Press.

Linde, J., Peters, Y., 2020. Responsiveness, Support, and Responsibility: How democratic responsiveness facilitates responsible government. *Party Politics* 26, 291–304. https://doi.org/10.1177/1354068818763986

Lopez-Cordova, J.E., Meissner, C.M., 2007. The Impact of International Trade on Democracy: A long-run perspective. *World Politics*. 60, 539–575.

Luther, S.L., in P.K., Luther, K.R., Müller-Rommel, F., 2002. *Political Parties in the New Europe: Political and Analytical Challenges*. Oxford: Oxford University Press.

Maatsch, A., 2017. Effectiveness of the European Semester: Explaining domestic consent and contestation. *Parliamentary Affairs* 70, 691–709. https://doi.org/10.1093/pa/gsx021

Maatsch, A., Cooper, I., 2017. Governance without Democracy? Analysing the role of parliaments in European economic governance after the crisis: Introduction to the Special Issue. *Parliamentary Affairs* 70, 645–654. https://doi.org/10.1093/pa/gsx018

Mair, P., 2008. The Challenge to Party Government. *West European Politics* 31, 211–234. https://doi.org/10.1080/01402380701835033

Mair, P., 2011. Bini Smaghi vs. the Parties: Representative government and institutional constraints, *Working Paper*. Fiesole: European University Institute.

Mair, P., 2013. Bini Smaghi vs. the Parties: Representative government and institutional constraints, in: *Politics in the Age of Austerity*. Cambridge: Polity Press, 143–168.

Mair, P., 2014. Representative versus Responsible Government, in: Biezen, I. (ed.), *On Parties, Party Systems and Democracy*. Colchester: ECPR Press, pp. 581–596.

Majone, G., 1994. The Rise of the Regulatory State in Europe. *West European Politics* 17, 77–101. https://doi.org/10.1080/01402389408425031

Manin, B., 1997. *The Principles of Representative Government, Themes in the Social Sciences.* Cambridge: Cambridge University Press. https://doi.org/10.1017/CBO9780511659935

March, J.G., Olsen, J.P., 2009. The Logic of Appropriateness, in: Goodin, R., Moran, M., Rein, M. (eds.), *The Oxford Handbook of Public Policy.* Oxford: Oxford University Press, pp. 689–708. https://doi.org/10.1093/oxfordhb/9780199548453.003.0034

Maricut, A., Puetter, U., 2018. Deciding on the European Semester: The European Council, the Council and the enduring asymmetry between economic and social policy issues. *Journal of European Public Policy* 25, 193–211. https://doi.org/10.1080/13501763.2017.1363271

Matthijs, M., 2016. Powerful Rules Governing the Euro: The perverse logic of German ideas. *Journal of European Public Policy* 23, 375–391. https://doi.org/10.1080/13501763.2015.1115535

Matthijs, M., 2017. Integration at What Price? The erosion of national democracy in the euro periphery. *Government and Opposition* 52, 266–294. https://doi.org/10.1017/gov.2016.50

Matthijs, M., Blyth, M., 2018. When Is It Rational to Learn the Wrong Lessons? Technocratic authority, social learning, and euro fragility. *Perspectives on Politics* 16, 110–126. https://doi.org/10.1017/S1537592717002171

Matthijs, M. 2020. Lessons and learnings from a decade of EU crises. *Journal of European Public Policy*, 27(8), 1127–1136.

McDonnell, D., Valbruzzi, M., 2014. Defining and Classifying Technocrat-led and Technocratic Governments. *European Journal of Political Research* 53, 654–671. https://doi.org/10.1111/1475-6765.12054

McKenna, B.J., Graham, P., 2000. Technocratic Discourse: A primer. *Journal of Technical Writing and Communication* 30, 223–251. https://doi.org/10.2190/56FY-V5TH-2U3U-MHQK

Mérand, F., 2021. *The Political Commissioner: A European ethnography.* New York: Oxford University Press.

Müller-Rommel, F., Vercesi, M., Berz, J., 2022. Changing Career Experiences: Less political, more technical, in: Müller-Rommel, F., Vercesi, M., Berz, J. (eds.), *Prime Ministers in Europe: Changing career experiences and profiles*, Palgrave Studies in Political Leadership. London: Springer International Publishing, pp. 101–133. https://doi.org/10.1007/978-3-030-90891-1_4

Newell, J.L., 2019. The Lega—Five-star government: Tanto fumo per poco arrosto? *Contemporary Italian Politics* 11, 1–4. https://doi.org/10.1080/23248823.2019.1577005

Oesch, D., 2015. Occupational Structure and Labor Market Change in Western Europe since 1990, in: Beramendi, P., Häusermann, S., Kitschelt, H., Kriesi, H. (eds.), *The Politics of Advanced Capitalism.* New York: Cambridge University Press, pp. 112–132.

Pappas, T.S., 2016. The Specter Haunting Europe: Distinguishing liberal democracy's challengers. *Journal of Democracy* 27, 22–36. https://doi.org/10.1353/jod.2016.0059

Pierson, P., 1996. The New Politics of the Welfare State. *World Politics* 48, 143–179. https://doi.org/10.1353/wp.1996.0004

Pontusson, J., Raess, D., 2012. How (and Why) Is This Time Different? The politics of economic crisis in Western Europe and the United States. *Annual Review of Political Science* 15, 13–33. https://doi.org/10.1146/annurev-polisci-031710-100955

Powell, G.B., 2004. The Quality of Democracy: The chain of responsiveness. *Journal of Democracy* 15, 91–105. https://doi.org/10.1353/jod.2004.0070

Randow, J., Speciale, A., 2018. The Inside Story of How Mario Draghi Saved the Euro. Bloomberg.com.

Rathgeb, P., Gruber-Risak, M., 2021. Deserving Austrians First: The impact of the radical right on the Austrian welfare state new nationalism and labor law. *Comparative Labor Law and Policy Journal* 42, 43–60.

Regan, A., 2017. The Imbalance of Capitalisms in the Eurozone: Can the north and south of Europe converge? *Comparative European Politics* 15, 969–990. https://doi.org/10.1057/cep.2015.5

Repubblica, La, 2011. Monti al Senato per la fiducia: il testo integrale del discorso https://www.repubblica.it/politica/2011/11/17/news/monti_al_senato_per_la_fiducia_il_testo_integrale_del_discorso-25168289/

Reuters, 2018. France's Macron Learns the Hard Way: Green taxes carry political risks. Reuters.

Riker, W. H., 1982. The two-party system and Duverger's law: An essay on the history of political science. *American political science review*, 76(4), 753–766.

Rixen, T., 2014. Ambitious Goals, Deficient Output: Tax and fiscal policies of the conservative–liberal government, 2009–13. *German Politics* 23, 304–321. https://doi.org/10.1080/09644008.2014.953487

Rixen, T., 2019. Administering the Surplus: The grand coalition's fiscal policy, 2013–17. *German Politics* 28, 392–411. https://doi.org/10.1080/09644008.2018.1488245

Robinson, P., 2005. Britain's Labour Government and Public Discourse, in: Schmidt, V.A., Robinson, P., Meyer, T. (eds.), *Public Discourse and Welfare State Reform: The social democratic experience.* Amsterdam: Friedrich Ebert Stiftung, pp. 51–68.

Rodrik, D., 2000. How Far Will International Economic Integration Go? *Journal of Economic Perspectives* 14, 177–186. https://doi.org/10.1257/jep.14.1.177

Rodrik, D., 2011. *The Globalization Paradox: Democracy and the future of the world economy.* WW Norton & Company.

Rokkan, S., 1977. Towards a Generalized Concept of Verzuiling: A preliminary note. *Political Studies* 25, 563–570. https://doi.org/10.1111/j.1467-9248.1977.tb00466.x

Ronchi, S., 2018. Which Roads (If Any) to Social Investment? The recalibration of EU welfare states at the crisis crossroads (2000–2014). *Journal of Social Policy* 47, 459–478. https://doi.org/10.1017/S0047279417000782

Rose, R., 2014. Responsible Party Government in a World of Interdependence. *West European Politics* 37, 253–269. https://doi.org/10.1080/01402382.2014.887874

Ruiz-Rufino, R., & Alonso, S., 2017. Democracy without choice: Citizens' perceptions of government autonomy during the Eurozone crisis. *European Journal of Political Research,* 56(2), 320–345.

Sartori, G., 1970. Concept Misformation in Comparative Politics. *American Political Science Review* 64, 1033–1053. https://doi.org/10.2307/1958356

Sartori, G., 1976. *Parties and Party Systems: A framework for analysis.* Cambridge University Press Archive.

Saward, M., 2006. The Representative Claim. *Contemporary Political Theory* 5, 297–318. https://doi.org/10.1057/palgrave.cpt.9300234

Saward, M., 2008. Making Representations: Modes and strategies of political parties. *European Review* 16, 271–286. https://doi.org/10.1017/S1062798708000252

Schäfer, A., Streeck, W., 2013. *Politics in the Age of Austerity.* Cambridge: Polity Press.

Scharpf, F.W., 1975. *Demokratietheorie zwischen Utopie und Anpassung.* Scriptor-Verlag.

Scharpf, F.W., 1991. *Crisis and Choice in European Social Democracy.* Ithaca and London: Cornell University Press.

Scharpf, F.W., 1998. Interdependence and Democratic Legitimation. *Working Paper* No. 98/2. Max-Planck-Institut für Gesellschaftsforschung.

Scharpf, F.W., 2011. Monetary Union, Fiscal Crisis and the Preemption of Democracy, SSRN *Scholarly Paper* No. ID 1852316. Rochester, NY: Social Science Research Network.

Scharpf, F.W., 2015. Political Legitimacy in a Non-optimal Currency Area, in: Cramme, O., Hobolt, S. B. (eds.), *Democratic Politics in a European Union Under Stress*. Oxford: Oxford University Press, pp. 19–47.

Schattschneider, E.E., 1942. *Party Government*. New Jersey: Transaction Publishers.

Schiavo-Campo, S., 2017. *Government Budgeting and Expenditure Management: Principles and international practice*. Routledge. https://doi.org/10.4324/9781315645872

Schmidt, M.G., 1995. The Parties-Do-Matter Hypothesis and the Case of the Federal Republic of Germany. *German Politics* 4, 1–21. https://doi.org/10.1080/09644009508404411

Schmidt, M.G., 1996. When Parties Matter: A review of the possibilities and limits of partisan influence on public policy. *European Journal of Political Research* 30, 155–183. https://doi.org/10.1111/j.1475-6765.1996.tb00673.x

Schmidt, V.A., 2008. Discursive Institutionalism: The explanatory power of ideas and discourse. *Annual Review of Political Science* 11, 303–326. https://doi.org/10.1146/annurev.polisci.11.060606.135342

Schmidt, V.A., 2010. Taking Ideas and Discourse Seriously: Explaining change through discursive institutionalism as the fourth 'new institutionalism'. *European Political Science Review* 2, 1–25. https://doi.org/10.1017/S175577390999021X

Schmidt, V.A., 2016. Reinterpreting the rules 'by stealth'in times of crisis: a discursive institutionalist analysis of the European Central Bank and the European Commission. *West European Politics*, 39(5), 1032-1052.

Schmidt, V.A., 2020a. *Europe's Crisis of Legitimacy: Governing by rules and ruling by numbers in the eurozone*. Oxford: Oxford University Press.

Schmidt, V.A., 2020b. Theorizing Institutional Change and Governance in European Responses to the Covid-19 Pandemic. *Journal of European Integration* 42, 1177–1193. https://doi.org/10.1080/07036337.2020.1853121

Schmitter, P.C., 2009. The Nature and Future of Comparative Politics. *European Political Science Review* 1, 33–61. https://doi.org/10.1017/S1755773909000010

Schmitter, P.C., 2011. The Future of 'Real-Existing' Democracy: Society and Economy in Central and Eastern Europe. *Journal of the Corvinus University of Budapest* 33, 399–428.

Schnabel, I., 2020. The Shadow of Fiscal Dominance: Misconceptions, perceptions and perspectives. Speech given at the Centre for European Reform and the Eurofi Financial Forum on 11 September 2020.

Schneider, S., Hurrelmann, A., Krell-Laluhová, Z., meier, F., Wiesner, A., Nullmeier, F., 2010. *Democracy's Deep Roots: Why the nation state remains legitimate*. New York: Palgrave-MacMillan.

Seeleib-Kaiser, M., 2016. The End of the Conservative German Welfare State Model. *Social Policy & Administration* 50, 219–240. https://doi.org/10.1111/spol.12212

Starke, P., 2006. The Politics of Welfare State Retrenchment: A literature review. *Social Policy & Administration* 40, 104–120. https://doi.org/10.1111/j.1467-9515.2006.00479.x

Starken, J., 2011. Economic Adjustment in a Monetary Union. Speech given at the Bank of Latvia annual conference, on 12 October 2011.

Steinmo, S., Tolbert, C.J., 1998. Do Institutions Really Matter?: Taxation in industrialized democracies. *Comparative Political Studies* 31, 165–187. https://doi.org/10.1177/0010414098031002002

Streeck, W., 2015. The Rise of the European Consolidation State. *Discussion paper* 15/1, Max-Planck-Institut für Gesellschaftsforschung.

Telegraph (The), 2014. Europe Is Slowly Strangling the Life Out of National Democracy. https://www.telegraph.co.uk/news/worldnews/europe/eu/10546394/Europe-is-slowly-strangling-the-life-out-of-national-democracy.html

Truchlewski, Z., 2020. 'Oh, What a Tangled Web We Weave': How tax linkages shape responsiveness in the United Kingdom and France. *Party Politics* 26, 280–290. https://doi.org/10.1177/1354068818764017

Tsatsanis, E., Lisi, M., Freire, A., 2021. The 'Lost Generation' and Its Political Discontents: Age-related divides in Southern Europe after the crisis. *South European Society and Politics* 26, 133–151. https://doi.org/10.1080/13608746.2021.2032936

Urbinati, N., 2014. *Democracy Disfigured.* Harvard University Press.

van Riet, A., 2021. Safe and Risky Sovereigns in the Euro Area Capital Market: Financial drivers of fiscal policies in Germany and Italy. *German Politics* 30, 441–461. https://doi.org/10.1080/09644008.2021.1881956

Veen, A.M. van der, 2011. *Ideas, Interests and Foreign Aid.* Cambridge: Cambridge University Press.

Verdun, A., 2015. A Historical Institutionalist Explanation of the EU's Responses to the Euro Area Financial Crisis. *Journal of European Public Policy* 22, 219–237. https://doi.org/10.1080/13501763.2014.994023

Verdun, A., Zeitlin, J., 2018. Introduction: The European Semester as a new architecture of EU socioeconomic governance in theory and practice. *Journal of European Public Policy* 25, 137–148. https://doi.org/10.1080/13501763.2017.1363807

Wasserfallen, F., Lehner, T., 2017. Mapping Contestation on Economic and Fiscal Integration: Evidence from new data. *EMU Choices Working Paper*, University of Salzburg 23.

Wasserfallen, F., Leuffen, D., Kudrna, Z., Degner, H., 2019. Analysing European Union Decision-Making during the Eurozone Crisis with New Data. *European Union Politics* 20, 3–23. https://doi.org/10.1177/1465116518814954

Zeitlin, J., Vanhercke, B., 2018. Socializing the European Semester: EU social and economic policy co-ordination in crisis and beyond. *Journal of European Public Policy* 25, 149–174. https://doi.org/10.1080/13501763.2017.1363269

Zelditch, M., 2001. Processes of Legitimation: Recent developments and new directions. *Social Psychology Quarterly* 64, 4–17. https://doi.org/10.2307/3090147

Index

For the benefit of digital users, indexed terms that span two pages (e.g., 52–53) may, on occasion, appear on only one of those pages.